I0181388

Other novels by Cort Fernald

Algonquin

Sisters' Secret

Keeper of an Ordinary

KEEPER

TRIAL & VENGEANCE

CORT FERNALD

Thanks to Sue Michels for the invaluable advice, support and assistance with editing, formatting text and creating the cover. Also, thanks to Tony Williams, JJ and Nebraska Novelists for critique help. Author inside photo courtesy of Torri Pantaleon. For more information: www. cortbooks.com

Keeper Trial & Vengeance/ Cort Fernald. -- 1st edition
ISBN-13: 978-0692908327
ISBN-10: 0692908323

CHAPTER 1

To Richard Rice: You are commanded to appear in the United States District Court ...

He read and reread the subpoena, his forehead propped on his palm, fingers gnarled in his sandy brown hair. The mug of coffee by his hand had gone cold.

Autumn winds frosted the corners of the kitchen windows.

The tri-fold document shook slightly in Rich's hand. He drew in a breath.

The rhythmic whir of a spinning wheel as his wife Gisele worked out on a stationary bike could be heard from the living room, adjacent to the kitchen.

... to testify before the court's grand jury. When you arrive, you must remain at the court until the judge or a court officer allows you to leave.

His gut churned.

The spinning stopped, and the bike beeped and went quiet.

Place: U.S. District Court, Nebraska. The Roman L. Hruska Federal Courthouse, 111 South 18th Plaza, Omaha.

Gisele breezed in, toweling off her arms and neck. The cheeks of her oval face glowed reddish. Spots of wetness showed on her gray cutoff sweatshirt. The tanned flesh of her flat, muscular stomach peeked out above her black cotton, three-quarter length yoga pants. She noticed Rich's tight expression and thousand-yard stare. Tilting her head, she leaned over his shoulder and looked at him. "You okay?" She smoothed down his hair.

He started. "Yeah, I'm fine."

"You don't look it." Her short honey-blonde hair was pulled back from her broad forehead by a white band. Gisele's left eye still showed faint greenish-yellow bruising—a reminder of the black eye Suka Franko had given her with a swipe of a MAC-11. Three white scars stood out visibly, scored across her golden cheek from the same vicious blow. Gisele looped the white towel over her neck and jerked open the refrigerator. "Don't you have an appointment with a lawyer this afternoon?" She took out a glass container of cranberry juice.

"Yeah, downtown." Rich sighed, swiveling on the stool at the kitchen island. He poured his cold coffee in the sink. "Guy with a weird name: Douglas Borodavka."

"Borodav—*wha*?" Gisele poured juice into a glass and leaned against the sink.

"Yup." He lifted the coffee pot.

"Mmmm." She spilled some juice as she drank and wiped her lower lip. "Don't forget, we have interviews for Tom's replacement."

"I'm aware of that." Rich refreshed his mug with hot coffee, adding sugar and milk. He tasted it, and satisfied, sat back on the stool. "I'm hoping we can reopen The Ordinary next week."

"We need money coming in. Are these the bartenders Daisy recommended?"

"Just one. The others responded to an ad in the *World-Herald*."

"I've been helping Jorge get the kitchen ready after the remodel. I think we're in good shape."

"I thought that, too, until that fucker walked in and handed me this." Rich waved the grand jury subpoena.

"You'll be fine," Gisele said walking over and rubbing Rich's neck. She sounded vague, worried. "It's just what the FBI guy said—they're covering their asses."

Rich shook his head, glancing up at her. "Covering their asses might get mine thrown in prison."

"Oh no, that's mine." She ruffled his hair, joking. "They aren't taking that from me." She downed her juice and rinsed the glass under the faucet. "I'm going to jump into the shower."

"Okay," Rich mumbled.

She kissed the back of his neck and left the kitchen.

The subpoena read, *You must also bring with you the following documents, electronically stored information, or objects.* It listed surveillance tapes and photos from The Ordinary bar before and after the shootout.

They didn't know about Nicky Franko's notebook, or the money in his black satchel. A stroke of luck, Rich realized. He got up and walked into the living room.

The spare bachelor décor of Rich's nine-hundred-square-foot flat, that he had shared with his dog

Roommate, had changed when Gisele moved from her mother's in Glencoe. After the shootout, there was no point in living apart. What Rich had feared would happen...had. The corner table, gun safe and bookcase remained much the same. But she had turned the far end of the room into a mini gym, with a stationary bike, a Nautilus machine, and a bench with a rack of free weights. The room was divided by a three-tier bookshelf topped by green plants.

Rich opened his laptop and let it boot up. Contractor bills and receipts from plumbers and electricians were piled on the table. They needed to be recorded in The Ordinary's spreadsheets.

Rich heard the shower and couldn't help but imagine Gisele's long and muscular body naked, stepping under the steaming spray. It stirred him. She had kept her swimmer's body in excellent shape. Gisele was on the good side of her 40s, when her definitive German features showed attractive lines of maturity. Her hair always appeared tasseled: not flyaway, but stylishly mussed, as if she were freshly loved.

Gisele's woman's touch had left Rich with half a table piled with his books, notes and pads with drafts of his book on human trafficking. The other half had Gisele's laptop and her neatly laid-out folders and papers. He was okay with it all. After all that had occurred with the shootout—the killing of his friend Tom Waller, the shooting of Lieutenant Lavender, the death of Roommate, the near destruction of The Ordinary—Rich had lost his bearings. Gisele had swept in and taken over. He had come to rely on her for stability.

He knew that shooting Dedmon, critically wounding the big Russian, Yuri, and the shooting death of Nicky Franko were justified. They had come to kill him. It was self-defense. Nonetheless, the killings bothered him. And somewhere out there, Nicky's mother Suka, maybe wounded, would be wanting to even the score. In the weeks since, he repeatedly woke in a sweat, remembering sighting her in the circle of the scope, steadying the dot, letting out a half-breath and squeezing the trigger.

The shower shut off, bringing Rich back. He leaned forward to the keyboard, opening the accounting application. Gisele was right. There was no money coming in from the bar, but lots going out. Jorge Ruiz, the cook, and his wife Carmelita, the cleaner, were still drawing paychecks; so was Daisy Lincoln. Daisy was Tom's girlfriend and the young black woman still grieved over her loss. Rich logged their hours for the week and scheduled the transfer of funds to their bank accounts. He glanced at the contractors' bills and sighed.

Gisele walked out of the bedroom in a thick white terry cloth robe, toweling her wet hair. She smelled fresh and warm.

"I'll feel a lot better when we reopen The Ordinary and see money coming in." Rich clicked off the accounting software.

"We're all right." Gisele bent forward and set the towel on the back of her head. She stood and wrapped it around her head like a turban. "We haven't even dented all that cash Nicky Franko left us."

"Left us?" Rich chuckled. "Bequeathed us."

"Call it what you will. With all the damage those Russian fuckers did to the bar, I am less and less squeamish about keeping their money to fix The Ordinary. Any coffee left?"

The Ordinary had once been a working man's bar with a wood floor, tables, a large-screen TV and a pool table in a side room, featuring beers, wine and some mixed drinks. Under Gisele's guiding hand, however, it had undergone a transformation and extensive repairs. The dimly lit classic tavern had become brighter and more colorful, featuring hanging lights, green leather upholstered booths along the window side, stained cherry wood paneling with matching circular tables and red oak floors with oriental throw rugs. Rich had to battle to keep the pool table. The bar top, which had been shot nearly to pieces, had been reconstructed close to its original polished mahogany look. The bar back mirror and multi-color display of liquor bottles had been replaced. A new polished steel and glass wine cooler set in the corner had yet to be restocked. Stainless steel fixtures under the bar, sink, ice chest and prep area were all new. Of course, the large screen TV and speakers had to be replaced. The surveillance system and computer under the bar had somehow escaped unscathed.

Gisele worked in the kitchen while Rich busied himself behind the bar, stocking glassware and supplies. The door opened.

"Are you the Keeper?"

Rich glanced up. "That's what they call me. Are you Carl?"

"I am."

"Pull up a stool, and let me get the paperwork." Rich looked back, taking a quick measure of Carl. He was older and rough-looking. Most people would've shaved for a job interview. His brown hair had a mix of gray and lay unevenly cut just over the tops of his ears. Carl moved his mouth in and out like a man missing his false teeth. Rich took a manila folder from under the bar by the computer and opened it as if reading, though he was actually studying Carl over the top of the page.

Carl settled himself on a stool and scanned the length of bar back. He wiped his mouth with his hand and dried the palm on his pants.

"Okay." Behind the bar, Rich stepped up to Carl. "Thanks for coming in. I've got your resume from the email you sent. Looks like you've worked at quite a few bars and restaurants, in a lot of different places."

"I been around." Carl twitched as he talked.

"Appears that way." Rich smiled. "You last worked in Rapid City. What brings you down here?"

"My wife. Ex-wife, for true. We're taking another shot at it." He wiped his mouth again, dragging his fingers slowly across his wet lips. "You got a real nice setup here. Your taps working?"

"Yeah. I had to replace one recently."

"I'm a little thirsty. It be okay you gave me a little pull?" His eyes pled.

Rich hesitated a second. "Oh, yeah. No problem." He reached under the counter and took out a pilsner glass and tilted it under the tap, tugging the long white handle.

Carl grinned with an open mouth, exhaling loudly.

Rich placed the glass on the back edge of the bar, on purpose.

Carl's hands shook reaching over the bar. He brought the glass to his lips and downed its golden contents in a couple of gulps. He set down the empty glass with a steady hand and a calm demeanor.

Rich watched, arms folded. "So tell me about yourself," he said, his voice flat.

"Wife and I are settling here. I'm an experienced mixologist and can run an efficient bar." Carl's thumb and forefinger went into his breast pocket, fishing out a cigarette.

"You can't smoke here."

Carl looked surprised. "You're not open."

"Doesn't matter. Have you got your Nebraska license?"

"Not yet." Carl carefully slid the cigarette back in the pack.

"I called some of your previous employers. They were so-so about you. No glowing reports, but nothing bad."

"Yeah, I figured. Some of those guys...they're jerks, y'know?"

"No, I don't know."

"I worked for good guys too."

"I see some long gaps in your employment history."

"County vacation. Not my fault," Carl smiled with one side of his mouth.

"Gotcha. Why not your fault?"

"Bitch shoulda never got me mad."

"Oh, okay. I know you're looking for fulltime, but if it doesn't work out, would you be available for part-time or fill-in?"

Carl looked crestfallen. "Well, if that's all you got."

"I'm interviewing others." Rich plucked the glass from the bar.

Carl's eyes followed the glass. "How about a refill?"

"No, Carl." Rich shook Carl's cold, moist hand. "I'll give you a call. And Carl...do me a favor, prop the door open to let the paint smell out. Thanks."

Less than ten minutes later, a middle-aged man strutted in wearing a tight Giorgio ribbed gray V-neck t-shirt and expensive jeans. His eyes immediately located the mirror behind the bar, and he greeted himself with a smirk. "I'm Chet," he said, his hand out to Rich.

"Hello, Chet. I'm Keeper. Let's sit at a table."

Chet turned a chair around and straddled it across from Rich. A heavy gust of Axe cologne blew Rich's way, almost choking him.

"You've worked at some pretty high-profile places." Rich read from Chet's resume.

"They want the best. I am the best." He smoothed back his long hair. "And, you know, I do pour a killer drink and bring in the ladies." He appeared to please himself with that.

Gisele came out of the kitchen and went to the side room.

"She work here?"

"Excuse me?"

"She's fine."

Over his shoulder, Rich saw Gisele working in the pool room. She bent over, sliding a box under a shelf. Her tight jeans showed her well-defined calves and thighs, leading up to the firm teardrop shape of her butt. Rich looked back and saw Chet leaning to the side, leering at Gisele.

"I'm going to like working here."

"That's my wife."

Chet sneered and nodded. "That's cool."

Rich had to fight the impulse to swing an open hand hard across Chet's smug face. Guys like Chet deserved no less.

"Get the hell out."

"What?"

"You heard me. Get the hell out of my bar, before I throw you out."

Chet tucked his smile into his cheek and shook his head. "Your loss, dude. I bring in the babes." He stood and flipped his hair. "You're missing out." He backed to the door.

Rich held up his left hand, a closed fist except for his little finger.

"What's that supposed to mean?"

"Goodbye."

Rich wadded Chet's resume and threw it after him as he went out the door.

"How're the interviews going?" Gisele wondered, coming up behind Rich and toting a box.

"Well, I've had a drunk and a Don Juan *play-ah*." He shuffled through papers in the folder. "I've one more before I have to go see the lawyer."

"Did you see the guy Daisy recommended?"

"He's next." Rich held up a resume. "Riku Suzuki ... Riku Costello Suzuki."

Gisele peering over his shoulder, murmured "Costello?"

"Yeah." Rich went on. "He's getting a fine arts degree, photography."

"That's cool."

"You talking about me?"

Standing before them was a tall, somewhat round young Asian man with thick black hair, wearing a striped dress shirt untucked over khaki slacks. He had a pudgy, pleasant face and an engaging smile that made his eyes disappear. He must've slipped through the open door.

"Riku?"

"Yes." He offered his hand.

"Take a seat, please." They shook. "This is my wife, Gisele."

"Very nice to meet you." Riku sat, folding his hands on the tabletop.

"You as well," Gisele replied, excusing herself. "I, ah, have some things to do in the kitchen."

"Daisy Lincoln recommended you. She said you're a student at Metro Community College."

"I was. I transferred to UNO in September."

"Still pursuing a fine arts degree?"

"Yes. Photography. I have two more years." He had no trace of an Asian accent.

"Good for you." Rich settled back in his chair, reading Riku's resume. "And your background working in a bar?"

"It's more like restaurant experience. My parents owned a Japanese restaurant."

"Which one?"

"Nagasaki Grill. It was a barbeque joint."

"You have a bartender's license?"

"I did." Riku calmly answered. "It expired about a year ago. I can renew it."

"I have to tell you, we're not a very sophisticated bar. We serve a variety of beers on tap, some domestics, the usual suspects, European imports and an assortment of craft brews from California, Oregon and Washington. A few mixed drinks and wine are pretty standard. No flaming or smoking drinks or any exotic concoctions."

Riku nodded, following Rich's description.

"Why do you want to work here?"

"I need a job, of course, and Daisy told me you were flexible about hours, so I'd be able to schedule classes around work."

"I would work with you on that as much as I could. But there'll be late nights on Fridays and Saturdays."

"I figured that."

"Your days off will more than likely be Monday and Tuesday."

"Works for me."

"You know Daisy is getting her license. Any issues working behind the bar with a woman?"

"Nope, none. She and I have classes together."

Rich studied Riku a minute. "Any other reason you would want to work here?"

Riku's chubby face broke wide with a grin. He rocked back, blushing. "Daisy said you and your wife were really cool."

Rich returned the smile. "Thanks for the compliment." Not a snap decision. The second that Riku had replied politely when meeting Gisele, Rich knew Riku was the right guy for the job. He slipped an application out of the folder and pushed it across the table. "I'd like to hire you. Fill this out, please."

"Thanks." Riku took the form and pulled a ballpoint pen from his pocket.

"And I'll need you to go downtown and apply for renewal of your bartender's license. They'll let you work while they process it. Also, I need you to take a drug test." He gave Riku a half-sheet. "I will be running a background check. You have anything I should know about?"

Riku's head came up quick. His face twisted in thought. "No, nothing but a couple of campus parking tickets." He went back to writing. "Which I paid."

"Good." Rich slapped both palms on the table. He stood. "I have an appointment and have to get going. Please fill out the application and hand it to my wife. Can you start on Saturday, around ten?"

"Yeah."

"Got any questions for me?"

"What are you going to pay me?"

"Sorry, I'm kind of rushed." Rich half-laughed. "It will be hourly, twelve dollars an hour to start. A thirty-two-hour week. You'll get time-and-a-half overtime or comp time, whichever you want. You'll have to work some holidays, but you'll be paid double-time, with eight hours a month PTO. And right now, we pool and split tips between bartenders and kitchen. How does that sound?"

"I like it."

"Good to have you onboard, Riku. See you Saturday."

They shook hands. Riku's round face cracked into a toothy smile.

Rich grabbed the door jamb and leaned into the kitchen. Gisele was organizing stock on shelves. "I hired him."

"I was eavesdropping. He's a good fit, but ..." Gisele stopped, looking hard at Rich.

"What?"

"Did you ask him?"

"Ask him what?"

"How he got his middle name...Costello?"

Rich chuckled. "No, I didn't. You can."

"Oh, no, not me. You're his boss."

Midafternoon traffic down Thirteenth Street reminded Rich of a boxing match between two old, overweight prize fighters. They went into a clinch at intersections, openly sparred for lanes between blocks, and then brawled fist-to-face the closer to downtown he drove. The address was on South Sixteenth, a short block of past-century buildings between Farnam and Harney streets. There was plenty of parking on the east side in front of an empty jeweler's shop in the 1880s Securities Building. Rich parked his Ford F-150 and pumped five quarters into the meter. An aging black man sat on the stoop of a vacant building across the street. He ate something out of a wrinkled, grease-splotched page of newspaper and then sucked the ends of each finger. He was skinny and resembled a bundle of sticks wrapped in a red flannel and baggy trousers.

The lawyer's office was on the third floor of Prince Tong's, a long-established Chinese restaurant with a dubious history. The ornate building, with its fake Arabic columns, was alleged to have housed an opium den. Rich found the narrow door next to the restaurant. A directory, defaced by spray-painted graffiti, listed Borodavka Law. Pushing open the door, Rich paused, staring up a narrow flight of stairs three stories steep.

"Holy crap."

With a deep breath, he started up the creaky wooden steps. The stairway reeked of boiled rice and sesame from the restaurant one wall away. By the time he neared the third-floor landing, he was all but breathless. “This guy has to be in the best shape of any lawyer I’ve ever seen.” He caught his breath and mounted the last steps. Green indoor/outdoor carpet, wrinkled, ripped and worn in spots, led down a hall with frosted glass doors to offices along the left. The walls were grim, gray and ugly.

And this is where they used to kick the gong around? he wondered.

Smells of cooking, dust and mold filled Rich’s nose. Halfway down the hall, he noticed the crisscrossed brass accordion gate of a small service elevator. Two of the offices were empty, with doors ajar and debris scattered about. On the frosted glass door of the middle office was written in faded gold lettering, *Douglas Borodavka, Lawyer, Criminal & Civil Law, Immigration & Notary.*

Rich rapped a knuckle on the glass.

“What?” replied a loud, impatient voice from inside.

“Mr. Borodav ... ka?”

A chair squeaked in the office, and heavy steps approached the door. The handle rattled and hinges creaked as the door pulled back. A large hairy face with droopy, red-rimmed eyes below a mass of long, oily, ill-kempt hair peered out.

“Who the hell are you?”

“Richard Rice. We had an appointment.”

“Oh shit, was that today?

Rich stood back. This hadn’t started well. Maybe he should turn and go.

The big man opened the door wide. “Come on in.”

Rich decided to chance it. He looked around the messy office and saw overflowing book cases and piles of folders on a pair of army-green metal filing cabinets that were dented as if they'd been in a traffic accident. Books, newspapers and magazines lay here and there across the floor. Last year's calendar, crooked family portraits and things resembling diplomas adorned the walls. The blurry windows could have used a damp cloth. Two mismatched chairs fronted a mess of a desk. Stale tobacco and Chinese cuisine made the air very close in the cramped office.

"Have a chair," Borodavka offered as he deftly maneuvered his bulk past the law books and legal briefs mounded around the desk. He knew his way about his office.

Rich brushed crumbs from the chair and settled in.

Borodavka had stuffed his pear-shaped frame into a brown dress shirt and brown slacks. He wore his gray tie loose under his open collar. His overgrown head of curly black hair was tied in the back. He had a monk's bald circle on top. He groaned, wedging it all into a desk chair. "So what can I do you for, Mr. Rice?"

"We talked on the phone. I have a subpoena to appear before a federal grand jury."

"Did you bring it?"

"Yeah." Rich pulled the thick letter from his back pocket.

Borodavka opened it and read, making growling sounds in the back of his throat. "Can't help ya. They won't let me prowl around in there." He handed back the letter to Rich.

"What?"

The lawyer held up a large hairy paw. “Hold on. Tell me what’s going on. Why’d you get a subpoena?”

Rich sighed. “I own The Ordinary, a bar in South Omaha. About three weeks ago, there was a shootout between—”

Borodavka leaned forward. “I remember that. I saw it on the news. A gang of Russians came in shooting up the place.” He made gun shapes with his hands. “Pow. Pow.” He stopped. “Didn’t some bad guys get killed? And wasn’t an Omaha cop critically injured?”

“Yeah, sort of like that. Omaha Police Lieutenant Lavender was shot. My friend Tom Waller got killed.”

“And the others?”

“A Russian Mafia character named Nicky Franko and a rogue cop were killed.”

“This is juicy. Why the hell were the Russians after you?”

“I’m a journalist from Chicago. I wrote investigative reports about Russian Mafia prostitution and human trafficking. Someone, presumably the Russians, took a shot at me. Cops said I should get out of Chicago. I left my wife with her mother in Glencoe and went underground. To survive, I bought a bar in South Omaha.”

“What’s the name of the bar?”

“The Ordinary.”

“Sorry, never been there. So why are you subpoenaed?”

“I guess they want to find out what happened.”

“Did you kill’em?” The lawyer put up his meaty hand. “Don’t answer that. You know how the grand jury works?”

“I came here to get answers, and all I’m getting are questions. No, not totally. I’m a journalist, I’ve covered preliminary hearings and inquests, but never a grand jury.”

"Okay. First, I'm going to tell you, if you're testifying, that's sort of a good thing."

"Sort of?"

"Yeah, sort of. If you were the target of the grand jury investigation, they wouldn't have you testify. You'd already be in jail."

"So, I'm in the clear?"

"Oh, hell no. They could turn around and make you the target of the investigation after you testify. You'd be screwed blue and tattooed, my friend." Borodavka smiled a smile that lacked an upper canine and lower incisor amongst a batch of crooked chompers. "Mind if I smoke?" He reached a hairy paw across to a briar pipe in a dirty ashtray.

"No, go ahead." Rich slumped forward in his chair, elbows on his knees, looking through his clasp hands to the carpet. What lay before him felt like a yoke resting heavily upon his shoulders.

The large lawyer tamped tobacco into the pipe bowl and then struck a kitchen match on the wall. From the gate count of black streaks, it wasn't the first match he had fired up and laid to his pipe. Between shallow draws under the flame and smoke, he said: "I'm going to tell you ... what a grand jury ... is all about. And you can ... call me Doug."

Rich straightened in the wooden back chair, crossing his legs, thankful that Borodavka smoked a pipe. Smoldering pipe tobacco was a preferable stink to frying and boiled rice.

"You can either thank or cuss out the English for our grand jury system. It goes back to the Magna Carta. Ever heard of that?"

"The English or the Magna Carta?"

Doug puffed, looking at Rich through clouds of blue smoke. "All right. I deserved that. A grand jury, like a preliminary hearing, is used to present evidence and determine if a crime has been committed and who, if anyone, should be bound over for trial."

"I'm testifying, but I'm not on trial?"

"Not *per se*." Borodavka rocked back in his desk chair and blew smoke toward the ceiling. "A grand jury hears evidence presented by the state or federal government to show the commission of a crime. There is no judge, only a sitting jury of thirteen- to twenty-odd people hearing the testimony." He paused. "I meant twenty-odd as in more than twenty, not twenty odd people."

"I understood. Can I counter other testimony?"

"Not really. No defense attorneys are allowed in the proceedings. That's why I said I couldn't help you. But actually, I can. There's a way."

"That's crazy. They can accuse me, and I can't defend myself."

Doug laughed and coughed on pipe smoke. "Technically no, but there are ways. And you're not being accused or tried. At least, not yet. If you don't want to answer a question, you can plead the Fifth Amendment and not incriminate yourself. But if you do that, you may as well stick out your wrists for the bracelets. Nothing screams guilty like refusing to answer a question." His belly shook as he laughed again. "We can put together a defense packet and give it to the prosecutor. I think I know who the prosecutor is, and he might supply the defense evidence for the jury to look at."

"Why don't they just put me on trial?"

“On what charge?”

“Murder, I guess.”

“You’d better hope it’s not murder.”

“Why’s that?”

“This is a death penalty state. In the case of multiple murders, the death penalty is automatic.”

“Are you saying ...?”

“That’s exactly what I’m saying.”

A stony silence fell between them.

“More than likely, it would be manslaughter.” Borodavka scratched himself thoughtfully, not bothering to disguise it. Rich’s eyes drifted up to the brown water stains on the ceiling, clouds in a sky of perforated white tiles, as he waited for the lawyer to finish his chores. “They may not have enough evidence. If I recall, the Russians came after you, right? And you were the only one to walk out.”

“Yeah.”

“So you didn’t instigate it. And who shot first?”

“They did.”

“Two of them were killed ...”

“And they killed Tom.”

“I remember something about your wife?”

“She was taken hostage at gunpoint by a Russian woman.”

“And you killed her?”

“The Russian woman? Yeah. No. I mean, I don’t know. I shot her, and she got away on a boat.”

“Is your wife all right?”

“Yeah. She got banged up, but she’s recovering.”

“That’s good. You gave a statement after?”

“I was interrogated by the FBI.”

"Well," Borodavka said slowly. "And you didn't get arrested?"

"Nope."

"Your weapons? Did they make you hand over your weapons?"

"Yeah, but they gave them back."

Borodavka rocked, puffed, rocked, puffed, transfixed by another brown stain, this one on the side wall. Rich watched him. The chair stopped. The big man leaned forward, his belly pressing against the desk. He stabbed at Rich with the wet, chewed stem of his pipe. "I'll be honest with you. You have a fifty-fifty chance of being indicted for multiple counts of manslaughter."

A cold shiver crept up Rich's spine. "I don't get it. I was defending myself."

"Sucks, doesn't it? But fifty-fifty odds with a grand jury are pretty damn good."

"Doesn't sound like it."

"Believe me, it is. Don't do anything stupid, like take off." Borodavka searched around the papers on his desk. He found a yellow pad and plucked a pen from a cup. He hunched over the pad. "Have you been deposed?"

"No."

He looked up. "Any other witnesses?"

"Lavender. He was the cop they shot up."

"That all? Come on, we need anyone and everyone."

"A Glencoe, Illinois Public Safety Officer named Terry."

"You need to be deposed." Borodavka tore off the top sheet from the pad. "We'll steal a march on them. You and your wife go to this address at that day and time. You'll give depositions to a paralegal. I'll get in touch with

Lavender. Try and give me more than Terry the Glencoe cop."

Rich took the offered sheet, glanced at it, and then folded it and tucked it in his breast pocket.

Borodavka squinted with one eye into the bowl of his now-dead pipe.

"We done?" Rich pulled himself up from the chair.

"For now. Don't freak out. If it was self-defense, well, that makes for a long and costly trial that they're not going to want." Borodavka tapped the pipe in the ashtray. "The U.S. District Attorney is a guy named Bernard Nutkis. A pretty decent guy. He may take this case. He'll take the defense packet we prepare. If the jury foreman wants to see it, Bernie'll give it to him."

"Thanks, Doug." They shook hands over the desk.

The lawyer held Rich's hand tight. "Oh, ah, how you going to pay me?"

"I used to pay cash for everything. I don't have a bank account, but my wife could ..." Rich gripped Borodavka's wrist in his left hand and pried his hand from the large man's grasp. "... could write you a check. What do I owe you?"

Borodavka laughed. "Just a little professional humor. In a case like this, I would want a thousand dollar retainer. That'll cover your depositions, incidentals and dinner at Prince Tong's. When can you get me a check?"

"I'll drop one off tomorrow."

"Far out. If I'm not here, slide it under the door."

Rich picked his way through books and debris, stopping at the door. "And do me a favor," he said.

"You name it."

"Don't tell my wife about the death penalty."

"Deal."

"Is there another way out of here?"

"You can use the elevator, if you don't mind walking through Prince Tong's kitchen."

"I'll pass."

"Call me the day after the depositions. We'll go over evidence."

"Thanks." Rich gave a two-finger salute and closed the glass door behind him. Out in the hall stood a Hispanic family, anxiously whispering. Nearby were a pair of women wearing hijabs with small babies astride their hips. Rich smiled and stepped between them toward the stairs. He reached the landing and paused, looking down. "I don't need to worry about falling down these stairs," he muttered to himself. "I feel like I already have."

CHAPTER 2

Russian snow—fat, white flakes—tumbled out of an inky blue sky, collecting around the edges of the windshield of a black Mercedes speeding over snow-swept streets. The flakes became droplets of water, sliding sideways over the curved glass until the wipers erased them. The sedan bumped off the Moskva River Bridge and into the innermost ring, Bulvarnoye Koltso, penetrating central Moscow. Flashing through a pool of illumination from a single streetlight, it wheeled onto Mokhovaya Street, toward the bright lights of Red Square.

Dark masses of first shift workers, huddled against the weather and cold at a corner stop, waited as the Elektricha lumbered up the street.

A young *Federal' naya sluzhba bezopasnosti* officer drove. The black and gold boards on his green uniform indicated his rank as captain. An amber glow from the dashboard lit his round face and non-regulation shaggy haircut. His eyes flicked to the rearview mirror and the lone passenger in the back seat.

"Are you warm enough, General?" the driver asked.

The dark figure turned from the window. A passing street light illuminated a man of advanced age with skin like parchment stretched taut over his face. He had thin gray patches of hair as fine as silk on the narrow and freckled crown of his head. His long face had hawk-like features set off by small, intense eyes. He was dressed in a heavy gray wool overcoat with a beige cashmere scarf around his spindly neck. A thick olive-green blanket lay across his legs. His brown leather-gloved hands were folded over a black mink Cossack hat on his lap.

"I am warm," he replied distantly, turning back to the window.

Swirling flurries danced in the iridescent beams of the sedan's headlights.

They drove along Mokhovaya Street, passing the red and green colored lights of Red Square and the Kremlin, approaching Lubyanka Square.

"Perhaps the General would like coffee?" The captain slowed at an intersection. "It has been a long day, sir."

Indeed, it had. The long day had turned to night and then the morning since the phone rang at the general's dacha in Ochakiv on the Black Sea. "You must come in," the message began. "Your grandson, Nikolai Franko, is dead. Your daughter, Irina Ilyich, is missing in the United States." The death of his grandson did not surprise the general. The boy's wild ways had caught up with him. But Irina? His only daughter. This troubled him.

A car had taken him from his dacha to Mykolayiv Air Base. They had seated him in the front section of a Federation Antonov An-12. The only passenger, he had arrived at Krasnogosk, east of Moscow, just as the snow came.

"Perhaps something stronger to warm your blood?"

"I need nothing to warm my blood."

The sedan entered the square. A late-autumn covering of snow dressed the central garden rotunda where, until recently, the statue of "Iron Feliks" Dzerzhinsky, father of the Cheka, had presided.

The imposing shadow of the neo-Renaissance Lubyanka building dominated the square. Silhouettes of construction cranes crisscrossed in the gray horizon atop the building. The general noticed yellow lighted windows along the third floor.

But a few years after the Great Patriotic War ended, Malenkov had thrown young Ivan Dimitri Franko into the lower depths of Lubyanka as a prisoner. Month upon month, he had sat in the small, dank basement cell, hearing the screams and denials of men being interrogated. When the shrieking stopped, the general knew the man lay broken or dead. He waited his turn. As a leader of the *vory v zakone*, he had been small time, running a smuggling operation across the Black Sea from Turkey and Greece to Odessa. Coffee, cigarettes and meat he sold out of his boat's hold on the docks of Sebastopol. Why did they want him?

One day he woke to a pair of eyes peering through the shoulder-high slit in the cell's rusted iron door. The door was hauled back with a metal screech, and in the light stood a stocky man in an ill-fitting suit flanked by NKVD guards. Blinking, his eyes aching, the general thought, *this man brings my death.* But it was Stalin who was dead, and a power struggle gripped the party. Malenkov needed friends. He made Ivan his protégé in the newly formed KGB. As thieves, they understood each other, and Malenkov preferred to surround himself with men indebted to him for their very lives.

Stalin's death prompted the ouster of Lavrenti Beria, known as "the bloodthirsty dwarf". Almost invisible, the general did Malenkov's bidding from his third-floor office in Lubyanka. Many did not know what had hit them, especially the dwarf. The state mourned the loss of such a great servant. No one knew why Beria, a war hero and confidante of Stalin, would ever think to take his own life. Let them wonder. They would never know that he was machine-gunned in a bed with the two seven-year-old Georgian girls whom he had just finished raping and strangling.

"Do you not hear the wails, the weeping, Captain?" the general murmured as they drove past Lubyanka.

"Excuse me, General?"

The black sedan crossed the square to Kuznetskiy. Most of the street fell under the shadow of the Central Children's Store and a row of Stalinist Gothic buildings. Turning left at Bank Moscow, they were suddenly caught in the white glare of a searchlight. The captain, blinded, shielded his eyes with his left hand. He braked the Mercedes, and it skidded slightly to a stop in the circle of light. Federation Special Forces in green flecktarn camo and black balaclavas surrounded the car. They leveled AK-12s at every window. A voice shouted for the captain to show identification.

The young officer let down the window. A small blizzard and cold air blasted in. He handed out his laminated identity card.

"Who's in the back?" an officer demanded.

"*Federal' naya sluzhba bezopasnosti* General Franko."

A flashlight lit up the general's face. The old man stared back, unblinking.

"Apologies, General." The light snapped off.

The general nodded.

"You may proceed." The Special Forces melted into the darkness.

The captain rolled up the window and drove forward slowly. "We worry about Chechens?"

The general grunted.

A square of light in the long, high, dark wall of the Federal Security Service complex led to an underground garage. The Mercedes turned at a downslope and entered the garage, which had been transformed into a staging area for a company of Special Forces. A squad lay about, some sleeping, some talking, others eating, on one side of a mottled green Ural 43206 light cargo truck. A ZZ Top song played on a small radio. *Every girl's crazy 'bout a sharp-dressed man.* The second squad stood ready to reinforce the squad on alert outside.

The captain parked in a far corner and stepped out. He slowly and deliberately put on his uniform cap and then pulled a wheelchair from the trunk. The general put on his Cossack hat, waiting as the captain readied the chair. The captain then bent down, lifted the general from the back seat, and placed him in the chair.

"Thank you, Captain," the general said as the young officer arranged the blanket on his legs.

"Yes, sir." The captain locked the sedan and pushed the general across the garage to an elevator. The garage reeked of petrol, onions, sausage and men's sweat. The Special Forces troops paid little attention as the captain keyed in a code at the elevator.

The general fully expected the doors to open on familiar green walls and a parquet floor like Lubyanka. Instead, he saw grimy brown linoleum and cement walls painted over multiple chipped layers of dirty beige. They rolled from the elevator. The high ceilings were a tangle of phone, electric and coaxial cables over, under and around twisting metal ductwork and hanging fluorescent lights.

The floor had been sectioned off into cubicles of blonde wood and glass about two meters high. Desks cluttered with papers, fat folders, computers and coffee cups occupied half of each cubicle. Cardboard boxes and filing cabinets filled most of the remaining space. In the majority of the cubicles, the only open area was a path from the entrance to a chair at the computer. At a far back wall were bank upon bank of computers, their screens flickering, rolling over columns of white numbers.

An assortment of narrow, short and stout filing cabinets had been stacked along the corridor. The smell of coffee and insecticide pervaded the floor.

A few bleary-eyed workers stood about, talking low or typing at computers. Heads turned as the general was wheeled past.

The captain's breath was visible in the air. The old man glanced over his shoulder. "Turn the heat up."

"Yes, General." There was no conviction in the captain's voice. He opened the door to a corner office and snapped on the lights. He pushed the general into the office and then removed the chair from behind the desk.

The old man glanced around the office disdainfully. "Take these police photos from the wall," the general said as the captain pushed him behind the desk. "Especially *Khuilo*." The pictures were all of the current Federation leadership. "But not that one." The general indicated a photo of a stocky man in an ill-fitting suit.

The captain removed the pictures, leaving clean squares of beige on the dirty wall. He piled the frames on a filing cabinet.

"And those rags, take them into the hallway," the general added, shaking his finger at a set of flags on short staffs. He unbuttoned his overcoat, pulled off his gloves, unwound his cashmere muffler and removed his hat, folding and placing each of them on the desk. He moved the keyboard closer. "Is there a folder, or a communique?"

"No folder, and communiques are pure Cold War, Ivan Dimitrovich," said a tall, angular, ashen-haired man in the doorway.

"Anatolyovich," a slight smile crossed the general's bony face. "I see the state still owns your soul."

"Yes, General." Anatoly sauntered in. "The Fifth Directorate has also a lien on my backside." The man had his hands deep in the pockets of his heavy brown wool trousers. He wore a threadbare gray cardigan sweater over a dingy white shirt with an ink stain on its breast pocket. "Although a sad occasion, I am happy to see my old friend."

"And I you." The general started tapping the keyboard and moving the mouse. "What is this nasty business with my daughter and grandson?"

"It's that key, General." Anatoly pointed.

The computer screen flashed Hewlett-Packard.

"This piece of western plastic doesn't fool me."

Anatoly held up a small thumb drive. "The information is all in here."

"More capitalist mumbo jumbo?"

"I don't recall the general being so faithful to the CCCP."

"You recall correctly, Anatoly."

The captain took the thumb drive and plugged it into a port on the tower.

"We received a encrypted email from our embassy in the United States," Anatoly explained, "stating that your grandson had been killed and Irina Ilyich, your only daughter, and the one they call Suka, had been shot and is now missing."

"May I, General?" The captain took the mouse, clicking on a file. The text of the embassy email came onscreen.

The general's face moved close to the screen. He squinted and read. "Omaha? And where is this Glencoe?"

Anatoly pulled his hands out of his pockets and sat on the corner of the desk. "Glencoe is north of Chicago."

"Ahhhh." The general nodded. "Was this a *Federal' naya sluzhba* operation?"

The tall man looked down and brushed lint off his pants. "You know better than that, General."

"Anatoly, no one knows better than I that my daughter is *Bratva* and that my grandson thought himself some kind of *pindos* rock'n'roll cowboy. I assume this affair is the result of that?"

Anatoly shrugged. "Rather—" He paused. "I have to say the truth. It is the result of that activity."

The general waved away the comment. "A man only needs honor, not laws. And since when do we obey the laws of western countries?"

"Oh, my *dachanik* friend. Times are different; our influence less. We strive to be most quiet in all that we do."

"Captain, I would like coffee now."

"Yes, General." The captain briskly left the office.

"We can talk now, Anatoly. Tell me all about it."

Anatoly retrieved the desk chair and sat across from the general. "I think you are aware that American newspapers have been printing things about *Bratva*'s activity—specifically, the prostitution and drugs. Not good. Instead of going underground and waiting for it to move past, Nikolai took it upon himself to try and eliminate the writer of these articles. He missed, wounding the man. The man then disappeared. Nikolai became obsessed with finding and killing him."

The old man pointed to his temple. "Birds flew about crazy in his bird cage." He shook his head. "And my Irina, what did she do?"

"She wisely went back to Toronto and waited out the storm."

"Then how did she get involved?"

"Nikolai tracked the man's wife and found them together. But they split up, and he lost track of the man."

"This is the writer, the man he wanted to kill?"

"Yes."

"Then how is it that this man killed him?"

"I am getting to there. Nikolai got the man's address in Omaha. He foolishly went to kill him. He informed his mother. Irina knew her *malysh* well and knew he would be in danger. She came down from Toronto."

"And it all went bad."

"Quite bad." Anatoly glanced away. "The man was prepared."

"Nikolai was alone?"

"No, no. He had a paid American and a Russian bodyguard."

"The paid American? Is he dead? And who was Nikolai's bodyguard?"

"Yes, the American is dead. His bodyguard was Yuri Grimansky."

"No? Yuri? His grandfather is *vory*. I knew him in the gulag. Is Yuri dead as well?"

"No. He is in an American hospital, critically wounded."

"This killer—this writer, you say—he must be a soldier. American special forces, CIA?"

Anatoly laughed silently. "No, General. A writer, yes, for newspapers."

"Terrible. And my Irina? Who shot her?"

"Same man." Anatoly pointed to his left and then across to his right as he spoke. "But in Glencoe, Chicago. A boat was sent, and just before she got aboard, the man shot her."

"Where is she now?"

The captain came in with a mug of steaming coffee and set it by the general's right hand.

"We do not know."

"Is she alive or dead?"

"We do not know."

The general slammed his fists hard on the desktop. "I do not want to hear what we don't know. I want to hear what we know."

Anatoly stood. His face hardened, but his eyes betrayed anger. "My friend, I can only communicate the information I receive."

The general clenched his fists and shook. "This is my family, Anatoly."

"General. You must control yourself. I only know what I am told."

"Is my daughter alive or dead?"

"We...do...not...know."

The captain raised the blinds on the window behind the desk. Darkness had lifted. But still came the snow, falling from low-hanging gray clouds above the jagged Moscow skyline.

"I want to know more about this man who killed by grandson." Placing his thin, bony hands on the mug, the general lifted it to his lips. It shook as he sipped.

The captain leaned in and clicked on an attachment. Various documents opened onscreen: LinkedIn, Facebook and South Suburban Newspaper files. "This is his photo."

The grainy image, taken by a telephoto lens from a distance, showed a man getting out of an automobile in a parking lot. He wore a flannel shirt and sunglasses. The left side profile was clearly visible.

"Who does that resemble?" The general muttered, replacing the mug.

"A Hollywood man."

"Yes, yes, an actor."

"Steve McQueen," the captain offered.

Both the general and Anatoly gave the young officer a dismissive look.

"His name?"

"Rice. His name is Richard Rice."

"Richard Rice. Richard Rice," the general muttered through clenched teeth. "What are we doing, Anatoly?"

The tall man let out a long breath. "What we are doing is not for the known world. I am having the embassy demand the return of Nikolai's body. The Americans are dragging their feet."

"Why? It is to their benefit to return Nikolai quickly and quietly."

"I agree. But they are examining the body, wondering if the newspaper writer should be tried for murder."

"Astounding," the general laughed, clapping. "The Americans seem intent on eating their own child."

"You recall the CIA Operative we killed in Kiev? Then we flew the body to Washington and planted it in his own bed."

"Yes, and when the wife came home, she thought he slept. But he never woke, and she realized he was dead."

"The wife was tried for murder."

"And let loose only when they found dry ice burns on his arms."

Anatoly glanced out the door of the office. "But now—now, we are accountants. Fancy bear accountants. We kill by computer."

"Find my daughter, Anatoly. If she is alive, bring her to me." The general leaned toward the onscreen image of Richard Rice. He grunted with a disdain as cold as the frost on the window glass. "And this writer...I will take care of him."

Two men wearing red foul-weather gear, offshore bibs, rubber boots and jackets worked feverishly to keep the long go-fast boat upright and pointed into the quickly rolling Lake Michigan swells. Rain, wind and spray came out of the night and lashed the deck as they plied the long paddles over the gunwales. The pointed bow climbed a high swell and then teetered amidships, crashing down into a deep trough between waves. After this, the boat was shut down and dark. Running lights, engine and all electrics had been turned off. They had powered into the white squall and gone black.

The sound of a woman moaning came from the bow cabin.

Water splashed left and right across the deck.

Smoke billowed out of the aft engine compartment.

"Shut the woman up, Mikhail," said a slight young man with a slender, bright face and long, wet black hair.

"We have to get through the storm."

An FBI helicopter trailing them had been forced to break off when the gust of the sudden white squall made flying unsafe. But the FBI boat had followed them into the storm. It was battling the waves not far behind.

The intensity of the wind and water threw the fiberglass go-fast boat up in the air, and it came crashing down into the waves.

To the left glowed the lights of Green Bay and surrounding towns. The two worked the paddles, keeping the long boat pointed into the waves.

Both men, tethered to the rails, held on as the boat went almost vertical and then dove to the bottom between two waves. Water crashed on the bow and washed over the boat. Up, up and then down fast they went, again and again.

A mile back, in the blackness after the wall of rain, red, green and white running lights zigzagged, trying to pick up the trail of the go-fast boat.

The moaning from the cabin grew louder.

“Can they see us?” One yelled into the ear of the other.

“I do not know, Alexi,” replied Mikhail, a stocky middle-aged man with close-cropped hair and a harsh, scarred face.

They looked back at the top of a swell.

“I don’t see their lights.” Alexi sounded anxious.

“Keep us pointed into the waves.”

They worked the long paddles for more than two hours, and the rain and white squall passed. Exhausted, they stowed the paddles and collapsed to the deck. Water sloshed about them. Smoke stopped coming out of the engine compartment.

The groaning from the cabin had become quieter.

“Have we lost them?”

“I think so.” Mikhail breathed hard. “You go down and see about the woman. I will power up.”

Alexi struggled to his feet, unhooking the tether. Crouching, he went hand over hand, battling the rolling of the boat. He made his way to the cabin door. Feeling his way down the short stairs, he stepped into ankle-deep water in the cabin.

“Mikhail?” he hissed. “Can I turn on the lights?”

In the darkness, she made a low, agonized sound.

"Shut the door."

Alexi reached back and pushed the cabin door closed. He found the light switch. The overhead light flickered a moment. He rubbed his eyes, adjusting to the brightness.

She had fallen off the leather seat and was lying in reddish water that flooded the cabin. Her wet orange hair stuck to her round head. She wore a cowboy boot on one foot and wool sock on the other. The front of her tan wool sweater had a single hole in a red blot between her shoulder and neck.

The bloody water confused Alexi. The wound seemed so small. He put his hands under the woman's shoulders to lift her. Then he recoiled and shivered. It felt like he had put his left hand in raw meat. Gritting his teeth, he heaved the small woman onto the leather seat.

She screamed.

Turning her sideways, Alexi saw the back of her shoulder. The bullet's exit wound was a mess of sharp gray bone and flesh surrounded by a large tattered circle of sweater. He lifted a cushion, pulled out a white metal first-aid kit and cut away her sweater and bra strap. Near as he could tell, it had gone in clean but then tumbled, coming out sideways through her shoulder. There wasn't much Alexi could do. He tore open a large bandage packet and placed it over the bloody area.

"How is she?" Mikhail called from the deck.

"Is bad," Alexi shouted, winding gauze about her neck and shoulder. "She needs a doctor."

"We're meeting someone at Anderson Point with petrol and a doctor. Shut the light, I'm coming down."

Alexi reached over, swiping off the switch. He continued to bandage her in the darkness.

Mikhail stepped down into the water. He closed the door and turned on the light. He pinched his eyes together until he could see. A look of horror crossed his face. "You must keep her alive. Do you know who this is?"

"No."

"Nicky's mother."

"The one they call Suka?" Panic made Alexi's voice crack.

"Yes, Suka Franko."

"If she dies, we're dead."

"You think I want *Bratva* after me?" Mikhail beat the sides of his head with the palms of his hands. "It's not just *Bratva*. You know who her father is?"

"No."

"He is ex-KGB, now FSB General Ivan Franko."

Alexi stopped bandaging. In the quiet, all that could be heard was the two men breathing.

"You bandage and stop the bleeding. I will get us under way," Mikhail said, coming to his senses.

"Did we lose the trailing boat?"

"I think so. I don't see lights."

"American FBI or *Russki Bratva*, we have trouble, my friend."

As if to underline their dire circumstances, Suka moaned.

With no concern for the light, Mikhail went back up to the deck, slamming the cabin door.

Alexi tied off the gauze. He closed and secured the first-aid kit. From an overhead cabinet, he pulled down a dry blanket, wrapping Suka and tying her securely to the leather seat.

The electric starter ground, but the engine didn't catch. Mikhail pressed the red button again, and the engine caught with a throaty growl. It idled a moment as Mikhail switched on the bilge pump.

Alexi snapped off the light and climbed to the deck. The rain and wind had passed. A star-flung deep blue sky lay ahead. Smoke seeped out the engine compartment.

"Hold on," Mikhail yelled over the engine noise.

Alexi grabbed for the hand rail.

When Mikhail pushed the lever forward, the boat lurched, bumping and splashing through the small waves. They kept the Door Peninsula to the left and within sight as they raced north. They passed Pilot Island Lighthouse.

Dead ahead, Alexi spotted a white ship playing its searchlight along the shoreline and shallows. He pointed, but Mikhail had seen it also.

"It's a Coast Guard Cutter." Mikhail throttled back and shut off the engine. "They must have come from Sturgeon Bay."

"What they look for?" wondered Alexi.

"Us, you fool."

Out in the shipping lanes, a long low-in-the-water lake freighter with a load of iron ore chugged south. The Coast Guard Cutter switched off its search light and came about, heading toward the freighter. The wake rocked the fiberglass speed boat and made it wallow.

Mikhail quickly started the engine and accelerated.

"Keep your eye on him, Alexi. If they see us, we will run for Escanaba, beach the boat and try to get away."

Alexi watched as the Coast Guard Cutter continued out to the freighter. Soon, they were past it.

"We're close," Mikhail shouted over the wind and engine noise. "Take the wheel."

Alexi stepped over as Mikhail moved back. He pulled out his mobile phone and pressed the power button. The screen lit up. He scrolled, tapped a number and put the phone to his ear.

"We are a half-hour out. You have a doctor?" He clicked off and dropped the phone in his pocket.

Mikhail crouched at the cabin door. "I don't hear her."

"Maybe she's dead," Alexi replied. Both men exchanged a look of fear.

A land mass slipped past to the left. On it were scattered house lights and a lighthouse with a weak, rotating light.

"That should be Washington Island. Pottawattamie Light," Mikhail remarked. "Next is St. Martin, then Summer Island."

Alexi slowed to one-third speed.

"See the darker water? That's the channel."

Alexi hauled the steering wheel to the left, easing off the throttle. The boat seemed to slip sideways.

"Slow, slow. This is Anderson Point. Stay in the dark water. There are sandbars."

Land loomed ahead as they weaved left and right, avoiding the bars. A light suddenly blinked from the shore.

"Turn." Mikhail hissed. "Here."

Alexi eased the boat toward shore.

"Cut engine."

He obeyed, and the aft end rose, pushing the boat toward the sound of waves on a beach.

"Grigori?" The voice came out of the dark.

"Zakhar?

A dark figure stood knee deep in the surf. The man grabbed the boat and guided it toward shore. "Mikhail? Where Grigori?"

"Dead. Killed on the dock. Did you bring doctor?"

"I have someone."

The bow scraped the sandy bottom.

"You have Suka?"

"Yes. She is hurt bad."

Zakhar took the bow rope and splashed to the beach, pulling the boat to shore.

Mikhail and Alexi went down to the cabin. The bilge pump had taken out the water, except for small, bloody puddles. Suka lay silent, wrapped in the blanket. Alexi put his ear to her mouth.

"Tell me she's alive."

"Shush."

"We'll never see home again."

"Will you shush?" Alexi straightened and looked down at Suka. "She's bad. But she still breathes."

They carried Suka up the cabin steps and laid her on the deck. She moved her head and groaned.

"Zakhar?"

"I am here."

They picked up Suka and eased the bundle feet first over the railing.

"I have her."

Both men jumped off the boat into the surf. They lowered her and, splashing, carried her to the beach. A black Cadillac Escalade with its hatch raised and interior light on was backed up to the beach. Inside were five ten-gallon gas cans. Zakhar pulled cans from the back, making room for Mikhail and Alexi to lay Suka down.

The side door opened, and a wide-shouldered man in a black tracksuit backed out, holding a gun on someone inside. Mikhail looked over.

"What is this?"

"Your doctor."

After the gunman, out climbed an older gray-haired woman in a heavy down coat. She pulled a backpack from inside the Escalade. "I told you, I'm not a doctor," she protested.

"Shut mouth." The man with the gun nudged her around to the back.

"I'm a nurse. There's only so much I can do."

Mikhail stood, hands on hips. He looked at Zakhar. "If she dies, we're dead men."

"You think I don't know this? Get the gas cans out, and let the nurse in."

The nurse, urged by the muzzle of the gun, got in. "You shoot me, you got no chance. What are you boys, Russian terrorists?"

"No, bank robbers," Alexi said, grabbing two gas cans and hustling down to the beach.

The others looked after him incredulously.

"We'll pay you."

"Not if you robbed a bank." The nurse unwrapped the blanket. She lifted one of Suka's eyelids and then pressed two fingers on the inside of her wrist. "Okay, she's a mess. Look, I'll try and stabilize her. But then you take me back to the clinic." She slipped on purple rubber gloves and cut away the bloody bandage from Suka's shoulder.

"She was shot." Zakhar said.

"No shit, Al Capone."

Alexi and Mikhail scuttled back with fuel cans. Then Alexi stayed aboard and began filling the tank.

"She going to live?" the man with the gun asked as the nurse cleaned and began dressing the wound.

"Her pupils are dilated. Her breath is shallow, and her pulse is high. She's in deep shock." With scissors, the nurse cut white tape and secured the dressing. "Near as I can tell, the bullet shattered her clavicle and rattled around, busting out her scapula. Hope she's not left-handed. She's lost a helluva lot of blood. But you're lucky, it missed some major arteries." From her backpack, the nurse pulled out a tube and a plastic packet filled with clear fluid. She unwrapped a long needle from a sterile package, swabbed an area on Suka's arm and jabbed the needle in. She connected the tube and secured it with tape. "You boys need to get her to a hospital pronto." She secured the IV packet on Suka's chest and rewrapped her in the blanket.

"You no worry. We do."

Zakhar lounged against the back of the Escalade, watching the nurse. Mikhail approached.

"So what do we do now?"

"You take Suka and—"

"You can bring her to the clinic," the nurse interrupted.

"Not your problem, woman," Zakhar shouted.

The man with the gun straightened, edging forward.

"Okay. Just take me back."

"Yeah. Yeah." Zakhar put a hand on Mikhail's shoulder, leading him away and walking a few steps toward the beach. "You continue hugging shore, going east. After the

Straits of Mackinac, steer true north to St. Ignace and Horseshoe Bay."

Mikhail listened, nodding.

Zakhar went on. "Once you near St. Martin Bay, there are two islands. Between the islands, a freighter waits. Is a saltie named *Alexander Pushkin*, out of Rotterdam. Approach on port side. Flash a light. A light will answer." Zakhar studied Mikhail a long moment. "You shake your head, but do you get it?"

"I get it. I get it."

The nurse climbed out of the back of the Escalade. The man took a step nearer, aiming his gun. She moved the gun aside, removing her gloves. "Quit aiming that thing at me." She pushed the gun away again. "I'm not going to give you any trouble."

Zakhar, with Mikhail following, went to the back of the Escalade. "We take Suka now."

"She'll be okay for a couple of hours." The nurse pulled the drawstring on her backpack. "You ought to leave her here. We could treat her at the clinic."

"You no worry about that."

Mikhail and Zakhar struggled carrying Suka down to the beach. She moaned.

"Alexi?"

"I'm here, Mikhail."

"We need your help."

The boat rocked slightly in the waves, but the men managed to raise her, get her aboard and take her down to the cabin. On deck, the two Russians stood catching their breath. Alexi went aft to the open engine compartment.

"You know what to do?" Zakhar pointed into Mikhail's face.

"I know."

"Keep your lights off," Zakhar added, looping his legs over the gunwale and splashing into the surf. "Coast Guard have small station at St. Ignace." He coiled the rope, threw it in and went to the front of the boat.

"Did you fix engine?"

"There's a bullet hole in twelfth cylinder." Alexi shut and clamped the engine compartment. "It spit fuel on the block and exhaust pipe, making smoke. But I put bolt in the hole."

"Is okay?"

Alexi rocked his head from side to side. "I think."

From the bow, Zakhar pushed the boat away from the beach.

A flash lit the shore, and a single shot reverberated over the water.

Alexi looked to shore and then to Mikhail. His big eyes gleamed in the stray light. Mikhail responded with an angry expression.

"Shut up, Alexi." He turned and punched the starter button with his thumb.

All during the night, Mikhail and Alexi traded the wheel as they sped through calm waters between the shore and the shipping lanes. Nearing exhaustion, they ran for hours, slowing only through the navigation channel in the Straits of Mackinac and under the bridge.

A thin band of gray light stretched across the eastern horizon as they entered St. Martin Bay. In the distance, Mikhail spotted the silhouette of a ship. They neared and saw small white lights fore and aft, with scattered lights on deck. As they approached the back of the freighter, they read its faded white lettering: *Alexander Pushkin, Rotterdam.* The bulk freighter, made for hard cargo, sat high in the water, looming many stories above. It had to be at least the length of three football pitches. Mikhail took the wheel of the go-fast boat and veered to the port side. He throttled back and drew close to the faded red and black hull of the freighter. From inside, they could hear the low rumble of engines.

"Get the light." Mikhail's voice echoed off the hull and water.

From a compartment, Alexi took out a long-handled mag light. He banged it against his palm to get it to work, aimed it up at the deck and clicked it on and off, over and over.

No response.

"Keep flashing."

Shadows gathered at the ship's railing above.

A light flashed. A rope came down. Mikhail cut the engine. Alexi grabbed the dangling rope. A motor sounded above, lowering a dinghy from the deck.

"Put the woman in the dinghy," a megaphone squawked.

Alexi tied the rope to a cleat and followed Mikhail down into the cabin. Suka could be heard breathing with a rasp. They carried her up and laid her on the deck.

The go-fast boat bounced up and down, banging against the heavy steel hull of the freighter. The dinghy hovered over the stern.

"Put the woman in the dinghy," the megaphone voice repeated.

"What about us?"

"You'll be taken care of."

The two men timed the up and down of the go-fast boat and the sway of the dinghy, placing Suka's body inside as soon as they got a chance. The deck motor immediately began raising the small boat. Alexi grabbed the cable and started to climb aboard. The motor stopped.

"Just the woman!" the megaphone barked.

The young man jumped back to the deck, and the motor started drawing the dinghy up.

Turbines loudly whined within the large freighter. The hull shuddered as the twin screws in back began to churn up the water. The dinghy swung over the railing. More dark figures gathered at the railing. The freighter moved.

"Hey!"

"What about us?"

The rope, cut from above, fell down to the boat.

Flashes lit up the shadows along the deck above. Automatic weapons ripped and popped. Bullets thumped into the fiberglass boat.

"Start the engine," Mikhail yelled.

But Alexi lay in a wet heap at the cabin steps.

Mikhail made a grab for the gunwale to vault over the side. He shook and shivered as bullets walked up his back and spurts of red blood spit out his back. A ball of yellow fire exploded around him. His face melted as his flesh burned. And then the lake took him down to the dark under the waves. He coughed. Cold water filled his mouth and lungs. He struggled and then went still.

His body bobbed to the surface. An open, unblinking eye stared at the heavy freighter as it lumbered toward dawn, leaving in its wake a sinking, burning wreck.

CHAPTER 3

A sad relic from the Eisenhower era, the four-story Roman L. Hruska Federal Courthouse stood like a sarcastic reminder of utilitarian architecture. With its cement, tinted glass and geometric block design done up in sooty slate over a parking garage, the building blighted South Eighteenth Street Plaza, west of downtown.

Rich steered his truck into the first-floor garage. Parking, he took his gray suit jacket from the hook over a side window. He tugged the cuffs of his white shirt out of the jacket's sleeves and wiggled the knot of his blue tie in the wing mirror. A manila folder, about two inches thick with papers, lay on the console. In his pocket were two thumb drives, additional evidence in his defense. Rich hefted the folder and then closed and locked the truck. It beeped as he pressed the button on his key fob. He paused, taking a deep breath and letting it out. "What the hell," he muttered as he shouldered open the heavy steel door and scuffed up the concrete stairs.

The main floor had a makeshift partition of fake wood paneling and two center screening stations. The stations were manned by a trio of U. S. Marshals. A number of people milled about on the other side of security.

"Afternoon, sir. May I inquire the reason for your appearance today?" The young marshal sounded straight out of the army.

"I'm appearing before the grand jury."

"You have a subpoena, sir?"

"Yes."

"May I see it?"

Rich opened the folder and took out the envelope with the subpoena.

"Would you take it out of the envelope, please?"

He put down the folder on a stainless steel table that separated the screening stations and pulled out the subpoena.

"And your identification as well."

Rich slipped his driver's license from his wallet and handed subpoena and license to the marshal.

The marshal looked over the subpoena and held up Rich's identification. "Would you remove your sunglasses, please?"

Rich did so.

"Seems in order. Please put the papers in one tub and the contents of your pockets in another." The marshal pointed to a stack of gray plastic tubs.

Rich put the folders in one tub and then emptied his pockets in another. He pushed them forward on a rolling conveyor through an X-ray machine.

"I also have a concealed carry."

This got the attention of a third marshal, who stepped forward, his hand on the butt of his sidearm.

"You'll have to surrender that, sir."

"I understand." Rich unclipped his holster and .32 from his belt.

"In a tray, sir."

Rich complied. He raised his hands and stepped through the screener. It beeped.

"Stand to the side, sir." The marshal waved a metal detecting wand around Rich. The third marshal stood back and watched, his hand on his sidearm. The wand beeped at Rich's waist.

"Open your jacket." It was just the tie clip. The marshal jerked his head to the side. "Thank you, sir. We will return your concealed carry when you conclude your business with the grand jury."

Rich put his keys, wallet, loose change and thumb drives back into his pockets. He picked up the folder. "Thank you."

The wide hallway of the courthouse had wood veneer walls, gray mottled marble and raised metal lettering above the courtrooms. The tan carpet had a pattern that could have been Joan Miro's bored doodles.

He spotted a young man standing just to the side of the hall's center. The man wore a blue tab collar dress shirt under a black four-button suit jacket. He had disdained the full suit, opting for black Levi 501s and desert boots.

"Mr. Rice?" He sidestepped into Rich's path.

Coming up short, Rich studied the man's smallish features. He had a cruel mouth and reckless eyes. "What do you want?"

"My name is Tom Crockett, from the *World-Herald.*"

"I've nothing to say."

"Just a couple of questions."

"No."

"You're a newspaper man, you know the drill."

"Sure I do." Rich eyed him. "Where's the tape recorder?"

"Excuse me?"

"Come on, show me."

Crockett lifted a narrow digital recorder from his breast pocket.

"If you're worth a shit, it's already running."

"I'm worth a shit."

Rich nodded. "Okay ... I'm testifying on the shootout at The Ordinary. This was self-defense. They came after me. I defended myself. I was told I am not the target of this grand jury." He stared at Crockett.

"That should be enough." The reporter clicked off the recorder. "Thanks. I saw your stories about Russian Mafia's human trafficking and prostitution on the Tribune wire. They were good."

"Thanks, brother." Rich started to leave, adding, "I'll give you an exclusive interview if they throw my ass in jail."

"You won't look good in orange." Crockett called after him.

The grand jury hearing room was at the end of the hallway. Benches between potted palms were set along the hall's windows. On a bench outside the hearing room sat Borodavka, reading over notes on a yellow notepad. A stack of folders were piled at his feet. The large man noticed Rich approach.

"Mr. Rice," he said, hand out, flashing the gaps in his smile. "Nice-looking suit."

"Thanks, Doug."

"Didn't know you had a suit."

"Every man should have at least two suits. Black and gray. One for marrying. The other for burying."

"Indeed. All a man needs." Borodavka patted a hairy hand on the folders. "Right here, I have thirteen folders with your deposition, your wife's deposition and statements from Lieutenant Lavender and Sergeant Terry Washington, Glencoe Public Safety. I've included screen prints from the surveillance cameras showing Nikolai Franko, Dedmon, Yuri Grimansky and what looks like someone's young daughter entering The Ordinary on the day of the shootout. There are screen prints during the shootout inside. You can see police arriving, setting up a perimeter and all that. I know you wanted me to include a screen print of you coming out. I didn't think it prudent. You have a rifle in your hand. That wouldn't help you."

"What about these thumb drives?" Rich held out his hand with the two drives in his palm.

"Here, I'll take them. I think we have all that." Rich spilled the drives into Borodavka's puffy hand. "I'm not sure we'll need them. Can't hurt. Once the bailiff calls you, I'll have her take these in and give them to the prosecutor. And if that folder you're carrying has the same info, you won't need to take it with you."

Rich put the folder on the bench next to his lawyer and then thrust his hands into his pockets and looked around, nervous.

"You'll be all right. I'll be out here during your testimony. If you get stumped or don't want to answer a question, you are allowed to ask for a brief recess to come out and talk to me."

Rich nodded. A middle-aged woman wearing a drawn and worried expression sat on the next bench. She was dressed in a plain brown pantsuit and clutched her purse tightly to her waist. Her hair needed a brush. She stared forward and down at the tan carpet.

"Lieutenant Lavender's wife," Borodavka whispered.

Two men sat on another bench. One was thin and wore a long black leather coat over a flat collar shirt. He had a pockmarked complexion and long oily black hair, neatly parted toward the right and combed side to side. The other was stocky and had close-cropped bottle-blond hair. His face looked as hard as a roughhewn plank. He sat bolt upright and, like his companion, watched Rich with cunning eyes.

Borodavka glanced from Rich to the two men. "They've been here since the morning," he said under his breath. "Russians."

"I figured," Rich murmured.

"Not sure if they're from the consul or not."

"Leather coat isn't. He looks like *Bratva.* The other one's maybe FSB." Rich smiled and waved.

They turned away.

"Lavender is in there now." Borodavka nodded toward the closed double doors of the grand jury hearing room.

"How long has he been testifying?"

"Nearly an hour." Borodavka slapped his thigh as if just remembering. "I've been trying to get the transcript of your FBI interrogation after the shooting, but they won't let go. It's in that black hole called 'an ongoing investigation'. You neglected to tell me you know Paul Bertoloni."

"Bertoloni? Yeah, I know him. Why?"

"I've known Paulie since he was a little leaguer." Borodavka smiled, folded his hands over his protruding belly and leaned back. "Ah, the Grover Little League."

"Paulie?"

The lawyer's wet eyes dreamily rolled up as if happily reminiscing about bygone summer days of baseball and glory.

Rich frowned. He was not in the mood. "Bertoloni's FBI. Young and ambitious. He's on the other side. What's that got to do with us?"

"He can be an ally."

"I don't know if I totally trust him."

Just then, the doors opened, and a bailiff came out. She was an older black woman with a mane of thick hair tied in the back and barrel of a body on two skinny legs. She wore her brown uniform tight, hugging her rolls and roundness. She held the door open, and Lieutenant Lavender rolled out in a wheelchair. He appeared physically spent.

The woman on the bench stood.

Rich walked over and met Lavender. "Lieutenant. It is good to see you."

He gave Rich a breathy smile. "Keeper, and you."

Rich leaned over and put his hand over Lavender's right hand, which sat on the armrest. He gave it a squeeze. "How's the prognosis?"

"A couple more months in this chair. Then I start rehab to see if I can walk again."

"You get away from him." Mrs. Lavender all but shrieked, coming up behind her husband's chair. Her voice cracked with emotion. "This is all your fault. You're responsible for him being crippled."

"Mary, stop." Lavender tried to catch his breath.

"Mrs. Lavender, I am very ..." Rich straightened.

"Just stay away from us. It's your fault he's like this."

"No, Mary, it's not his ..."

She jerked the chair back, a vicious look on her face.

"Mrs...."

"Keep away from us." She wheeled the lieutenant away.

Rich watched them go down the hallway. He turned and went back to Borodavka. Out of the corner of his eye, he saw the Russians snickering.

"Maybe I should've warned you about that," the lawyer said. "She gave me the death stare when I got here."

The bailiff came up behind Rich. "Mr. Rice?"

"Yes?"

"We'll be ready for you in about ten minutes."

"Okay."

"Bailiff?" said Borodavka. "Would you please take these in when my client testifies?"

She saw the stack of defense packets. "I ain't carrying those."

"I'll help," Rich said.

"I called the prosecutor's office, and they are aware we're supplying these."

The bailiff cocked a hip and cast flinty eyes at the stack, then at Rich, then at Borodavka.

The lawyer offered a gap-tooth smile.

She pulled her head back with an expression like something smelled bad. "Okay, okay, you don't need to be giving me that nasty-ass grin. I'll be back in a few, and we'll carry them in." She returned to the courtroom. The door closed with a loud click.

"May I see one?" The leather-clad Russian stood at Rich's shoulder.

Rich gave him a sidelong glance. "Not on your life."

"Whoa." The Russian's hands went up. "Shouldn't be talking about lives." He smirked. "Have it your way." He ambled back to the bench with the other Russian.

Rich paced, his head down, brows pulled together and mouth tensed. Borodavka watched him pass, then re-pass. "Mr. Rice?"

He didn't hear.

"Rich?" the lawyer said again, a little louder.

No response.

"Stop it." Borodavka reached out and grabbed Rich's sleeve.

"What?"

"You're going to be all right."

"I wish I could believe you."

"I understand you're nervous about testifying. But believe me. You will be all right."

"The law's on my side?"

Borodavka smiled, and his belly shook with a chuckle. "The law is a fickle girl. She's got memory and smarticles. She's supposed to defend the weak."

"If you made that up to reassure me…it didn't."

"One thing, Rich. Juries rarely indict someone they like."

"Mr. Richard Rice?" The bailiff called from the courtroom door. "We're ready for you now."

The two Russians rose and started for the courtroom. The bailiff gave them a cross look. "Just Mr. Rice."

"We come too," the hard Russian said.

The bailiff's hand went up. "Oh no, you don't."

"Why that?"

"These are closed proceedings, Boris."

"I not understand. America is land of free."

"And you're free to go, so get your ass out of here."

The Russians relented and slouched back to the bench. "My name not Boris. Why she call me Boris?"

Rich hefted two thirds of the folders and started across the hall.

"Bailiff?" Borodavka waved his hand, pointing to the remaining pile of folders.

The bailiff let her head fall back. "Okay. Okay."

Rich held the door with his foot as the bailiff went and picked up the folders.

"Thanks," she said, going through the open door. "Follow me."

Rich trailed behind her, entering the large and brightly lit courtroom.

He was met by the usual blonde wood veneer courtroom setting of gallery seats and a low partition separating spectators from the open court. Here, however, there was only one spectator. There was a large jury box on one side, and a judge's bench towered along the back wall. But there was no judge. In the jury box, groups of people stood and casually talked in low tones. Two attorney's tables fronted the short wall. The table to the left had empty chairs and nothing on it; the opposite table had papers and folders and three people about it, one seated and two standing. A woman sat at a small table with recording equipment. She stared off into the distance, waiting. Sound was muted, and the whole room smelled of furniture polish and carpet cleaner. Rich's attention fixed on a single straight-back blonde wood chair with armrests. It sat in the middle of the floor below the judge's high bench.

Such a familiar setting, yet it was eerie. No judge presided from the bench above. No defense team sat at the other table. And the one person sitting in the gallery—FBI Agent Paul Bertoloni. He lounged in a padded chair in the far corner and greeted Rich with a closed smile and upraised eyebrows.

"Put those on the table." The bailiff held open the gate with her hip.

A tall, extremely well-dressed man with a shaved head turned from the woman with whom he was talking. His three-piece tailored blue-striped suit must've cost a lavish sum. He had an icy bearing and ruined any chance at being good-looking with his chiseled scowl. He fixed the bailiff with a chilly gaze.

"What's all this, Bailiff?"

"I dunno." She dropped her stack with a thud on the table, among folders and notepads. "Came from his lawyer." She jerked her thumb toward Rich.

"You are Mr. Rice?"

"Yeah." Rich placed his pile of folders on the table.

"What the hell are these?"

"They're defense packets." The tall man's tone got Rich's back up. "My lawyer informed the district attorney's office we would be supplying them."

"And your lawyer is ...?"

"Douglas Borodavka."

"Oh, Christ," he mumbled. "I don't have to take these."

Rich stood as tall as the man and regarded him eye to eye. "We know that. My lawyer said the district attorney was a decent guy and would consider it." Rich said this more as a challenge than a statement. They stared at each other a long moment.

"Mr. Rice, it would be a grievous error for you to consider these proceedings as anything less than serious, very serious. Am I clear?"

They held each other's gaze longer. His cologne put a stink like insecticide in Rich's nostrils. Then the lawyer blinked.

"Crystal," Rich finally replied.

The tall man gathered himself. "I am U.S. District Attorney Bernard Nutkis." His introduction sounded more a boast rather than salutation. "We've got a lot of ground to cover, Mr. Rice, and it seems we've started with a stumble." He picked up the top folder and leafed through. "What's in here?"

"Depositions from me, from my wife ..."

"And screenshots of the location and statements." He slapped the folder closed. "We have all this."

"I understand that. I'm just not sure what you have would be helpful to me."

"Okay. We're wasting time. Molly?" The tall man did a half-turn. "Would you and Bill take these folders and distribute them among the jurors?"

A petite woman, her black hair in a tight bun, wearing a black and white female business suit, picked up half the folders. The young man, in white shirt and tie, took those remaining. They crossed to the jury box.

"Would you take a seat, Mr. Rice?" Nutkis indicated the single chair in the well of the courtroom, below the judge's bench.

Rich unbuttoned his suit jacket, sat and looked about. The pit of his stomach quivered. He sat alone, deep in his thoughts and miles away from the swirl of activity in the courtroom. Jurors took the folders and settled into their seats. Things were starting to fall into place. Nutkis bent over the table and arranged papers. The room seemed too bright. Bertoloni leisurely slumped in the back. The bailiff stood by the door. Balanced on the ball of his foot, Rich's right knee bounced double-time. He clutched his knee and rearranged his legs, hoping no one had noticed. He scanned the jurors. They were a blur of faces: white, black, brown, maybe Asian, men and women of all ages. His throat was parched.

The woman and young man returned to the district attorney's table.

"I think we are about ready to begin," Nutkis said loudly, bringing the courtroom to order. "Ladies and gentlemen of the jury, the folders handed to you are what are called 'defense packets'. These were provided by Mr. Rice and his attorney. They contain evidentiary material that Mr. Rice believes will aid in his testimony. You are not required to refer to these materials. However, in an effort to get to the truth of the events pertaining to the activities in question, it might be prudent to give the materials a glance." Nutkis paused. "Oh, and by the way, Mr. Rice, at this point, you are not the target of this grand jury's investigation. You are here to testify on the events of the day so we may determine if the law has been violated. However, you do understand that your status can change?"

"Yes, I do." Rich realized he had the armrests of the chair gripped in fists. He let loose, rubbing his hands together, and tried to relax.

"Jury Foreman, would you swear in the witness?"

A bespectacled mid-twenties black man with a short haircut, who wore a blue and yellow argyle sweater vest over a salmon-colored dress shirt, stood in the corner of the jury box. Rich started to rise.

"You can stay in your chair," the foreman said.

"Do you solemnly swear," he read from a notecard, "that you will not reveal, by your words or conduct, and will keep secret any matter about which you may be interrogated or that you have observed during the proceedings of the grand jury, and that you will answer truthfully the questions asked of you by the grand jury, or under its direction, so help you God?"

"Yes," Rich replied.

"Most people say 'I do'—but yes will suffice," said Nutkis. "Thank you, Foreman." He swung around from behind the table and took two long strides to the center of the courtroom. He held a notepad in his hand. "For the court, would you state your full name?"

"I'm Richard—" Rich froze, panicked. He realized he had nearly rattled off his customary glib greeting: *I'm Richard, Rich, Richie, don't call me Dick, Rice.* That would not have gone over well. He recalled Borodavka's last comment: *Juries rarely indict someone they like.* His breath came shallow. He forced himself to breathe.

"Mr. Rice?" Nutkis tilted his head, eying Rich.

"Sorry. My name is Richard Vere Rice."

"And, Mr. Rice, you are the owner and operator of The Ordinary, a drinking establishment on Vinton at Sixteenth Street in Omaha."

"No and yes."

Nutkis appeared surprised by Rich's response. "Excuse me?"

"No," Rich explained. "I do not own The Ordinary. It is owned by my wife, Gisele, under her maiden name, Gisele Esslin. But yes, I do operate The Ordinary, managing a staff of five people. And I live in the flat over the bar."

"Quite, quite. I misspoke."

Rich mentally clicked one wooden bead to his side of the scoreboard. "Would you like me to explain?"

"For the jury, yes."

"I was living underground and couldn't have my name on anything that might be traceable."

"We may be jumping ahead, but the reason for this is...?"

Rich would let the tall prosecutor lead the dance for this song, but he wasn't going to get cheek to cheek. "This was because I had to leave the Chicago area suddenly, after an assassination attempt."

Nutkis scanned his notepad while pinching his lower lip. "The assassination attempt was in the parking lot of the *Park Forest Daily*. You were working there as a journalist at the time, correct?"

"Yes."

"Who told you to leave Chicago?"

"The shooter was fairly persuasive." A tittering rippled over the jury box. "Actually, it was a guy named Dedmon." Rich ran his hand through his hair. "I can't recall his first name. Anyway, he led me to believe he worked with the Chicago Police. But I just did not trust the guy completely."

"We'll come back to Mr. Dedmon." Nutkis struck a thoughtful pose and took a relaxed amble toward the jury box. "You were wounded in the assassination attempt."

"Yes."

"Were you badly injured?"

"It was an odd kind of wound. I bent forward just as the bullet was fired. It got me in the shoulder." Rich twisted in his seat, tracing with his finger the path of the bullet down his right side. "Then it went down my ribs and came out just above my hip."

"What do you think was the reason for the attempt on your life?"

"I was writing a series of exposes on Russian Mafia activities in human trafficking, drugs and prostitution in the Chicago area."

"What got you started on that?"

"Oh," Rich sighed. "Well." He rubbed the back of his neck. "That's a long story."

Nutkis folded his arms and leaned his hip against the jury box. "We don't have a time limit on your testimony."

"Okay." Rich resettled in his seat. "My editor at the *Park Forest Daily* was Bill More. Good editor. Good guy. I worked late one night, and Bill introduced me to a friend of his from high school—a guy named Mike Smith. Smith was a sad character. His wife had been abducted, raped and brutally murdered. They found her dismembered body in a park in West Des Moines, Iowa."

"Unfortunate," Nutkis muttered, sounding impatient. "How does this figure in the assassination attempt?"

"I warned you it was a long story." Rich smiled, though the joke got no response from the blank faces of the jurors. He looked doubtfully at the district attorney, thinking, *a lawyer never asks a question he doesn't know the answer to.* He continued. "They never found out who did that to

Smith's wife. After a while, the guy tried to get back into life. He attended his high-school reunion. There, he learned of an ex-girlfriend and her younger sister who had been kidnapped and raped by a father, his son and two others. This was when they were in high school, and the girls had never reported the crime. Smith had an inkling that the rapists were his classmates. And he found out that they'd done the same thing to a lot of other girls. He set out to expose them." Rich cleared his throat. "Is there any water, or something to drink?"

"Sure. Molly, would you get Mr. Rice some water?"

The woman at the table poured a glass of water from a pitcher and carried it to Rich.

"Thank you." He took the glass and drank. Refreshed, he started again. "Smith tracked down the father and son. The father was the state superintendent of education, a political bigwig. Smith then was killed under suspicious circumstances. I imagine they thought they were done with anyone uncovering their activities after they killed him. But Smith had left a notebook with my editor, Bill More. When he was killed, Bill looked at the notebook. It was filled with information about all that these guys had done over the years. So I was assigned to investigate and write the whole sordid story." Rich took another drink. The glass shook slightly in his hand. He brought it down from his mouth and held it with two hands on his lap. "Turns out there was a connection between the father and the Russian Mafia in the Chicago area. The Russians were supplying girls for sex parties. The more I looked into it, the deeper I got into the Russians' activities. That's what I wrote about."

"Not to the delight of the Russians, I would venture."

"Of course not. The more I investigated, the more contacts I made inside *Bratva*, which is what they call their mafia. It forced the Chicago cops to get off their butts and kick in some doors on North Shore brothels and other houses of prostitution."

Nutkis pushed off from the jury box and strolled across the courtroom, vaguely focused on a high spot on the opposite wall. He spoke as if thinking out loud. "That, no doubt, sparked the anger of the Russians."

Is he playing dumb? Rich thought. "Yes, it did. Especially angry was Irina Suka Franko, the woman who ran the sex operations for *Bratva* in the Midwest."

"Ah." Nutkis did a slow turn on his heel. "Suka Franko." He pointed to the jurors. "There's a piece of the puzzle we recognize. Go on, Mr. Rice."

"One of Suka's gang was Nikolai Franko, her son. I was later informed that it was Nicky Franko who tried to shoot me in Park Forest."

Nutkis stopped and faced Rich. "So you came to Omaha? Any particular reason?"

"No, none really. I sort of knew the area. My wife stayed on in Glencoe with her ailing mother. I figured she'd be safe since I was the one they wanted. The paper put out a false story claiming I had been critically injured, implying I had died. That's when I went off-the-grid."

"You bought a bar in South Omaha. Why?" Nutkis shrugged like it was the most outlandish thing he had ever heard.

"My wife bought the bar, remember? We thought that I would manage the bar and live upstairs, with nothing under my name. We didn't have enough money for me to just hide out. And if I took a job somewhere, I could be found."

"And by 'off-the-grid', you are referring to becoming anonymous, going by the name 'Keeper'."

"Pretty much." Rich finished the water and placed the glass on the floor to the side. "Everything was cash and burner phones. No one knew my real name. I was Keeper. I trusted no one. Well, other than my wife. All communication on the 'net was over the dark web, using Tor and Telegram. I never believed my communications were safe, even with a new phone every week—not with cell-site simulators and IMSI catchers. I was always on the lookout. Sometimes I wasn't sure if I even existed any more. You walk on the edge of the shadows. This is not a glamorous world; no one would enjoy living in it."

Nutkis tossed his notepad onto the table and sat on the edge. "You must not have felt completely safe. Otherwise, you wouldn't have gotten in contact with the FBI."

"I didn't. I knew they were looking for me."

"They?"

That's another bead on my side, Rich told himself. "The Russians, *Bratva*, Suka Franko, God knows who else." He saw an opening and sliced through. "That's why I started working with the FBI task force."

"Working with?" Nutkis recognized that Rich had played a good bounce.

Bertoloni straightened in his seat in the back.

"Yeah, I was working with the FBI. In many ways, my situation overlapped with the work of their Russian Mafia task force. They wanted to catch Suka doing something more criminal than prostitution. I wanted Suka and Nicky caught and no longer gunning for me."

Some jurors smiled, nodded. A few others scribbled notes.

"How, then, would you characterize your *work* with the FBI?" Nutkis tried to twist all the juice out of the word *work*.

"Agent Bertoloni..." Rich gave a tip of his head to the gallery. "...and I met on numerous occasions. Bertoloni came to The Ordinary to see the setup. Lieutenant Lavender was brought in from Omaha PD, and we shared information."

With each statement, Rich thought he had scored in the game.

"And where is it that you met?"

"The FBI regional office in Omaha."

Nutkis did not like the direct answer. He might have been hoping for some forgetfulness. "So what happened after that?"

"Actually, not much. The Ordinary started doing business. I kept a very low profile. There were frequent Omaha Police drive-bys, and I would check in with the FBI weekly."

"Did the FBI, through Agent Bertoloni, or the Omaha Police, offer you money for your services in their investigation?"

"No money, just protection. But I never asked for money."

"So you couldn't say you were ever in the employ of the FBI or Omaha Police."

"Seriously? No informant wants it known that they are in the employ of the FBI or Omaha PD." Rich glanced over, giving the jurors a comic face. "I did provide critical information, and I worked in concert with the task force's investigation. I acted in a manner indicative of an informant and a part of the FBI's task force." Rich leaned back in the chair. This was a statement that Borodavka had urged him to somehow weave into his testimony.

Nutkis went to the table, leaned over some papers, leafing through and reading. He put his finger on something. "But you weren't totally forthcoming with information, were you?"

"What do you mean?" Rich feigned ignorance, but he knew the reason behind the DA's question.

"I mean, the FBI requested certain information in your possession that you refused to provide."

"If you're referring to my sources for the news stories on the Russians, as a journalist, I am not giving up my sources."

Nutkis stood tall behind the attorney's table. He tugged the bottom of his blue pin-striped vest and turned up the volume. "You wouldn't cooperate, and yet, you expected the full protection of law enforcement."

Rich raised his tone and slowed the cadence to emphasize each word.. "I gave them more information and more leads than they had before. How long would they have protected me once I no longer had information they wanted? Besides, I had a feeling all along that Bertoloni and the FBI were just waiting for the Russians to find me. I was being used, like bait in a trap."

The prosecutor had no follow-up. Silence fell over the courtroom. Rich gazed around. Some of the jurors tilted their heads together, sharing whispers.

"Give us a moment." Nutkis sat, conferring with the other two at the table.

Rich got up and refilled his glass from the water pitcher.

"Okay, Mr. Rice, if you would be seated."

As Rich sat, Nutkis rose.

"If need be, we can debate the previous point at a later date. Going back to our timeline—once The Ordinary opened, things calmed down."

"Yes." Rich placed the glass on the floor and folded his hands together, waiting on more questions.

"Did you believe things had blown over?"

"Sort of, but I knew it was too soon. I did think I was the least of the Russians' worries."

"So what changed?"

Rich clenched his teeth and pulled his lips tight. He dropped his head.

"Answer, please."

"I made a mistake," he replied quietly.

A slight smile spoiled Nutkis' scowling face. He walked up, confronting Rich.

"A mistake?" The tall man looked like he thought the advantage had shifted. "Such a cautious man as you, a mistake? What did you do?"

Rich turned in his chair, facing the jurors in the box. He assayed each face, making eye contact with each of them as he answered.

"I had been on the run for months and months. I'm not ashamed to say I was frightened and lonely. I had not seen my wife in all that time. I am sure the members of the jury can understand what a terrible time it was for me."

Nutkis' arms went to his hips, realizing his play had been intercepted.

"I thought maybe the Russians had forgotten about me. I set up a meeting with my wife in Dubuque, Iowa."

"And that was a mistake?"

"I didn't know they were staking out my wife at her mother's house in Glencoe. Nicky Franko and Yuri Grimansky followed her as she drove out from Chicago," Rich continued, answering to the jury.

"How come they didn't shoot you then?"

"Not for want of trying. They did take a couple of shots at us—the last day we were there. We got away. I think they didn't know what I was driving. When Gisele and I split up, Nicky and Yuri followed her car, thinking I might be with her."

"You were in the clear?"

"I knew it was temporary."

"How is it than that they found you in Omaha?

"They got a letter my wife sent me."

"It had your Omaha address?"

"Yes, it did."

"Were you aware of this?"

"I had a pretty good idea. It smelled like Nicky Franko's work. Someone inserted an envelope in my wife's letter. The envelope had a torn 100-ruble note. Then, the following day, I got a priority letter with a torn copy of the newspaper story, the one that said I had been critically injured in an assassination attempt."

"And they showed up?"

"Not until the day after that."

"Perhaps I should have asked sooner, but what is your background in this type of thing. You seem to be comfortable with weapons and handling yourself in dangerous situations."

Rich shrugged. “Well, usual sort of background. I served in the Oregon National Guard with my friend Tom Waller. My father was a veteran, starting out doing special ops in Southeast Asia. In Oregon we camped, hunted, all that sort of thing.”

“Your father was pretty *gung-ho* then.”

“No, he was Airborne, not Marines. And he was pretty vocal in not wanting his son to go through anything like he went through. He had some interesting friends. One guy who was a *LRP*, Long Range Patrol. The stories that guy would tell about going down in *VC* tunnels and setting up a jungle ambush on the NVA was pretty thrilling stuff to a kid.”

“So you grew up with a lot of weapons.”

“Not really. Dad had a healthy respect for weapons. He always said it’s the last tool you reach for, and only after all else has failed. When you pick up a weapon, he told me, you had better be prepared to use it”

“Mr. Rice, I’d like you to hold right there. We are getting into key testimony. It’s closing on three o’clock, and I think we should break for the day. We will reconvene tomorrow at nine. Is that acceptable to you, Mr. Rice?”

“Yeah, I guess.”

“Please be advised these are secret proceedings and are not to be discussed with anyone.” Nutkis showed Rich his back and dismissed him quickly. “Thank you, Mr. Rice.”

Rich stood, stretched and walked through the courtroom, up the aisle in the gallery. Bertoloni had left.

Borodavka sat at the same bench, munching on a sandwich and reading the newspaper. When Rich came out of the courtroom, he glanced up. “I got hungry.”

"What're you eating?"

"A ham sandwich. How'd it go in there?"

"Kind of rough. You were right about the direction the prosecutor wants to take with his questions."

The Russians were gone.

"Were you able to work in the points we discussed?"

"Yeah, I did."

"Are you done?" Borodavka wrapped up the other half of the sandwich, folded the newspaper and put the bundle into his brown leather valise. He raked crumbs out of his beard with his hand and got up.

"No, I have to be back tomorrow at nine."

They started to walk out.

"Think you can give me a ride to my office? I took a cab to get here."

"Sure."

"Wear your black suit tomorrow."

All the way back to The Ordinary, Rich's testimony played over and over in his head. The prosecutor's questions and Rich's responses wound out on an endless loop. He tried to picture the people in the jury box, but they seemed a blur of skeptical faces and accusing eyes, like a painter's smeared canvas. He had gotten in the necessary defense points: that he had provided information to the FBI and participated in the investigation. Borodavka had prepped him well. But was it enough? Nutkis had tried but didn't seem able to discredit Rich's testimony. Meanwhile, Rich had been open and forthright and could only hope the jury appreciated that. There was no science to a jury, and ultimately, it would be they who determined if he would be indicted.

Borodavka had cautioned him not to be too loud or too forceful. "Defense is subtle, not a loud objection. A brief, strong wind bends the tree, but after it passes, the tree stands tall again. Defense is built brick by brick," he had said. "Eventually, all of the bricks become a wall. That wall is solid and reflects the shadow of a doubt."

Borodavka's crazy-ass Zen comments wearied Rich, although they made sense to him. His head ached. He could not believe how physically drained testifying had left him. There was more to come tomorrow. *That's when the shooting starts.*

He opened the back gate with the remote and pulled into the gravel lot behind The Ordinary. Gisele's Accord was parked on one side. Rich shut off his truck and just sat. Tomorrow would be another round of testimony, this one all about the shootout. He started to think of what to say. Slowly, like a marathoner the morning after a race, he climbed out of his truck. Cold autumn air stung his lungs coming in and steamed on the way out. He retrieved the folder from the seat and slung his suit jacket over his shoulder. He slammed the door and paused. His eyes drifted to a small mound of bare dirt by the dumpster. Roommate, his Boston terrier, lay there. He missed that dog.

Rich opened the back door to The Ordinary and stood in the warm kitchen. Jorge's hard work showed here: the place was restored, clean and ready-to-go. Something in the oven smelled good. A vacuum cleaner ran up and back in the pool room. Easy, light music played. Adele, Gisele's choice. In the doorway, he saw Daisy instructing Riku behind the bar. The slender young black woman was putting him through the paces: where was this, how do you pour that, step it up, step it up. *Lessons should not be done with smiles, though*, Rich thought.

Gisele worked at a table in the center of the barroom, alternating between her laptop and papers while talking with Jorge, who was seated next to her.

The vacuum shut off, and Jorge's wife, Carmelita, bent and wound up the cord. Rose, Carmelita's younger sister, came out of the restrooms, a wet rag in one hand, toting a yellow plastic bucket of gray water in the other.

Rich went to the table.

"Richie," Gisele glanced up. "I was getting worried about you."

"*Jefe*."

"I had to take my lawyer back to his office." He slapped the folder on the table, pulled out a chair and laid his suit jacket over the back. "What smells so good in the kitchen?"

"*Ay*, the pizza!" Jorge jumped up.

Rich collapsed into the chair.

Gisele's eyes conveyed concern. "How'd it go?"

"Okay, I guess. This was the first half; the final half is tomorrow."

"Tomorrow?"

"Yeah, we mostly covered the backstory."

"Oh, baby. I'm sorry."

"Ha. Yeah, me too."

Jorge came out of the kitchen with a large round platter. He set it on the corner of the bar. "Pizza, she ready."

"Hungry?" Gisele asked, getting up.

"I suppose. Right now I'm too tired to think and wondering if a handful of aspirin will help."

"Hey, boss," Daisy greeted.

"Keeper," Riku echoed.

Rich nodded.

They gathered around the pizza and slid long triangular slices onto plates.

The remodel of The Ordinary was just about complete. The bar was rebuilt; everything seemed ready for the reopening.

Gisele placed a plate with a single slice of pizza before Rich. He looked at it. "Thanks, Gis."

She sat across from him, watching him while she took a bite. "Jorge and I ..." She yelped, opened her mouth and fanned it with her hand. "It's hot. Well, we've been working on the menu: expanding the old menu, adding more sandwiches and soups, and chili now that it's cold outside."

"I miss it," he said.

"What?"

"Square-cut Chicago pizza. I miss it."

"Oh, me too." Gisele wiped her fingers with a paper napkin. "Anything else happen in court?"

"I can't say much." He heaved a deep sigh. "But I was able to get my points in. I think I did okay. It's not up to me. Everything will come down to what the jury decides."

"Want something to drink, boss?"

"Yeah, Daisy. A Seven Up would do."

"Mrs. Rice?"

"I would like a glass of wine. Cabernet."

"'Mrs. Rice'?" Rich gave Gisele a teasing look.

"They still don't know what to call me." She smiled. "Sometimes I'm *la patrona*, Mrs. Keeper, *jefa*, even Ms. Boss. Mostly it's Mrs. Rice, and even that gets caught their throats."

"They'll loosen up."

"I know. I'm not concerned about it." Gisele hungrily finished off her slice. "I'm pretty sure we can open this Saturday." She keyed up a picture on the laptop and turned it toward Rich. "I've taken out a series of ads in the alternative newspaper. They promised a little write-up and calendar listing. Channel Four said they'd do a piece on the news if we bought an ad running in rotation. I think it's a good deal."

"Sounds okay to me. Did you get leaflets out to Metro Community College? Guess we don't have to keep a low profile anymore."

"Yeah. You didn't hear me, did you? Channel Four wants to do an interview with you."

"No."

"It would be a short thing."

"No."

Daisy came up with Gisele's wine and Rich's soft drink.

"I'm not doing it." He took the glass. "Thanks, Daisy."

"But ..."

"No. You do it, and have everybody else with you."

Gisele said nothing, staring at Rich over the rim of her wine glass. She was clearly perturbed.

Rich picked up his slice, took another small bite and then dropped it on the plate. He had no appetite.

"We can talk about it later," said Gisele.

"We can talk about it forever. I'm not going on camera."

Gisele, with slow and exaggerated movements, set her wine glass down on the table. She seemed to know that she had pushed Rich just a little too far. “I have ideas for adding more special nights, with poetry readings, karaoke, stuff like that.”

He cut her off, pulling himself up. “”I’m going upstairs. I have to be in court at nine tomorrow.”

“Are you all right?”

“No.”

“We were going to knock off in an hour,” Gisele said. “I’ll be up after I lock up.”

“Okay.” Rich’s voice seemed to come from far off. He picked up the folder, took his coat off the chair and walked through the kitchen and out the back. Frigid wind caught him as he climbed up the iron stairs outside. Daylight rushed away from dusk. He unlocked the door to the flat and walked in. He listened for, and was disappointed not to hear, a scramble of claws as Roommate came running up to greet him. Roommate was dead, buried in the back, gone forever. He went through the kitchen and put the folder on the table. The large living room was still, half-lit gray with the diminishing light. He went to the couch and collapsed, staring out the row of windows as the far sky went deeper blue. A yellow glow speckled the western cityscape. The room filled with shadows and brightness as Rich sat parsed between darkness and light.

CHAPTER 4

Rich slipped on his black suit jacket, watching his lawyer maneuver his bulk out of Rich's truck and carefully down its step. "Did you just break a sweat?" he asked.

"What?" Borodavka breathlessly replied. He dragged his brown leather valise out of the truck and loudly hocked phlegm up his windpipe.

Rich turned away toward the parking garage door. He had no desire to know what his lawyer did after clearing his throat.

"Wait up," the big fellow said, waddling to Rich at the door.

People bustled through the lobby of the courthouse, with just a short line waiting at security. The marshals appeared to recognize Rich. His concealed carry didn't faze them as he handed it over. Borodavka beeped, having forgotten to put his loose change in a gray plastic tub. He beeped again. This time, his key ring had registered. He beeped yet one more time, and it was either the metal in his pipe or his belt buckle. With a weary look, the marshals waved him through.

They walked down to the grand jury courtroom. "You'd make a terrible terrorist," Rich told him.

No Russians sat outside.

"We're early." Borodavka dropped his valise with a sigh, and encamped on the bench. He appeared distracted. The district attorney advanced with long strides toward the courtroom. The tall man wore an impeccably tailored gray suit with an iridescent Blue Jay blue tie. Behind him, his assistants hop-stepped to keep up. The scowl kept many people at bay.

"Nutkis!" Borodavka cried out.

Rich spun about. "Are you crazy? That's the prosecutor..."

"Wart," the district attorney cried in reply, his scowl replaced by a wide smile.

They enthusiastically shook hands.

"Is that little Molly?"

The young woman's face flushed.

"It is," Nutkis beamed. "My little litigator."

"Dad! Hello, Mr. Borodavka." Molly wore a simple claret-colored dress highlighted by her jet-black hair.

"It's good to see you, Ms. Nutkis."

She glanced away with a tiny smile.

Rich took a step back from the convivial circle. This serpent's nest of lawyers gave him the creeps.

"We may be losing Molly."

"Private practice?"

"No, nuptials."

"Nuptials? That is wonderful. Congratulations," Borodavka grinned. "Anyone we know?"

Nutkis looked quickly over his shoulder at Rich. "Oh yes, but I am not allowed to say." He added, "Mr. Rice, perhaps you should go into the courtroom."

Rich caught the hint. "With pleasure."

"I will be out here if you need me," Borodavka advised.

Rich entered the empty courtroom. The stenographer busied herself setting up. A few jurors lounged in the jury box, chatting. Rich wasn't sure if he should go sit in the chair below the judge's bench or wait in the gallery to be called. He started down the aisle.

"You don't need to go there yet."

It was Bertoloni, in the same corner seat, last row. Today, he favored a blue suit, white shirt and red-striped tie.

Rich went over and sat, leaving an empty seat between them. "I didn't think they allowed spectators."

"They don't. I'm not really here." He showed a row of white teeth, giving his boyish face an impish quality.

"Did you testify?"

"Already did."

"Saw Lieutenant Lavender yesterday."

"I did too. That's really a shame."

"Shame?"

"I think one of those bullets nicked his spine. I doubt he'll walk again."

"Who else has testified?"

"You know I can't tell you."

"Thought I would try."

"Don't blame you. We did have a Skyped session with Grimansky from the hospital. He was anything but helpful."

Nutkis came striding in and, for a moment, still wore a broad grin. By the second row, he had his courtroom scowl on full display. Molly, trailing him, cast a glance over to the young FBI agent, smiling a smile that said more than just hello. Bertoloni responded with some teeth, but shyly. He suppressed it when Rich gave him a sideways glance.

"Show time." He leaned across and spoke to Rich in a hushed tone. "We need to talk."

"Who? Me and you?"

"No, I'm sorry to tell you—my boss, Special Agent Jejune, and a couple of others."

"You can come by on Thursdays, visiting hours."

Bertoloni chuckled, and his face lit up. "You crack me up. I heard your round-one testimony. You landed some blows but got punched once or twice. Still, I had you on points."

"I'm a rank outsider. This guy bobs and weaves. Punchers luck."

"You got some leather on him. He'll jab, jab, jab. Make him stand and fight. Rumble, young man."

"Why do we need to meet?"

The light dimmed in Bertoloni's expression. "We've got some news on Suka Franko."

"Really?" Rich's eyes narrowed. "She alive?"

"We can't talk here."

"She's not dead."

"I can't say no to that." Bertoloni swayed back. "And there are other players involved."

"*Bratva*? Or ...?"

"Mr. Rice," Nutkis called from the courtroom well. "Would you please take the stand?"

Bertoloni's face went blank. "Bigger."

Rich half-stood and froze. "Bigger?"

"We are waiting, Mr. Rice."

Bertoloni pressed his lips tightly together and nodded.

Dazed a little, Rich made his way to the front of the courtroom.

"If you will be seated." Nutkis twiddled a pen in his hand, reading from a notepad. "May I remind you that you are still under oath?"

Rich unbuttoned his suitcoat and took a seat. He pushed aside Bertoloni's comments and forced a greeting smile toward the jurors, readying himself for the prosecutor's questions. Yesterday, he had been plagued by nerves and apprehension. Today, he had mentally prepared himself to testify.

The black jury foreman, who wore a beige cable knit sweater, was busily shining the lenses of his glasses with a tissue. He examined them for specks against the bright fluorescent lights of the courtroom and then slipped them on, blinking.

A tripod with a large cardboard floorplan diagram of The Ordinary, including the first-floor bar and second-floor flat, had been set up to Rich's left. There were red *X*s and blue *O*s at various points. Rich checked it over, understanding the red marks must indicate the bodies of Dedmon, Nicky Franko and Yuri Grimansky and one other person, while the blue *O*s were he, Tom Waller and Lieutenant Larry Lavender, Omaha Police.

The towering attorney strolled from behind the table. “The jury will recall we adjourned yesterday with Mr. Rice testifying that he received items in the mail that indicated to him elements of the Russian Mafia had discovered his whereabouts in Omaha.” He looked up from the notepad. “Is that accurate, Mr. Rice?”

“Yes. I received a letter from my wife with a torn 100-ruble note. And the next day, I got a priority letter with a copy of the newspaper clipping about the attempt on my life.”

“Did you expect Nicky Franko?”

“After taking a couple of shots at me and my wife, Gisele in Dubuque, I thought he might turn up.”

“What did you do to prepare?”

“I notified FBI Agent Bertoloni.” Rich looked to the agent in the gallery. “And had to leave a voicemail message.” His tone was tinged with sarcasm. “Then I called and spoke with Omaha PD Lieutenant Lavender.”

“Let’s hold on that point and talk for a moment about your personal protection. You have a permit and concealed carry for a Glock 32 and a short-barrel Smith & Wesson .32 caliber.” Nutkis reached for a folder on the table, opened it and read from its contents. “You also own a twelve-gauge shotgun, a Bushmaster semi-automatic and...” Nutkis paused. “And heirlooms?”

Rich squirmed in his chair. “Yeah, heirlooms.”

“What does that mean?”

“I have a 1903 Springfield rifle with scope and a Colt 1911 .45 automatic. These were left to me by my father. He was Airborne and liaised with the French in Indochina. He acted as an advisor in the early days of Vietnam.”

"Indeed. Do you tote this mini-arsenal around with you?"

"No. I wear the .32 on my belt, alternating with the Glock, depending on where I am going and what I'm doing. I wear the .45 in a shoulder holster when I work in The Ordinary. The shotgun is under the bar with a box of shells. The Springfield and Bushmaster are in a gun safe in my flat upstairs."

"So it is safe to say, you're always armed."

"Yes."

"I wanted to step back and review, for the jury, what protection you had. Events will speed up from here, and you will no doubt reference certain weapons."

Nutkis sorted through papers and folders. He pointed to a folder across the table, and his assistant handed it over. "Sorry for the delay. I needed to refer to the FBI interrogation. So, Mr. Rice, you had armed yourself and considered a confrontation with the Russian Mafia imminent. If I may ask, why didn't you just run?"

"It crossed my mind. Honestly though, I was tired of running, hiding, looking over my shoulder, telling lies. It seemed inevitable." Rich paused, studying his hands. "I guess I thought it was time to end it, one way or another."

"The day after you received the news clipping, into The Ordinary walked the Russian Mafia."

"Correct. Lieutenant Lavender happened to be there, responding to my call from the day before."

"And who else was present?"

"Tom Waller and I were behind the bar. Jorge Ruiz was in the kitchen. There were a few customers."

"Who was it, exactly, that entered?"

"Nicky Franko, Yuri Grimansky, Dedmon and some underage girl."

Nutkis went to the tripod display and spoke to the jury. "You may refer to the government's folder, exhibit 21. These are the same as the surveillance camera screenshots provided by the defense, and they are shown here in blowup display."

Some jurors opened folders.

"Where is Dedmon?" Nutkis asked.

"He's the red *X*, by the door."

"And this is?"

"That's Grimansky. The other two are Nicky Franko and the girl."

Nutkis pointed to a blue *O* behind the bar. "This, then, is you?"

"No, that's Tom Waller, then me, and in the corner there is Lieutenant Lavender. He was seated at a table."

"Mr. Rice, did you have any indication that Nicky Franko, or any of the others, was armed?"

"Yuri, the big Russian, wore a long black leather coat. Nicky flashed the butt of a revolver tucked Mexican-style in his belt. Didn't know about Dedmon. And the girl wore nothing more than a skimpy dress. Her weapons were very evident."

A couple of the male jurors snorted in laughter.

"You're saying she was armed?"

"I was making a joke. She wore a short, flimsy dress."

"Please refrain from joking. We are trying to get to the truth." Nutkis' scowl sank deeper into his face. "You were armed. Lieutenant Lavender was armed. Tom Waller was armed."

"No, Tom was not armed, nor was Jorge."

"Assuming Dedmon was also armed, it was three against two. What happened after that?"

"I tried to clear the place. I had Jorge take the customers out the back. I made Nicky send the underage girl out."

"Lavender stayed. Tom Waller stayed."

"Yes," Rich said. Tom had wanted to go, but Rich had asked him to say. He wished now that he had sent him away, but it might be damning to say that. He said nothing, knowing it would live with him the rest of his life. "They didn't know Lavender. He sat in the corner and nonchalantly talked on his mobile phone. He was actually calling Omaha PD. Within five or ten minutes, a couple of prowl cars showed up outside."

"Can we go back? You said Tom Waller was unarmed."

"Yes. I signaled him that I would get him a gun."

"Okay. Then how did it all start?"

Rich took in a deep breath. "We were at a standoff, jawing back and forth." He glanced at the jury. "I had a feeling it might end as a standoff."

"Why did you think that?"

"He, Nicky, knew I would be armed. He probably thought Tom was armed as well. He was mouthy and full of bravado, and those aren't the types you need to worry about in a fight. It was Dedmon and Yuri, who stood there silent—they were my concern. No one had a clear advantage. We were at an impasse."

"This Russian, Nicky Franko, he seemed to hold you in high regard."

"No, I don't think so." Rich tilted his head back, looking at Nutkis. "No, not in the least."

"Your description of the exchange appears to—"

"Appears to what? Have you informed the jury what Nicky Franko did for a living?" Rich counted the sins on his fingers. "Drug trafficking, gambling and extortion are probably the more likeable aspects of Nicky Franko. Make no mistake, he and his mother, Suka, made most of their money trafficking in women and young boys, kidnapping girls—and I mean young girls, twelve years old and younger. They would buy them from other traffickers or snatch them from villages in Eastern Europe, the Middle East or small towns in the United States. They would threaten to kill their families, beat the girls and turn them into prostitutes. They bought and sold human beings like cattle at an auction. And when their looks were gone and their bodies spent and they weren't earning, they would kill them and get another girl for that dirty mattress in the narrow cubicle."

"But you seemed—"

"I looked into Nicky's dead eyes and saw no soul. I knew what he was all about. He was a despicable person, immoral, without an ounce of humanity."

Nutkis struggled with his words. "I believe he respected you."

"No, he didn't. You're mistaking envy for respect. He liked The Ordinary, a bar I built. He wanted it. He had nothing, and he knew it. His life went from one desperate circumstance to another. He saw I wasn't scared to face him." Rich paused and half-smiled. "I had a weapon, and he knew I wouldn't hesitate to use it and end his miserable life."

Nutkis spoke quickly, working to get off this line of questioning. "So how, then, did it blow up?"

"I don't want this to sound like I'm blaming anyone. Lavender saw the Omaha PD cars outside. He miscalculated the scene and the actors. He stood, with his service weapon out, and loudly ordered Nicky, Yuri and Dedmon to put their hands on the bar. I took that chance to toss Tom the .32 while I pulled the shotgun from under the bar."

"They didn't put their hands on the bar, did they?"

"No." Rich looked down and then up. "All hell broke loose. Yuri brought out a black Kalashnikov with no butt stock from under his coat. He shot the hell out of Lieutenant Lavender. I yelled to Tom, telling him to take out Yuri. I put two loads of double-ought steel shot into Dedmon at the door."

"Stop there." Nutkis had his hand up. "Lavender is shot and critically wounded." He pointed to the blue *O* in the corner. "You kill Dedmon." He then pointed to the red *X* at the doorway.

Rich did not like Nutkis' implication. "I shot Dedmon while Tom took a couple of shots at Yuri, hitting him in the shoulder. Yuri then wheeled and unloaded the magazine into Tom, shooting him to death."

"I'm still talking about Dedmon. You killed Dedmon."

"I put the steel shot into him to knock him out of the fight."

"You did more than knock him out of the fight—you killed him. Correct?"

"I shot at him."

"You shot to kill?"

Rich went silent, exhaling through his nose. He knew where Nutkis was headed with his questions.

"Answer the question, Mr. Rice."

"I shot him to even up the odds. I assumed he was armed, like the others."

"You killed him but weren't sure he even carried a weapon?" Nutkis made it sound cold-blooded.

"I shot Dedmon, yes."

"With the sole intent of killing him," Nutkis pressed.

Rich squirmed under the pressure. He had never trusted Dedmon. He was a rogue cop, working for Chicago PD and the Russians. Images of the shootout ran wildly through his brain.

"I am waiting for an answer, Mr. Rice. Did you shoot to kill Dedmon?"

Nutkis had him cornered. Rich knew how bad it looked. His hand was forced. "This is the place where I invoke my Fifth Amendment rights. You're trying to make me decline to answer." He stopped a moment. "But you know what? Since you say we're here for the truth ... the truth is I shot Dedmon. And if he got killed ... tough shit."

A ripple of hushed conversation cascaded over the jury box. The foreman waved his hand to quiet the jurors.

"Moving on," Nutkis interjected. "Lavender is wounded. Grimansky wounded. Dedmon and Waller shot to death. That leaves you and Nicky Franko."

The bastard, Rich thought. *He just wanted me to take the Fifth.*

"What did you do after this?"

"I ducked behind the bar. Yuri was wounded but still shooting. He and Nicky turned over tables as cover."

"And then?"

"We picked and potted at each other. Yuri shot the bar-back to pieces."

"You were wounded?"

"In the arm."

"Shot?"

"Flying glass tore through my left bicep." Rich rubbed his upper arm. "Still healing."

"Another stand-off?"

"I could see cops showing up outside and snipers on the roof across the street." Rich wiped his hands together. "I just wanted to hold on. I was down to the .45 after running out of shotgun shells. But Nicky forced Yuri to jump the bar to finish me off."

"Grimansky leaped over the bar and …"

"And landed wrong, on his back, on a broken whiskey bottle."

"Did he come after you?"

"No, he was incapacitated, like a bug pinned to a display. It gave me a chance to wrestle the Kalashnikov from him."

Nutkis approached the jury. "Grimansky was found behind the bar, wounded severely, and yes, unable to move due to wounds to his lower spine, left thigh, right thigh and either shoulder." Lolling his head to the side, the prosecutor wondered aloud. "Unusual pattern to the wounds, wouldn't you agree, Mr. Rice?"

"He got knocked out of the action and couldn't shoot at me anymore."

Nutkis opened a manila folder. "Forensics reported the wounds to Grimansky's right shoulder were from a .32, which Tom Waller fired. But the wounds to Grimansky's legs and left shoulder were from a 5.45 round fired at close range. The Kalashnikov AK-47 fires a 7.62 round. But the model found at the scene of the shooting, a Kalashnikov 74, takes the 5.45 round. My question is, why didn't you just kill him ... like Dedmon?"

"Because I wanted him alive. He was going to stand trial for killing Tom."

"He will, though maybe not here. He's a foreign national, and the Russian Federation has already requested his return." Nutkis flipped the folder on the table. "I am curious, Mr. Rice. Did you pat down Grimansky for other weapons?"

"I didn't have time. I was getting shot at by Nicky."

"Grimansky had a 9mm automatic in a shoulder holster, a knife on his belt, a derringer in his boot. Had his wounds not prevented him, he would have retrieved one of those weapons and surely killed you."

"I wish I had known that. I was running out of ammo for my .45." Rich considered it quietly and then stepped off. "You react instinctively in a situation like this. I needed to take him out, like Dedmon. With all that was going on I wasn't thinking clearly. If I had thought it through, I would've knocked him unconscious and searched for other weapons. Certainly, I would've looked for another magazine for the Kalashnikov."

"And at this point, you are almost out of ammo."

"Yes."

"Again, I am wondering: did it ever occur to you to flee?" Nutkis shrugged. "Break for the front door and let the police handle it?"

"Nicky was between me and the door."

"Still, you might've got out."

Rich's eyes went to the carpet. He put his hands together as if in prayer, touching his lips to his fingertips. He thought before he spoke. "Flight, instead of fight? Now? Looking back, after all that has happened—that makes a helluva lot of sense. Though, in that moment, I had no other thought but to finish it alive or end up dead. I told you, I considered the confrontation inevitable. Nicky Franko had missed me once and had been chasing after me for almost a year. Twenty-four seven, I lived with the reality—the certainty—that the Russian Mafia was looking for me. They wanted me dead. And here he was, shooting to kill me. I had only one choice."

Members of the jury listened intently, seeming to hang on Rich's explanation.

"Your judgement, as this situation unfolded, is what we, the grand jury, seek to understand. Somewhere in there lies the truth. So, go on. You were running out of ammunition. What was your next move?"

"I had to get upstairs. The Glock, Springfield and Bushmaster were in the gun safe upstairs."

Nutkis nodded, following along.

"I took a shot and got Nicky's head down. Then I ran for the dumbwaiter."

"Dumbwaiter?"

"The downstairs and upstairs are connected by an old dumbwaiter shaft. There was a ladder instead of an elevator to the kitchen pantry in the upstairs flat. I ran for it and climbed to the second floor."

Nutkis went over to the diagram and pointed to the dumbwaiter. "Did Nicky follow you?"

"It was pretty smoky in there, but he found the dumbwaiter."

"Was there time to reload?"

"No, he was after me pretty quick, climbing the dumbwaiter. I got to the second floor. My dog, Roommate, was yapping. I tried to shoo him away and crossed the kitchen to the safe. I had time to open the safe and get the Glock. He was right there, behind a door, firing at me. I fired back, but there were only five rounds in the magazine. I hadn't reloaded the Glock since the last time I fired it."

"You were out of ammo."

"Yeah." Rich massaged his forehead. It was wet. "Sorry, it's all coming back to me," he said to the jury. "Nicky heard the receiver lock and ran in. We fought, and he dropped me with a chair. I don't know why he didn't shoot me right then. My dog barked at him, and Nicky kicked him across the room."

A woman on the jury sucked in her breath.

"I tried to get up, and Nicky put a boot in my face and laid me out. I was losing consciousness and thought: I'm done. I'm dead. He, Nicky, pulled out his phone and took a picture of me laying there. He laughed and said he was going to kill me but, first, he wanted to send a text to his mother, Suka Franko. She was outside my wife's house in Glencoe. If he didn't send a text, his mother would assume he was killed, and she would then kill my wife."

"And yet, here you are. What happened?" Nutkis wanted to know.

"Roommate, recovered from the kick and ran at Nicky, latching onto his leg." Rich pulled his thumb and forefinger along his eyes, to the bridge of his nose. The muscles in his chin quivered. “Nicky dropped his phone, and his gun fell as he grabbed for Roommate. He got hold of my dog and broke his neck like a farmer killing chickens.” Rich snapped his fingers.

The same woman in the jury gave an agonized cry.

“You’re half-conscious. Your dog is dead.”

“I got pissed-off. It helped clear my head. There was a filet knife that had been on the table. It was knocked to the floor in the fight. I grabbed it and stuck it into Nicky’s knee. It didn’t go through his knee right away. I twisted it and pushed it all the way through. It must’ve hurt like hell.”

“Then you had the upper hand?”

“I don’t know about upper hand, but I had a chance. I got the gun and pinned Nicky with my knee on his chest, holding the gun on him.”

“Then you killed him.”

“No,” Rich emphatically said. “No.”

“He was shot through the chest, puncturing his aorta. You killed him.”

“No. I hated the son of a bitch. He had come to kill me. He had destroyed my life. But I did not kill him.”

Nutkis’ scowl changed to disbelief. His arms flung outward to the ceiling. “Mr. Rice, how are we supposed to believe anything you say? You shoot Dedmon twice in the belly. He is dead. You have a gun on Nicky Franko, point blank. You fire, and you kill him.”

“I did not.” Rich’s anger welled up and overflowed. “At that moment, I realized that I couldn’t kill him. Racing through my mind was that Suka Franko was going to kill Gisele. I thought maybe I could barter Nicky’s life for Gisele. Let them kill me, but not Gisele. I drew back, and as

I did, Nicky grabbed for the gun. He got the barrel." Rich pantomimed holding the gun on Nicky. "But, with me moving back and him pulling forward—the gun went off."

Nutkis let his arms fall and slap his sides. His head dropped, and he shook his head from side to side, staring at the floor.

"I did not kill Nicky Franko."

"No? Are you certain?"

"Yes. I did not intend to kill him."

In a moment, Nutkis seemed to pull himself together. Speaking to the jury, he said, "Jurors will refer to forensics exhibit 25."

Jurors opened folders.

"There were powder burns on the inside of Nikolai Franko's left wrist and forearm. Also, powder burns on his left suit jacket sleeve." Nutkis rustled through papers. "The bullet that killed Nicky Franko was from a .357. The bullet went through the second floor and was dug out of the first floor. The bullet matched Franko's gun."

"So...?" Rich began. The prosecutor's comments bewildered him. This was a let-up. Nutkis had been throwing fastballs and curves, and now he started Rich off with a change-up so hittable and slow that you could almost stroll alongside it.

"So, nothing, Mr. Rice. I want to know what happened after that." Nutkis sounded irritated.

"Well, I watched him die." Rich spoke softly to the jury. "I have to say, I had no satisfaction in that, nor any regret in his death. I was half-crazed with the last thing Nicky had said—that his mother, Suka Franko was outside my wife's house in Glencoe and would kill her if she knew Nicky was dead."

"What did you do then?"

"The phone was on the floor, with my picture and Nicky's text. He hadn't sent it. I made a decision: I was going to Glencoe to save Gisele. I sent the text, which I knew would buy me a couple of hours. Then I went through Nicky's pockets for his car keys. I planned to take Nicky's hot rod."

"Why didn't you let the FBI handle it?"

"Have you not been listening to all I've said?" Rich enunciated each word. "Where was the FBI? They were no help."

"It's ten hours to Chicago. How did you think you would get there quickly enough?"

"I figured I would get a bucketful of tickets speeding through Iowa. I didn't care. I would get there as soon as I could."

"Well, in this instance, you were helped by the FBI, weren't you?"

"Yes, I was. They arranged an escort with Iowa State Troopers. I was across the state in a few hours."

Nutkis turned his hand and looked at his wristwatch. "We are close to lunch. I would like to adjourn and reconvene at one o'clock. Is that all right?"

"Yeah."

"Okay, we are in recess and will pick up the testimony after lunch." Nutkis started stacking folders.

Rich didn't see Bertoloni in the gallery as he walked out of the courtroom. The guy came and went like a ghost. Borodavka stood by the door.

"Lunch?"

"Yeah, until one."

"We're close to La Casa, great place to eat."

"Sure, let's go."

Borodavka did most of the talking while devouring a platter of calzones. Rich picked at his soup and half-sandwich, listening. Borodavka asked about Nutkis' line of questioning and how Rich had responded. He nodded and stuffed his face. "You've done well, dodging only one question." The lawyer chewed. "Got a read on what the jury thinks?"

"I think they are on my side. I've heard a laugh or two when I made a joke."

"Don't play a jury for laughs. It's like teasing a circus bear. It may seem tame, until a paw full of claws slashes your face. Be ready for their questions."

"They can ask questions?"

"It'll come through the jury foreman." His knife and fork rang and clattered as he carved up the last of the calzone. It looked a bloody mess. A large piece went straight into his mouth. "Mmmmph, they'll, mmmmph, ask odd stuff, like how'd it feel pulling the trigger. Don't respond like it's weird to ask. Make them think it's the best question you ever heard."

"What's with you and Nutkis?"

"Blue Jays."

"The baseball team?"

Wet, chewed fragments of food exploded out of Borodavka's laughing, bearded mouth-hole. "Blue Jays. Creighton law. Same class." He wiped his mouth along his sleeve.

"Oh," was all Rich said, noticing calzone shrapnel floating in his soup.

The red pile disappeared from the big lawyer's plate with alacrity. He mopped up with bread and then leisurely groomed his beard, enjoying the residue of lunch from shirtfront to eyebrows. "Yesterday, you told me you set up our defense. Hammer it hard this afternoon. It may be your last chance."

Rich pushed his soup bowl to the center of the table.

Back on the stand, he faced Nutkis.

"You got to Glencoe. What did you find?"

"A police barricade and two cops telling me there's a hostage situation."

"What'd you do?"

"I'm not thinking rationally. I ran the police barricade and drove down the block to my mother-in-law's house, where my wife was."

"And?"

"There's a black Mercedes in front of Gisele's. And remember, I'm driving Nicky Franko's car."

"Go on."

"I stopped about twenty yards from the Mercedes. Suka Franko and her bodyguard jumped out of the Mercedes. She must've thought it was Nicky."

"Did they have your wife?"

"Yeah, I saw her in the Mercedes. She tried to get away, and they pushed her back inside." Rich clenched his fists. "I got really pissed, but I kept my cool."

"You let them get close?"

"I did, and then I stepped out. They froze. Suka wanted to know where Nicky was."

"You said?"

"I said he was dead."

"She didn't take it well, did she?"

"No, not at all. I had the Glock. The bodyguard went into his coat, I assumed for a gun. So I tapped him twice in the middle of the chest."

"Jury will note forensics exhibit 27. The bodyguard, Dimitri Karpov, was indeed reaching for a weapon, which was found on his body. Go on."

"Suka grabbed a MAC-11 and let loose at me. Some Glencoe cops pulled up."

"One of them was Officer Terry Williams, correct?"

"Yes. Then Suka took off in the Mercedes. I convinced Terry to follow. I had also taken the Springfield, and now Officer Williams and I pursued Suka. We followed her to the community beach."

"The community beach is on Lake Michigan. Why do you think she went there?"

"We couldn't figure it out. It was a dead-end. Suka apparently had a boat coming to pick her up. But we didn't know that."

"And what did you do then?"

"Suka was at the end of the pier and I set up behind some pilings. We yelled at her to let Gisele go. But she wasn't about to do that. So I hoped to get a shot, knocking Suka out and allowing Gisele to escape."

"What about the boat?"

"It was one of the long speed boats, the ones that race. It was coming fast from the south. We weren't sure, but once it was obvious the boat was for Suka, I put a couple of rounds into the engine compartment."

"And into the driver?"

"I took him out."

"You killed him."

"I guess. I tried to stop the boat from taking Suka and Gisele."

"You guess?" Nutkis made an exaggerated display of disbelief. "Jury will note Grigori Cheknovski was shot in the temple and fell over the side. His body was recovered from Lake Michigan."

"You expect me to be sorry for him?" Rich countered. "They were going to take my wife."

"Just acknowledge you shot the driver."

"I tried to stop the boat and Suka's escape with my wife as a hostage."

"You then shot her—Suka Franko."

"Yes, I took a shot at her. Suka lost her grip on Gisele, and I was able to get to her."

"What happened to Suka?"

"Some guys grabbed her and pulled her onboard the boat. It took off, headed north. I had Gisele. I was done with it."

"You rescued your wife."

"Yes."

Nutkis took up a position in the well of the open courtroom. "For the jury, let's recap. You personally shot, wounded or killed ... James Dedmon, Nicky Franko, Yuri Grimansky, the bodyguard, Grigori Cheknovski ... and possibly Suka Franko."

"What about Tom Waller? What about Lieutenant Lavender? He may be in a wheelchair for the rest of his life."

"What about them, Mr. Rice? We're concerned with your killing spree."

"Killing spree? Are you trying to pin a murder rap on me?"

"Murder?" Nutkis took a haughty air. "No, not murder, just the possibility of three counts of manslaughter. And other counts of aggravated assault, assault with a deadly weapon and impeding officers in the performance of their duties. Theft of evidence. Leaving the scene of a homicide. Crossing state lines to commit a crime. And just a fantastic cornucopia of statues and felonies and misdemeanors, oh my."

The tall man stopped and spun about. "Perhaps you are not aware, Mr. Rice, that the death penalty was reinstated in the last election."

"And?" Rich squirmed in his chair.

"And," Nutkis started walking about again. "Multiple murders are an automatic death penalty."

Rich let Nutkis strut, like a peacock in full bloom of his feathery hyperbole. Though his belly churned, he calmly countered: "The whole situation was self-defense. You know that. That is what the evidence points to. But more importantly, I was working with the FBI as a key part in the plans of their task force. I was used as bait to lure *Bratva* out of the shadows. The information that I supplied the FBI helped them and Omaha and Chicago Police to arrest members of *Bratva*"—Rich swung over to the jury—"at deadly risk to my life and the life of my wife, Gisele. I believe I come under the protection of qualified immunity."

"Wait." Nutkis' hand went up. "You think you can claim qualified immunity for all the shootings and laws you broke?"

Members of the jury whispered amongst themselves, sharing confused expressions. Rich caught the jurors seeming misunderstanding and exploited it before Nutkis noticed.

"Perhaps the jury doesn't know, but qualified immunity," he explained, "is used by members of law enforcement, the FBI and city or state police when a shooting occurs during performance of their duty. It protects members of law enforcement and those that work with them."

"But you're not FBI," Nutkis objected. "You're not even Omaha PD."

"No, I'm none of those. What I am is a person that provided key information, worked with and acted in concert with the FBI task force in the investigation and apprehending of members of *Bratva*, the Russian Mafia. This, at considerable risk to my life."

Nutkis' eyes went to the ceiling, and he turned away with his hands in the air.

The courtroom became silent for a long time. Nutkis sat, his chin in his hands. His scowl seemed to be simmering.

Rich calmly waited, confident. He had repeated the lynch pin of his defense and was certain that he'd sold it to the jury.

"Well, I've no more questions for the witness at this time," Nutkis said, lacing his fingers atop his bald head and slouching down in his seat. "If the jury has any questions, you may ask Mr. Rice."

Jurors talked in small knots. Some wrote notes and passed them to the black foreman. When he had gathered the notes, he stood. "Mr. Rice, what injuries did your wife suffer as a result of the kidnapping?"

"She was pistol-whipped by Suka Franko, suffering a black eye and lacerations across her cheek."

The answer alarmed the foreman. "Is she okay?"

"Yes. There was no damage to orbital bone around her eye socket, but her face will be scarred for life."

The foreman shuffled through notes, asking, "And your property, The Ordinary, was it destroyed?"

"It was pretty well shot up."

"Are you planning to repair it, and what will that cost you?"

"We already are. Insurance will cover most of the damage. I have a fifteen-thousand-dollar deductible, but overall, the cost of repairs will be between twenty-five and thirty thousand dollars."

Someone in the jury murmured, "Oh my God."

"Why did you shoot to kill Suka Franko? Could you have put a gun on her and demanded she let your wife go?"

"I did ... but ..." Rich looked at each member of the jury as he answered. "She had a gun to my wife's head. She had no intention of negotiating, nor releasing Gisele. Remember, she was shooting at me and Officer Williams as well. And I wonder, would any of you not shoot to kill under similar circumstances?"

Some jurors wriggled in their seats. A short Asian woman stood and handed over a note to the foreman. He opened it and then said to her: "I can't ask him that." She looked disappointed.

"Go ahead," Rich volunteered. "If you have another question, I am more than willing to respond."

The foreman gave a pained look. "Okay." He read. "Were you really mad when the Russian killed your dog?"

Rich kept a serious expression, glancing from the foreman to the Asian woman. “Yes. I was very angry. My dog was named Roommate, and he was my only friend while I was hiding out.”

The Asian woman smiled and nodded.

“He was a stray, a Boston Terrier.” Rich studied his hands, playing it up. “He saved my life. I buried him in the back. Every day, I miss him.”

“Oh,” the woman quietly said, her face contorted to the verge of tears.

“Any more questions for Mr. Rice?” The foreman checked each juror. “We would like to call Agent Bertoloni back to the stand if that’s possible.”

Bertoloni rose from his seat in the last row of the gallery.

Nutkis unslouched himself and rose. “Mr. Rice, you are excused. If the grand jury requires further testimony, you will be notified.”

Rich paused, opening the partition gate. “When will I know the verdict?”

“The jury will deliberate and deliver a True Bill or No Bill, and the law will proceed from there.”

Rich passed Bertoloni. The FBI agent gave him a half-smile, and muttered out of the side of his mouth, “Thanks, pal. I thought I’d be done by the afternoon.”

“That it?” Borodavka rose up from the bench as Rich exited the courtroom.

“Apparently.”

“How’d it go?”

“Well, I was able to work into my testimony that I should be given qualified immunity.”

“Good. Good.”

Nutkis' daughter Molly approached. She was probably a click or two over five feet, very petite and trim-looking in a snug claret shift. Rich had hardly noticed her in the courtroom. She wore her black hair loose, and it fell above her shoulders. Her cherry-red lipstick and dark mascara was an attractive contrast against her pale complexion, giving her small face a luminescent quality.

"Hey, Moll."

"Mr. Borodavka. I wanted to talk to Mr. Rice a moment, if that's all right with you."

"Sure, shoot."

"I just want to let you know what happens next with the grand jury. Your testimony prompted questions, so the jury will call back witnesses or discuss previous testimony." She spoke to Rich with an all-business tone, but her eyes were busy roving over his face. "Once the members of the jury are satisfied that they've heard all the needed testimony and evidence, they will go into deliberations. After deliberations, they will come in with a verdict. You heard my father mention a True Bill or No Bill." She smiled. Her hand lightly touched Rich's elbow. "A True Bill means that a quorum of twelve or more jurors have voted to tender an indictment."

"We don't want that." Borodavka said.

"Of course not. It means charges will be filed and a trial scheduled. However, if the jury brings in No Bill, which will mean the testimony and evidence did not indicate the commission of a crime. Or, there were extenuating circumstances involved. So, no indictment, no trial."

"What's the likelihood of No Bill, Molly?" Borodavka wanted to know.

She pursed her very red lips and thought. "I couldn't say, even if I was at liberty to tell you, Mr. Borodavka. But, off the record, the strong self-defense aspect and Mr. Rice's contention of a qualified immunity, which protects law enforcement and those who aid them in their investigations, was a good play and seemed to carry considerable weight." The young woman silently looked up at Rich, then said, "If I were on that grand jury and you said what you said about giving your life to save your wife...well..."

"How long until I know the outcome?" Rich asked.

"Could be tomorrow, next week, a couple of weeks. We will notify your lawyer. Thank you for the frankness of your testimony." Her eyes lingered a moment longer on Rich. She smiled, spun on a high heel and went back to the courtroom.

She walked like a model, one foot in front of the other. Rich watched her, wondering.

Borodavka clamped a large hairy hand on Rich's shoulder. "You're just going to have to sit tight a little longer."

CHAPTER 5

Ship's Master Pavel Vovchenko swayed with the bridge as the cumbersome freighter eased out of the calm waters at the mouth of the St. Lawrence Seaway. With a heading of due east, the shadows on the ship reached long. Clouds above glowed pink, and the sky turned an icy kind of blue.

"Weatherpak reports a cyclone in the mid-Atlantic," said Chief Mate Pularski. "We should have clear skies, but rough seas over the Banks."

"Thanks, Chief," Vovchenko replied. Over fifty, overweight, of average height, with a bad kitchen-style fringe haircut, Pavel only cared about one thing—bringing his ship to port. His expressions were limited to impatience and pain, and his emotional range stretched from angry to not so angry. He had bad guts, made worse by that woman onboard.

The TS *Alexander Pushkin* was a large tramp freighter registered in Rotterdam, sailing out of St. Petersburg, under the flag of the Kozmos Corporation. Its keel was laid at Lomonosov Shipworks in 1984. At 67,000 tons and 164 meters in length, with a 27-meter beam, the *Pushkin* had a max draught of 10.66 meters. It had three cargo booms: fore, aft and amidships. Its seven holds were filled with a variety of cargo, from medical machinery and electronics in the forward holds to plastics and pumps, engines and factory machinery in the other holds. The cargo was destined for Russian Federation markets, and international sanctions dictated what they could include.

Old by merchant standards, the *Pushkin* could make eighteen knots powered by its twin seven-cylinder marine diesels burning bunker fuel. On all decks, the ship smelled of boiling tar. At fourteen knots, the bulkheads vibrated and loose rivets rattled while the entire ship creaked and threatened to split in two. The *Pushkin* required a crew of thirteen to run at sea. A cross section of seafaring nations were represented among the crew. A large group were Russian or Ukrainian like Vovchenko; but the chief mate was Polish, and the third mate German. The ship had an American engineering chief with an Australian his second, a Canadian electrotech officer, a Greek sailing officer and the rest were Chinese, African, Italian and God-only-knows what else.

In its early days, the *Pushkin* had sailed as a cargo-passenger freighter with six well-appointed staterooms below the bridge at deck level. Now, though, traversing the North Atlantic out of Lomonosov and St. Petersburg, down the St. Lawrence to the port of Duluth-Superior five times a season, the freighter rarely carried passengers.

However, on this return voyage, the *Pushkin* did have one guest: the woman picked up two nights before. They had taken her aboard and carried her to the stateroom. The engine department wiper, Gonzalez, had been a corpsman in the American Navy. Pavel ordered him to attend to her.

Vovchenko had received signals from Russia telling him to stop the ship and wait for a boat with a passenger to transfer. He did not want to know any more. Her presence on ship worried Pavel. The ship's manifest had to be doctored to list a passenger. He wondered if they could clear C-TPAT and customs. MSSIS would have noticed that the *Pushkin* had stopped for more than five hours as they waited for the small boat. He'd fabricate a story about balloon freight shifting, needing blocking in the hold. He entered this into the ship's log.

"Chief, radio Gonzalez to meet me in the crew's lounge."

"Aye." The chief unclipped a walkie-talkie from his belt and called the engine room.

"Take the bridge."

Vovchenko slipped on his foul-weather jacket and left the bridge. A cold, salty wet wind blew as the ship's master made his way down the ladder to the passenger deck. The throb and bump of the engine sounded louder below. He opened the hatch and dogged it behind him. A French-language radio station played low in a corner of the crew's lounge. Someone lay sprawled and snoring on a padded bench. Gonzalez sat at a round table, drinking coffee and reading a well-worn copy of *El Mundo*.

"How's our passenger?"

Gonzalez was a large man with a round head of close-cropped black hair. His arms were tattooed from his wrists to the short sleeves of his t-shirt. "Why am I her babysitter?"

Pavel unzipped his jacket and went to the coffee urn. “Because you are the only one in the crew with any medical training.”

“Am I getting extra pay?”

Pavel sipped and drew back from the hot black coffee. He stood across from Gonzalez. “Kozmos won’t give you an extra ruble.”

“*Mierda*, why should I do anything for her?”

“It wasn’t Kozmos that ordered us to stop and pick her up.”

“Yeah? Who then?”

“An organization that used to be the KGB.”

Gonzalez lowered his newspaper and raised his eyebrows. “What’s that old spunker got to do with spies and shit?”

“No idea.” Pavel replied, though he did have an idea why. “It’s not bad to have them owe you a favor.”

The Mexican stood and shook his shoulders loose. “I looked in on her this morning and at noon. She slept. I left lunch. Let me get some food out, and we’ll go see her.”

Gonzalez opened the refrigerator and assembled a meal from plastic containers. He microwaved a plate and put together a tray. “We just need the first-aid kit, and we’re ready.”

The ship’s master pulled the large medical kit from the locker. He tried to close the locker, but the latch had been sprung. “When are you boys going to get it? There’s nothing worth stealing in this locker.”

“Tell that damn Chinaman. He sees a Red Cross and thinks it means dope.”

The passageway to the staterooms rocked with the ship. Vovchenko followed Gonzalez. Pavel moved slowly, heavily, not eager to meet his passenger. Gonzalez balanced the tray on one hand, knocking.

"Bosun, ma'am." He waited. "I'm with ship's master. We're coming in." Gonzalez glanced back at Pavel and pushed open the door.

The stateroom was dark, a curtain pulled across the round porthole. The only light came from the head, its door ajar.

"Turning on the lamp, ma'am."

Suka lay on the bunk under a disarray of woolen blankets. She appeared to be sleeping.

The stateroom resembled a motel room, with bunk, bedside table, bureau, chair and narrow desk. All the comforts, except a television.

Gonzalez set the tray down next to another on the desk. The other had crumbs, crust from a sandwich, an empty soft drink can and a wadded-up paper napkin.

"She's eating, at least."

"Missus Franko," Pavel said loudly, hands in the pockets of his jacket. "Missus Franko. We have your supper."

"Aaaaaaaa," Suka groaned, rolling over. "*Khto ebat' ty.*"

"No no, Missus." Gonzalez rushed to her bunk and gently turned her onto her right side. "You can't lie on that side. You're hurt."

"We speak English on this ship," Pavel said. "We all understand it."

Suka's eyes focused on him. "Who're you?"

"I am Ship's Master Pavel Vovchenko."

"I don't give a fuck. Bring me the captain."

"Missus Franko, I am the captain."

Suka glared at Gonzalez. "Why is this fucking greaser pawing me?"

"He's a corpsman, tending to your wound."

"What boat am I on? Where are you taking me?"

"You are aboard the *Alexander Pushkin.* We are headed to Lomonosov, St. Petersburg."

"Vovchenko." Suka's face clouded over. "Where are you from, Vovchenko?"

"The Black Sea, Odessa."

"Ah, then you know my family."

Pavel broke his gaze with Suka and glanced about the stateroom. "You, your family, are not unknown to me."

Gonzalez carefully pulled off the bandages on Suka's left shoulder. He grimaced, dropping pus-yellow gauze pads covered with dried blood into the garbage can under the bedside table. "*Que malo,*" he muttered.

Suka breathed heavily, grinding her teeth as Gonzalez ripped off the bandages. She looked the worse for wear. Her orange hair lay matted and greasy. Her face appeared old without makeup.

Pavel watched, reticent, as the Mexican cleaned the wound and redressed it.

The bosun taped a fresh dressing and then wound an elastic bandage around Suka's left arm and body.

"You fucking greaser, how the fuck am I to eat with one fucking hand?"

"You'll manage," Gonzalez closed up the first-aid kit and helped Suka to sit up. He placed the tray on her lap.

Pavel said nothing.

"How much longer until we reach port?" Suka wanted to know, taking a spoonful of stew to her mouth.

"Late autumn weather," Pavel began. "The North Atlantic is unpredictable."

"Did I ask you about the weather?" Suka shouted, sputtering out food.

Vovchenko's expression tightened. He did not react. "With good weather, we will be in port in nine, maybe ten days."

"I will hold you to that, Vovchenko." Suka bit off the corner of a bread roll. "I want reports on our position every day. You understand? Your life may depend on it."

"Aye."

"And I want a mobile phone."

"You'll get no signal out here. We're not close to Russia."

"Just give me the phone. Now leave me."

Vovchenko's eyes betrayed the anger burning in his belly. "Come, Gonzalez."

The bosun handed Suka some capsules. "These aspirin will help with the pain. Two every four hours." He took the lunch tray and handed the first-aid kit to Pavel.

Out in the passageway, Gonzalez turned to Pavel. "She needs someone better than me—a real *medico*, a surgeon, Captain."

"Tell me about the wound."

"I can keep it clean, but," Gonzalez shrugged. "The bones are shattered. She needs surgery."

"We don't reach St. Petersburg for nine days."

"She'll have permanent damage to her shoulder and may not be able to use her left arm."

"There is nothing I can do about that. You've never set a broken bone?"

"Arm *si*, shoulder no," Gonzalez pled. "You don't know how many bones there are in the shoulder. She needs a surgeon."

Pavel threw out his arms. "There is nothing I can do."

"Ah, she's a *puta*."

"The name Suka fits."

Gonzalez grabbed his crotch and said: "I'll spread her *culo* and ..."

The first-aid kit crashed to the deck as Pavel seized fistfuls of Gonzalez's shirt and slammed him hard up against the bulkhead. The tray fell from the Mexican's hands. The ship's master's eyes blazed, startling Gonzalez.

"Captain!"

"Now, you listen to me. If you so much as touch a hair on that woman's head, I will kick your ass over the side."

"*Tranquillo*."

"You feed her. You treat her wound. You do nothing else, *comprende*?"

"*Si si*, yeah."

Vovchenko eased off, but only just. "And tell the rest of the crew, nobody lays a finger on her."

"That's a red flag to Youssef."

"You and that Moroccan will find yourselves treading water off Iceland as the *Pushkin* steams on. Only question then is how long you can stay afloat before hypothermia kills you." The captain roughly let loose of Gonzalez and stepped back. The fire smoldered still in his eyes.

"Okay, Captain."

"Now pick up this shit and take it to the galley."

Sullen, Gonzalez smoothed out the creases in his shirt and bent down, cleaning dishes from the deck.

Vovchenko shot him one last look and then climbed the ladder to the deck. He pulled from his pocket a bottle of pink sludge and drank to the dregs, pitching the empty into the dark, boiling sea. A blast of hot air blew into Pavel's face. *A dead man's wind*, he thought. Pavel entered the bridge, startling Pularski. The chief frantically waved away blue smoke and spit on the burning end of a thick blunt. The bridge reeked of the herb.

"Chief, what you do in your quarters, I don't care. Not on my bridge, okay?"

Vovchenko unzipped his foul-weather jacket and settled into the captain's chair. He stared out of the windows as multicolored instrument lights burned and blinked among computer screens flickering across the bridge. The lights cast the dark room in an eerie hue.

Darkness enveloped the ship. Running lights and deck lights glowed. They sailed through the calm waters of the Canadian Maritimes. After Cape Breton Island, Saito Pierce and Miquelon, the *Pushkin* would sail into the open seas of the North Atlantic.

This voyage had started all wrong. Cargo had sat on the dock with the threat of a longshoreman strike. They were late out of Duluth-Superior. Then the signal to pick up that woman had come just as the *Pushkin* entered the Soo Locks. He might be getting too old for the sea.

Third Officer Mueller had night watch. He wouldn't relieve Pavel for another three hours. The tension clawed up from the captain's gut. His stomach growled and gurgled.

"Coffee, Captain?" Pularski asked, handing Pavel an INTERCEPT weather update.

"No, no coffee," Vovchenko responded. "If you're going below, get me a hot tea and a bottle of the pink stuff."

"Aye. You have the bridge." Pularski ducked through the hatchway.

Pavel read the weather report: clear skies, temperatures zero to minus two Celsius, winds east, northeast six to eight knots, swells seven to ten meters. A sharp pang shot across the captain's abdomen. He massaged his belly, hoping it would pass.

The ship's master saw nothing of his special passenger for days. Bosun Gonzalez reported that the woman had become stronger, her wound healing well, and her attitude worse than ever. But, without surgery, he was certain she would lose function of her left arm. Pavel could only shrug. Then later that day, she came to the bridge.

"Vovchenko," Suka Franko barked. "Where's my phone?"

Pavel turned about in his captain's chair. "You're not permitted on the bridge."

"You said you had a phone." The middle-aged woman had cleaned up and washed her orange hair. She had a comb in her hand. Yet, she wore the same dirty, ripped and blood-stained clothing. She swayed awkwardly on her feet, unsettled by roll of the ship. Her left shoulder was visibly lower than the right, her arm bandaged tight against her body.

The captain looked her up and down. "You need clothing."

As Pavel slipped off the captain's chair, pain stabbed through his stomach. He fought to hide it. "Missus Franko." He stood before the short woman. "We are in the middle of the Atlantic. You'll not get MTS, MegaFon or any other service out here." He put a hand on her right shoulder. "Is your wound healing?"

Suka violently jerked her shoulder away. Wincing, she said in a strained voice: "Don't play me, Captain. Give me a phone, and let me know when I can use it."

"I will check ship's stores." Pavel rubbed his stomach just under his sternum. "Meanwhile, Missus Franko, go back to your stateroom. I will have clothes brought to you." His solicitous smile was met with a sneer.

"My phone," Suka shouted. "Who do you think owns Kozmos, Captain?" She banged the hatch as she left the bridge.

Vovchenko steadied himself on the back of the captain's chair and leaned forward, massaging his gut.

"You all right?" asked Third Officer Mueller, a pony-tailed German.

"I'm okay, Mueller. Radio the engine room and tell Gonzalez to get Missus Franko some clothing. And have him check stores for an extra mobile phone."

"Aye."

Pavel straightened and took out a pink bottle. He unscrewed the cap and slugged a couple of thick gulps. "Wait. Mueller, have Gonzalez meet me in my quarters."

The captain sat on the edge of his bunk, his head in his hands. Suffering Jesus, in brass on a wood crucifix, vibrated from a hook on the bulkhead at the head of his bunk. A red-beaded rosary swayed with the movement of the freighter. Multi-colored plastic bags with American brand names lined the opposite bulkhead. A single lamp lit a desk littered with charts and books. A framed picture of a stout middle-aged woman dwarfed by two grown adolescents, one in a dark blue Federation naval uniform, was cocked toward the bunk. A knock sounded on the door. "Come," Pavel growled.

Gonzalez entered. He had a bundle of clothing under one arm and a mobile phone in a plastic case in his hand. "The kraut said you wanted to see me."

"Yes. I see you have clothing and a phone for Missus Franko."

"I was on my way."

"How is it going?"

"How is it going? I don't talk to her. I come in, and she just bellows and bawls at me. I do what I have to do and *vamoose*."

Pavel rubbed his forehead. "Thank you, Gonzalez."

"She's like that movie, with the *viejo mama* on a train."

"I don't know what you're talking about. But ..." The captain let out a long breath. "I need to know if you, or anyone in the crew, has something to, you know, to keep Missus Franko calm?" Pavel glanced up, giving Gonzalez a questioning look.

The Mexican shifted his weight from one foot to the other. "I ... don't know, Captain."

Pavel exploded. "Don't give me that shit, Gonzalez."

"Well, if the Chinaman hasn't stolen it, I might know where I can get something."

"Get it. Don't kill her. Just keep her quiet."

"Understood."

"And don't fuck her."

Gonzalez loosed a hearty laugh. "Captain, no man on this crew would stick his dick in that bitch—including Youssef."

"What about the Aussie?"

"Him? We don't let him walk too close behind us. Know what I mean?" Gonzalez left the stateroom, chuckling.

Days passed, and no one saw Suka Franko above deck. The *Pushkin* steamed on, crossing the North Atlantic and entering the North Sea. But one night, as the ship plowed through spray and pea-soup fog so thick the captain could hardly see the bow from the bridge, Pavel noticed a lone figure staggering forward across the nodding deck. The orange hair gave her away. Fog horns wailed. Lights glowed like blurred orbs. Flags whipped and snapped. Metal clanged against metal on the ship's deck. Chief Pularski concentrated intently on the radar screen. Suka careened drunkenly about the deck until the pitch sent her tumbling against the leg of the crane amidships. She yelped, looped her good arm around the crane and clung desperately.

She brayed into the wind and fog.

Pularski looked up. "What is she saying?"

"Something about a Nicky." Pavel replied. "Nicky, Nicky her *malchik*."

"Who is Nicky?"

"I don't know. Listen, now she is vowing revenge. She says she's going to kill someone named Rice."

The chief visibly shivered.

"Get Gonzalez on deck to collect her."

"He's not going to want to leave the warm engine room."

Pavel's guts twisted into a knot, nearly doubling him over. "Just do it."

"Aye." The chief pressed the talk button on the walkie-talkie.

The *Pushkin* sailed through the North Sea, entering the Skagerrak Strait. At five knots, they slipped smoothly past anchored freighters, moored cruise ships, sailboats and the busy docks.

Pavel was on the bridge reading Viktor Pelevin's *S.N.U.F.F.* when there was a soft knock on the hatchway. The captain and Third Mate Mueller exchanged looks. The hatch opened, and in shuffled Suka Franko. She wore baggy dungarees and a bulky white cable knit sweater. Her head was bowed, and her left arm hung limp at her side.

"Captain, forgive me." She spoke almost in a whisper. "I don't know why, but I have been very sleepy." The woman's whole demeanor had changed.

"It's the sea air."

"What day is it? Where are we?"

"Crossing Kattegat Bay. We will be in the Baltic Sea in a few hours. In thirty-six hours, we will be docking in St. Petersburg. Our mooring has been changed from Lomonosov." Pavel went to a tray by the radio bay. "These signals came in for you." He handed Suka a sheaf of papers.

Suka took the signals in her right hand. Her expression appeared slack and dull. Like a sleepwalker, she shuffled back to the hatchway.

Vovchenko beamed. "In a few hours, you can use your mobile phone. You should get a signal."

"Uh huh."

Pavel turned to Mueller. "What did the Mexican give her?"

"Captain?" The mate stared straight ahead, smiling.

"Never mind. Tell Gonzalez to ween her off whatever he's slipping her. She must be Suka Franko when we dock. Understood?"

Dirty snow dressed the jagged ridges on either side of the Gulf of Finland. The early morning arctic sun burned white, and shadows cut across the ship's deck. It reminded Ship's Master Vovchenko that winter would soon close down St. Petersburg and the surrounding ports.

"Signal, Captain," Mueller said. "Pilot launch is coming alongside."

"Get some crew down there to bring the pilot aboard and up to the bridge."

"Aye."

This crossing could not end soon enough for Vovchenko. The pilot would take the helm and steer the *Pushkin* to its assigned mooring at the mouth of the River Neva. Once Suka Franko was off ship and the cargo off-loaded, the captain and his irritable bowels might be able to relax.

"Pavel Vovchenko!" called out a short, chubby round-faced man in a bundle of a coat and topped off by a thick woolen watch cap.

Pavel wheeled. "Evgeni." The captain hugged the short man. "You son of a bitch, you've no idea how happy I am to see you."

"I can imagine. You and the *Pushkin* have been the subject of much conversation."

"What? Why?"

"First, Mister, input this course and stay in the starboard channel." Mueller took the computer tablet that

Evgeni handed him. “And I want to see your C-TPAT and customs manifest.”

Pavel went to the ship’s papers and opened a folder. ‘Why do you need to see this?”

Evgeni took the customs form and ripped into it into quarters.

“Evgeni.”

He put the torn document in a pocket inside his coat and pulled out a C-TPAT form. “Put this in your notebook. Don’t read, just put it in.”

“I don’t understand.”

“You are better not to understand. Where is your MSSIS?”

“It’s there.”

Evgeni went to the computer and plugged in a thumb drive. “That will take a minute. You have the woman?”

“Yes.”

“She is well? She lives?”

“Yes. Evgeni, what is this all about?”

“It is about keeping you alive, my old friend. Where are your log books?”

Pavel pointed and fell into the captain’s chair, resigned.

Evgeni quickly leafed back through the log book. He tore out a page and wadded it up, pushing it into his pocket. He tore out another page, and another, and then slapped the log book closed. “I will need to see the woman. Where is she?” The chubby man pulled the thumb drive from the computer.

“She—she is on the passenger deck, in a stateroom.” Pavel felt a spasm in his innards. He patted his pocket. No bottle.

"Have someone meet me on the passenger deck and take me to her." Evgeni stopped at the door of the bridge. "And the crew that took care of the boatmen. Send them to me as well."

The pilot did not return to the bridge until the *Pushkin* neared the mouth of the Neva River.

"She is well?" Pavel's question was more in hope than in need of an answer.

Evgeni shifted his small black eyes to Pavel and nodded. "All ahead one quarter, Mister." The pilot took the tablet from Mueller.

A trio of tugboats buzzed about like water bugs, preparing to meet the *Pushkin*. Fore, aft and amidships, the tugs nudged the big freighter along.

"All stop, Mister."

St. Petersburg at the Neva River inlet was a bustling port with cranes and storage buildings along either bank. Squat and smeared black oil tanks dotted the hillsides.

"Deck crew, Mueller," Pavel murmured.

"Aye." The mate called over the walkie-talkie.

The tugs nosed the *Pushkin* to the dock. Containers and cargo packs were piled high on the hard stands. Trucks drove on access roads. Men on bicycles flitted here and there. Fork lifts wheeled about, taking palettes off cargo bays and putting them onto trucks. Thick braided mooring ropes dangled over the side of the *Pushkin* and were pulled to iron cleats and secured.

"Pavel," Evgeni said, motioning the ship's master to the dockside windows on the bridge.

Below, on the dock, a very old man in a wheelchair, attended by a green-uniformed Federation officer, waited in front of a black Mercedes sedan.

"I am going to take your manifests, bills of lading and notebook. I will get it to the Port Facility Officer. He will clear you through customs and port security."

Pavel nodded.

"Don't leave the ship until they are gone."

Cranes on rails, looking like hungry dinosaurs, rumbled forward as crew members opened access to the cargo holds.

"Pavel?" Evgeni grabbed his friend's coat collar. "Contact me in two weeks—if you are still alive. We will drink, no?" Evgeni tucked the ship's notebook under his arm and scuttled off the bridge.

Pavel had seen the old man before—when he was a boy in Odessa, standing in a bread line and clutching his mother's heavy wool skirt. A gray GAZ Volga V-12 had pulled up to the curb. Out stepped a tall, slender man in a green Soviet army uniform with red-trimming. The Order of Lenin and other medals dangled from his chest. He wore a high-peaked officer's cap with shiny black visor just above his brows. He pulled off his brown kid leather gloves slowly, finger by finger, and then held the pair in one hand.

"Avert your eyes," Pavel's mother hissed.

But the boy could not look away.

The man's long, bony face with its half-lidded eyes coldly studied each of the people huddled along the wall waiting to purchase bread. His thin lips were drawn in a tight line. Meanwhile, his driver pushed past people and disappeared into the bread shop.

The man's eyes fell on Pavel. His eyes and expression did not change as he idly slapped his gloves into the palm of his free hand.

"Does he hate us, mama?" Pavel asked.

"Shhhh, *malyutka*." She clamped her hand over his mouth.

The driver came out with an armload of fresh bread loaves and milk and eggs in a basket. He put the food into the back of the sedan and sat behind the wheel.

"There'll be less for us," someone muttered in the line.

When the driver had opened the rear door, Pavel noticed a small girl sitting inside. Even then she had that look.

The man eyed the people in line with a last disdainful sweep. He smirked, turned and climbed into the back of the sedan. The engine started up and the gray GAZ drove off.

The ship's master watched the activity along the port. Soon he saw Evgeni helping Suka Franko down the gangway. The orange-haired woman walked with difficulty, off balance, her left side dragging. She went to the old man in the wheelchair and fell to her knees. He stroked her head. The officer stood by until the man gave him a sign. He helped Suka Franko to her feet and brought her around to the rear door of the Mercedes. Evgeni bent low, talking into the ear of the man in the chair. He then darted off down the pier to the port authority office. Soon, the officer returned and pushed the man to the other side of the Mercedes.

A knife-sharp pain sliced across Pavel's lower belly. He spun about and made fast for the head.

The Ordinary reopened Saturday with little fanfare and not a lot of enthusiasm from one of its principals. Two days of testifying in front of the grand jury, combined with the anxiety of waiting for a verdict on indictment, tempered any eagerness Rich might have mustered. Gisele, on the other hand, having invested so much time redesigning and rebuilding the bar, could barely contain her excitement at the reopening. Jorge, Daisy and Riku were also anxious to open the doors again.

The neighborhood regulars returned, along with those curious to see the inside of the building after the shootout.

"I seens the inside the next day," Stephen, a local, said. "I didn't see no way you could put it back together."

Rich set a draught beer on a circular cardboard coaster in front of Stephen. "How's it look?"

The middle-aged man, with a studious frown, glanced left and then right and sipped his beer. "Looks great."

Daisy and Gisele waited tables while Riku and Rich tended bar and Jorge manned the kitchen. Gisele had pushed for staff uniforms, which Rich resisted, preferring white shirts and black pants. They settled on white shirts with dark jackets.

A mix of big beat and northern soul played just below the volume of conversation. Golden State battled Cleveland on the big-screen television.

Gisele tapped in an order on the POS computer screen.

"What do you need, babe?" Rich asked.

"Five blended margaritas." She blew a strand of blonde hair off her forehead.

"Five?"

"One for me."

"Not now, maybe later," Rich said with a grin.

"I know...bars and brothels serve the customers first."

Rich went to the service bay and started filling the blender.

"Hey, Keeper?"

"Yeah, Stephen."

"Who's the new gal? The blonde."

"My wife." Rich couldn't suppress a smile.

"No shit? When did you get married?"

"Long time ago. Hey, Tom ..." Rich stopped himself, realizing he had called Riku by Tom's name. It came back to him, the image of his friend shot dead. It disoriented him for a moment. "Crap," he snarled, punching the button and rocking the blender.

"Hey, Keeper?"

"Yeah?"

"Do you serve women?"

Rich hesitated for a couple of Mississippis, watching Stephen's very bad poker face. "No, we don't serve women. You got to bring your own."

"Aw, you're too sharp," Stephen laughed. "Hey, smile, Keeper. TV's here."

Coming into the bar was a smartly dressed woman and burly man with a video camera on his shoulder. A red circle with a white number four decal indicated that they were from Channel Four.

"Gisele? Did you call them?" Rich whispered into her ear as she leaned over the bar.

"No," Gisele took the tray of drinks.

"Talk to them. Get Daisy to spell me on the bar."

A light was activated on the camera, and the videographer panned across the bar.

Rich wiped his hands and ducked under the bar. Straightening, he came face to face with a microphone, female reporter and camera. The light burned bright, but that wasn't the reason Rich put his hand up.

"Are you the Keeper?" the woman wanted to know as she stuck the microphone up Rich's nose.

"You need to talk to her." Rich pointed across the bar to Gisele, who was placing the margaritas around a table. "She's the owner."

"But weren't you the one in the gunfight with the Russians?"

Gisele walked up. The reporter and videographer turned. Rich slipped away into the kitchen.

Jorge put two plates of nachos and tacos on the counter and rang a small bell. "*Jefe*," he said, back at the grill and poking a pair of sizzling hamburgers with a spatula. "*Que pasa*?"

"Just getting off the bar for a break." Rich peeked around the corner. Gisele stood in the center of the light, talking and gesturing quite animatedly.

"You're hiding," Jorge couldn't suppress a laugh.

'No, I'm not. Just taking a break."

"Okay, okay," the cook shrugged. "What you say."

Once the TV camera and reporter had left, Rich returned to the bar until last call, when he shooed Stephen away and locked the door behind him. The two weary ladies sat at the bar, while a tired Riku cleaned up the service trays and sinks as Rich checked stocks for the next day.

"Is it always like this?" Gisele wondered aloud.

"Sometimes it's busy," Daisy said.

"Want that drink now?" Rich asked Gisele.

"Yeah, a glass of wine would be wonderful—if I can gather the strength to raise it."

CHAPTER 6

Eppley Airfield is usually an easy airport. It takes 15 to 20 minutes from the car park ticketing and through TSA's friendly frisk to the gate. But that's on a good day. On a bad day, it can take as much as an hour and forty-five minutes to get from parking to boarding. Rich split the difference, reaching the gate for his Chicago flight in a little over half an hour.

He settled into the left-side seat on the long, narrow CRJ700 puddle-jumper to O'Hare. The single-aisle cabin configuration—three seats across, two on the right and single seats on the left—suited Rich. He'd selected an over-the-wing seat when he bought his ticket online. The Missouri River disappeared behind as the jet liner climbed steeply up through light, scattered snow flurries.

An hour long flight, Rich was scheduled to land in Chicago before noon. That allowed him enough time to rent a car and drive down the 90 Expressway to a Holiday Inn on West Harrison and then get to the FBI regional campus for a one o'clock meeting with Special Agent Bertoloni and his boss, Special Agent-in-Charge Jejune.

Bertoloni had called the day following Rich's grand jury testimony. He reminded Rich that they needed to meet; there was new information about Suka Franko. Rich didn't tell Gisele for fear of worrying her. As far as she knew, this was a wrap up of the shooting incident and investigation. But Rich knew that, if the FBI was requesting a meeting, he and Gisele were not out of danger.

The small jet touched down and taxied to the gate. Rich pulled his carry-on from the overhead bin and filed out. He thanked the lone flight attendant, a middle-aged woman with a sagging face and haggard expression, and ducked under the top of the fuselage door.

People on the go bustled up and down the terminal. Electric people-movers beeped, and groups of travelers clustered below overhead departure screens.

Rich knew his way and weaved through the people down a level to the rental car shuttle buses. He pressed Gisele on his contacts and put his phone to the side of his face.

"Hey, I was just thinking of you!" Gisele answered with a bubbling laugh.

"You were? Good thoughts?"

"Yeahhhhhh." She extended the *h* at the end, losing it to her breath, sounding soft and erotic.

"I'm on the next flight home."

"I wish, but you have that meeting."

"I know. Hold that thought, though."

"Why is it they want to see you?"

Rich paused at the head of a down escalator. "I'm not sure." He stepped on. "It may have something to do with wrapping-up the investigation."

"See if they can tell you what's going to happen with the grand jury."

"They wouldn't know. The grand jury is still hearing testimony, I think."

"Oh, that reminds me."

Rich could hear Gisele rummaging through papers.

"I got this … subpoena," she continued. "Some guy dropped it off at The Ordinary."

"They have your deposition. I don't understand why they would subpoena you."

"I'm supposed to testify tomorrow."

"That's pretty quick. You're my wife—you can't testify against me."

"Well, I wouldn't."

"Go see Borodavka."

"That horrible man?"

"He's not horrible … just … just a bit … eccentric."

"Eccentric in a gross, slovenly sort of way."

"Messy people are considered very creative." Rich assured her.

Silence. Rich imagined Gisele crinkling her nose, making the repulsed face he always found cute and disarming.

Rich exited to the outside. A bitingly cold wind, reeking of diesel, hit his face. The noise of cars, buses, taxis and police whistles made hearing difficult. He spoke louder. "Gisele, let me call you back." She said something he couldn't make out. "Go see Borodavka. I've got to go. Love you." He clicked off.

The green shuttle bus to the rental car lot stood with open door. Rich climbed the steps and took a seat.

Within an hour, he was maneuvering his compact rental car through the confusion of turns and exits and on ramps to get on 90 South toward Chicago. Once on 90 and settled in a lane, he pulled out his phone and called Gisele.

"Come on, hon, answer." The call went to voicemail. "Hi, it's me. I'm on my way to my hotel, and then I'll have to jet to the FBI regional office. I won't have a chance to call you until this evening. Go see Borodavka. Love you."

His reserved room was ready at the Holiday Inn on West Harrison. He had enough time to drop his bag, freshen up, change his t-shirt to a dress shirt and join up with the early afternoon city traffic.

The FBI regional headquarters on Roosevelt Road in the West Loop comprised a three-building complex, with a 10-story office made of blue-tinted glass and precast concrete. A black wrought-iron fence surrounded the 12-acre grassy expanse. Security procedures were similar, if not tighter, than those of the regional office in Omaha. Rich parked and went into the security screening station on the right side of the bright and airy wood-and-glass lobby.

"You found us," Bertoloni said, entering.

"Nice squat," Rich said, taking the orange visitor's pass handed to him by a security officer. He looped the lanyard over his head, settling the pass on his chest.

The agent held the door open. "Yeah, it'll do." Rich went through the door to the lobby. Bertoloni motioned toward the elevators. "The bureau was spread out all over Chicago, in small offices dealing with specific investigations and tasks." The agent wore a standard-issue blue suit and blue-striped tie, his jacket unbuttoned with hands casually in pants pockets. "We've still got satellite locations in

Rockford and other spots." The elevator doors closed. "Most offices have been centralized to this location."

"Why are we meeting, and who's running it?"

Bertoloni looked at Rich with mock surprise. "You're not interested in touring the temple?" He waited a second. "I'm kidding you. My boss, Jejune, is lead. He'll get you up-to-speed."

"How come you couldn't have just called me?"

They exited the elevator and walked down a wide, brightly lit corridor with a neutral off-green carpet. Television monitors mounted high on the wall along the corridor played CNN news. A display of framed black-and-white pictures with old-time gangsters with hands up to G-men leveling Thompson submachine guns celebrated the FBI's past glory.

"Jejune thought it best to meet with you in person."

They reached a door with a red oak veneer that led to a large corner office. The glass of the door, painted white on the corridor side, read, *Anton Jejune, Special Agent-in-Charge Criminal Investigation Division, International Operations Divisions.* Bertoloni stopped, his hand on the door knob. "Happy happy," he joked and then opened the door and motioned Rich in.

The office was conference room-sized, with file cabinets and book cases on the glass wall side and a round table, a short black leather couch and a wall-mounted television monitor on the opposite side. This all led to the oversized cherry wood desk squarely before a bank of windows. The desk looked too neat, holding only a banker's light, blotter and computer monitor. A small, balding man sat hunched over a pile of papers, reading and signing.

Rich strode in, recognizing Jejune, whom he had last seen across a steel table in the basement interrogation room of the Wilmette Police Department. Out of the corner of his eye, Rich noticed another man. His facial structure appeared western, though his skin tone was subcontinental from Asia. He wore an out-of-season beige suit and sat in an outsized chair to the other side of Jejune's desk. His expression was impassive; his legs were crossed and his fingers laced under his chin.

Agent Bertoloni closed the door.

Jejune glanced up. "Thank you, agent. Mr. Rice." Jejune stood. "It is good to see you."

Rich didn't think it so good, but he let that go and shook the shorter man's outstretched hand. "Uh huh."

Jejune's office smelled of leather and had a stunning vista through one-way glass to the east, with squat, square-top buildings and the Union Pacific and Metra rail lines. On a clear day, his view was deep into the Heart of Chicago and beyond.

"Please, do take a seat."

Rich sat in a padded chair, not directly across from the special agent.

Bertoloni lowered his long frame onto the couch.

"Have they been keeping you busy with the grand jury?"

"In a manner of speaking, yes."

"Not too taxing, I hope." Jejune's offered smile was devoid of sincerity.

"Not taxing, so much as anxious. I've no idea how it will turn out. And frankly, I am afraid I might get indicted."

Jejune cast a glance over to Bertoloni. "So he doesn't know."

"No, not as yet."

"Know what?" Rich wanted to know.

"In good time, Mr. Rice." Jejune repeated his false smile. "Let me just tell you that your anxiety is unfounded."

"I just learned my wife was subpoenaed."

Jejune looked surprised. "Say again?"

"My wife, she said she got a subpoena."

The special agent's head jerked over, and he cast sharp eyes at Bertoloni. "Did you know about this?"

"News to me."

"Look into it. Find out what that district attorney is playing at."

"Will do."

"What's going on?"

"Mr. Rice, your wife being subpoenaed to testify is a surprise to us. And frankly," Jejune leaned back in his chair, "I don't know why the district attorney would do that."

"Rich," Bertoloni chimed in. "I'll find out why and let you know. This might just be a due diligence thing, and she'll come in and back up what you said."

"All right."

"We have more pressing issues to discuss." Jejune interrupted.

Jejune had made no attempt to introduce the man observing to the side. Rich stared at him, taking his measure. Some men cannot match another man's stare. They become self-conscious, look away or distract themselves. This man, with his blank expression, did not look away but held Rich with cold, steady eyes. Rich realized that he was being measured himself.

"I didn't catch your name," he said to the man.

"It wasn't thrown," he replied.

Thrown? Rich wondered.

"Mr. Rice," Jejune said, tapping on the computer keyboard, "before we get fully into it, I wanted to let you know that the second satchel you turned over, the one with Nicky Franko's phone, yielded a trove of valuable information that has helped us tie up loose ends. The phone, though damaged, yielded a contact list that has proved invaluable."

For a brief moment, Rich experienced a pang of guilt, though he managed to acknowledge Jejune's comments with a nod. He would not tell them about the address book he had held back or the large quantity of money in Nicky's second satchel which Rich had kept. Much of the money had been used to repair the damage done to The Ordinary. These were, in his opinion, the spoils of war. "So you had no problems with encryption?"

"Not from that phone. All his contacts came up."

"Nikolai Franko wasn't the brightest amongst the Russian Mafia."

"Not sure if you are interested, but we've been scuffling with the Russian Federation over a couple of things. They have requested—" Jejune paused, looked at Rich with a bemused expression. "I needn't sugarcoat this. You've a good idea how the Russians are."

"Yes, a very good idea."

"They have been yelling and screaming for the return of Nikolai Franko's body, the body of the speed boat driver and that of Suka Franko's bodyguard. We're doing the diplomatic 'Oh by all means' expediting ASAWP ... As Soon as We Please. They also want Yuri Grimansky, who is lying in the hospital, returned. The Federation swears it plans to try him."

"Justice will be served," Bertoloni added in a sarcastic tone.

Jejune nodded with a pained smile. "They want all the *Bratva* we are holding in Cook County jail. And all the weapons we confiscated. But get this: they want, I mean really want, Nicky Franko's souped-up '51 Mercury."

"All those crap Russian rockabilly CDs also?" Rich joked. He wondered why they would want the car back.

Jejune's round, fleshy face almost broke into a grin. "Yeah, but the kicker is that they want you extradited, to stand trial for murder."

The room fell silent.

At once, Rich wondered if the meeting hadn't been a setup. "And we're not doing that. Right?"

Jejune went serious. "No. Let me repeat that. No." Seeing relief wash over Rich's face, he gave a half-smile. "You've already faced American justice and testified to the grand jury. Let's move on."

The wall-mounted television monitor flickered, and a picture of Jejune's icon-littered computer desktop came up.

"We will be sharing information that must not leave this room."

"Why are you doing that?"

Jejune's head tipped to one side with a resigned look. "I'll be candid. You were largely left in the dark before. The results were a couple of innocent people shot and killed, others put in jeopardy and a big flap with our Russian friends. It is our feeling that, if you have a better idea of what we are dealing with, you will be less likely to take matters into your own hands."

"You've been a loose cannon, Rich," Bertoloni said.

Rich didn't buy it. "Like hell, I have. Cannons get loose fighting your battles."

Bertoloni brought his hands and shoulders up.

"We've no problem with what happened before. We don't want it to happen again." Jejune worked his computer, and a grainy photo of a grassy area on the edge of a beach came up.

"This is Anderson Point. It lies on the western shore of Lake Michigan, across from the entrance to Green Bay and Escanaba Harbor," the agent explained. "The morning following Suka Franko's escape from Glencoe, a body was found up from the beach. The body was that of Frances Knudsen, fifty-three, a nurse at the clinic in town. Mrs. Knudsen was shot once in the back of the head, execution-style."

Rich started to add it up.

"At the scene were gauze dressings and a pair of bloody purple surgical gloves." Jejune turned to Rich. "The gloves and dressings were sent to the FBI lab for processing."

"I've a fairly good idea who they will match."

"As do we." Jejune changed the picture to a narrow stretch of sandy beach. "See the line there?"

Rich nodded.

"It doesn't show up well in this picture, but it is a deep groove, something the keel of a speed boat would leave if pulled up to shore."

"So the boat that took Suka Franko off the pier in Glencoe must've stopped there."

"Without a doubt."

"And I hit her."

"Yes, but we don't know what damage you did."

"Enough to have them get a nurse to patch her up."

"True."

"That's a pretty far piece from Glencoe. They must've been running out of fuel."

"You would think." Jejune again changed pictures to one with red jerry cans strewn about the beach. "Apparently, they refueled and continued on."

"To where?"

"Not back to Chicago," Bertoloni put in.

"The Coast Guard had been alerted and searched along Door County and the Upper Peninsula for a spot where they might hold up until things cooled down."

Rich was warming to Jejune, letting go some of his resentment over the interrogation. He seemed genuinely forthcoming and, in a small way, respectful of Rich.

"What about Canada?"

"Our thinking also. Nearest port is Sudbury," Jejune agreed. "But, a day later, we got a report of two bodies found among the wreckage of a boat. The debris was located in St. Martin Bay, an inlet a few miles east of the Straits of Mackinac." The special agent tapped his computer and showed a picture of boat parts floating about a body face down in the water. "Hope that isn't too graphic."

"Doesn't bother me."

Bertoloni picked up the tale. "The bodies were a couple of Russians with temporary visas and Chicago addresses. And yes, both are on the Russian Mafia database. The wreckage was fiberglass, consistent with a go-fast boat."

"Mr. Rice, they were shot numerous times and burned."

Rich started to speak.

Jejune nodded. "I know what you're going to ask. No, there wasn't a third body of a woman."

"She couldn't have just vanished."

"Of course not," Jejune replied. "We were forced to contact our friends." He said *friends* with an ironic turn, casting a quick glance to the silent man.

Rich now knew who and what he was.

"You want to pick it up from there?"

The man continued staring at Rich while slowly shaking his head.

"Okay," Jejune said. He clicked and up came a photo of a large three-boom freighter. "We received information from satellite surveillance that a freighter had stopped for over five hours in St. Martin's Bay, near the site of the wreckage and bodies. I'm doing a helluva lot of talking." Jejune got up and opened a brown compact refrigerator by the filing cabinet. He held up a bottle of water.

"Anyone else?"

"No."

"The ship onscreen is the TS *Alexander Pushkin*, a Russian freighter that left Duluth-Superior the previous day." He unscrewed the cap and drank. "All freighter traffic on the Great Lakes is tracked by MSSIS satellites, especially those with international registry. But, Homeland Security also tracks all freighter traffic in and out of US ports. We staged a work stoppage with the longshoremen. Homeland Security took the opportunity to look over the cargo that the *Pushkin* was loading to ensure it did not violate international sanctions." Jejune sidestepped around his desk and sat. "The *Pushkin* is owned by Kozmos Corporation, a Russian Federation import company with, we believe, ties to the Russian Mafia."

"They picked up Suka Franko?"

"That's our assumption. The *Pushkin* sailed out of the Great Lakes and crossed the Atlantic. Ten days later, three days ago, she docked in St. Petersburg."

"You're telling me Suka is still alive."

"We're fairly certain." Jejune turned to the silent man. "Should I go on?"

The man slid expressionless eyes from Jejune to Rich. "Let him know the whole story." His voice was flat and unemotional. Rich detected an accent, but he wasn't sure from where.

"Like I said, nothing leaves this room."

"Okay."

"You are, I believe, aware who Suka Franko's father is?"

"Is?" Rich did not like that. "He's Ivan Franko, *vory* and then recruited to the NKVD, which morphed into the KGB. But, is he still alive?"

"Yes."

"He's got to be in his nineties."

"Ninety-three to be exact. Alive and kicking." Jejune hesitated. "Sources at the St. Petersburg docks informed our friends that the *Pushkin* was met by Ivan Franko."

"Shit," Rich said under his breath. He had a clearer picture now.

"Yes." Jejune's eyebrows arched. "Shit indeed. We got a report that Ivan Franko traveled to Moscow from his dacha outside of Odessa the day after Nikolai Franko was shot and his daughter, Irina Suka Franko, was wounded. He went to the Federal Security Service complex in Moscow."

Rich jumped out of his chair. “Shit,” he said with more emphasis, pacing the room. “You’re telling me Suka Franko survived and will, no doubt, come after me—and, and, her father is involved and bringing down the whole of the Russian FSB.”

Jejune exchanged a look and sigh with Bertoloni.

Rich stopped mid-step. “Why? Why are you telling me this? You kept me in the dark before.”

“I told you: we want to avoid innocent people getting killed.”

“Before, they just wanted to scare me off or shut me up. But now, with Nicky Franko killed ... they will want a pound of flesh.”

“We left you in place last time, knowing they would come.”

“So I really was bait.” Rich looked at his hands. They shook.

“Unfortunately, that is true. Though now, we need you fully apprized and aware of the overall situation.”

“Aware that the Russian Mafia and Federation state agencies are out to kill me.”

Jejune retreated into the padded depth of his desk chair, hands clasped before his chest. His voice dropped, and he spoke without inflection. “We cannot have a repeat of the barroom gunfight. You have to report anything suspicious so we can head it off before someone dies.”

“I can’t keep running the rest of my life.” Rich gathered himself and returned to his chair. He slowly sat, all but resigned.

"We don't want you dangling in the wind, like a *Vaild Kaard*." The comment from the silent man startled the other three.

"*Vaild Kaard*? What does that mean?"

"Means--Cowboy."

"You don't fully trust me, do you Mr. Rice?" Jejune added. "But, in this instance, you've little choice. We'll be there. The Russians can be cold and calculating, although, in these circumstances, they are reacting emotionally. That may be their fatal mistake."

"Or my fatal end."

"When things appear most dire, opportunities arise." The dark man swayed forward in his chair, the window light putting half his face in shadow. "We have a score to settle with General Franko from his NKVD and Second Directorate days. These uncharacteristic familial actions could offer us a chance for payback."

"You have Agent Bertoloni's number. He is in constant contact with me. You have the Omaha regional office number. Anything out of the ordinary, let us know." Jejune chuckled. "Didn't mean to make a pun."

"Rich, I'll check in frequently." Bertoloni added.

"Do you have questions, Mr. Rice?"

They looked at Rich.

"I thought I had my life back. I thought it was over. Gisele and I could run The Ordinary and live upstairs. I could be a stringer for a newspaper. I would have time to finish my book on human trafficking in the United States. I can't believe how foolish I was to think that. And it goes on. Now I have to digest all this."

Rich got back to his hotel too late for lunch, too early for dinner. He called Gisele and got voicemail. He left a message.

Mulling the meaning of the FBI meeting over and over in his mind, he stared out the eastside window into the Loop as the gray light faded to dark. The late autumn wind whipped off the lake and rattled the glass. He stood restless, fidgety. Behind him, the television filled the silence with jabber. Rich had to get out. Pulling his head through a heavy, hooded maroon sweatshirt with the old Monmouth University logo, he left the room with the light and television on.

He hunched to the biting wind in his face. Lingering at the intersection, he waited for the light to cross Harrison Street Bridge over the tannery-brown Chicago River. Cars filled the westbound lanes, heading to the suburbs. Rich ambled north on Wacker Drive between the sheer cliffs of concrete and glass. The dark river moved imperceptibly with windy ripples crisscrossing the surface. He dodged people on the street. They shied away from his probing eyes. He studied the faces swarming past. Rich's thoughts were confused, damaged as he struggled to get back the solidarity of purpose that had kept him alive when on the run. He would not slip from sight and return to anonymity.

Dark shapes of noisy cars passed, with headlights splitting the night and steam from grates and the sewer. They were shunted along, stoplight to stoplight. Neon glowed multi-colors on both sides of the street, over stores and restaurants. He passed the smells of coffee from cafes, liquor from bars and frying from restaurants. None of it dispelled his anxiety, though he was getting hungry. Clusters of people talked and laughed. Rich walked on.

He took out his phone and tried Gisele. It went to voicemail. He left no message.

Past the Housing Authority of Cook County building, Rich found a Greek sandwich shop tucked into the FedEx Shipping Center across from the Federal Reserve Bank. He walked into the narrow, brightly lit gyro shop. There were small tables along the wall opposite the glass displays.

"What I get you, chief?" asked an older Greek in shirt sleeves and stained apron. The shop was humid and pungent of onions.

Rich studied the hand-painted menu mounted on the back wall. "I'll have a half gyro."

"To take away?"

"No, I'll eat it here."

"What else I get you?"

"Bag of chips and soda." Rich paid.

"I bring to you, chief." The Greek said at the register.

Rich gingerly sat, his back to the light, looking out the front window at the shadows of passersby. No one saw him. No one looked.

"You enjoy." The Greek placed before Rich a red plastic basket with a gyro on hard roll, a yellow bag of potato chips and red can of Coke.

"Thanks." Rich bit into the roll. The meat tasted peppery and warm. He snatched a paper napkin from a chrome dispenser and ate in silence, not wanting to think about anything.

Returning to his hotel room, Rich called Gisele. After three rings, it went to voicemail. It was past eight o'clock. He knew Jorge would be at The Ordinary.

"Jorge, is Gisele there?" He listened. "When did she leave?" He waited, idly clicking the remote control through the television channels. "When she gets back, let her know I called and ask her to call me. Thanks."

He stared out the hotel window at the lights of the city, trying to fight poisonous thoughts. "She's just got her phone turned off." Or: "she just needs some quiet time." There was nothing to worry about. He tossed his phone on the bed and lay down to watch television.

His phone buzzed, waking him. *Gisele,* he thought, feeling for the phone. "Gisele?" he sleepily answered. "Oh, sorry, Daisy. I thought you were. Huh? No, I haven't either." Rich sat up and turned off the television. "Just put the bank bag upstairs. I'll be back tomorrow. Thanks." He carefully laid the phone on the bed and swung his legs to the floor, shuffling to the bathroom.

He splashed water on his face and leaned close to the mirror. *Maybe she went to her mother's,* he thought. *She would've called.*

It was half past two in the morning—too late to phone his mother-in-law, Mrs. Esslin. He would try in the morning, before his flight. Switching off the bathroom light, he fell back into bed. Knowing the worry would keep sleep away, he turned on the television.

He called Gisele at first light. Voicemail.

"*Frau Esslin? Es ist heir Richard. Wie gehts? Ja, ja, gutt. Um, sprechen sie English, bitte?*" Rich said as he stuffed clothing into his carry-on bag. "Is Gisele there?" He waited. "Have you heard from her?" Rich grew impatient. "No, I haven't. Did she call you? Okay. I haven't heard from her, and I'm sort of worried. Sorry to wake you. Yes, I will let you know. *Vielen dank. Auf Wiedersehen.*"

Driving to O'Hare, Rich did his best to dissuade himself from worry. He would get home, and Gisele will be upstairs. She hadn't realized that her phone battery was dead. Maybe she misplaced her phone.

He returned the rental car and waited inside for the shuttle bus to the terminal. The anxiety made him antsy. He paced about the rental car office. When the green bus pulled up outside, Rich let the others go before him. As the last, he dashed from the warm office, through the foggy chill, to the bus. He sidestepped down the narrow aisle to an available seat. The bus doors shut, and with a loud diesel growl and cloud of black smoke, the bus started forward. Staring out the window at the cars, terminal and people, Rich distracted himself from wondering. Everything was fine, he was sure of it.

Rich got to his gate and called The Ordinary. Jorge answered.

"Jorge, is Mrs. Rice there? Maybe upstairs? Could you go upstairs and see? Call me back. *Gracias.*"

Pacing around the gate, Rich waited for his phone to vibrate. They started boarding his flight. He waited. At the final boarding call, he felt his phone in his pocket.

"Yeah, Jorge. What? She's not there? When did you last see her?" Rich handed his boarding pass to be scanned. "Yesterday. What did you say? She was going ... okay, I'll call Borodavka." Rich started down the gangway. "If she comes in, have her call me, right away. I'll be back this afternoon. Thanks, *amigo.*" Rich pressed the phone icon and ducked into the airplane cabin. He gave the flight attendant a quick, cursory smile and found his seat. He did not know how he could handle the inflight hour with Gisele's whereabouts unknown. He strapped in.

"Excuse me." He held his hand up. The passing flight attendant stopped and bent down. "Can I make a call before me take off?"

"No, I'm sorry, sir. We are about to push back from the gate. You'll have to switch off your phone and any other electronic devices."

"Can't I use my phone once we're in the air?"

"This plane is not equipped for that."

"I need to make a call."

"Sir, we'll be in Omaha in little over an hour. I am sure it can wait." She smiled a well-practiced smile.

Rich teetered on the verge of losing his temper, knowing that, if he did, he would be taken off the plane. With clenched teeth and tight jaw, he nodded. The flight attendant moved away.

He stared out the window at the layer of white clouds below. Thoughts crept back again and again: *Is this the Russians? Do they have Gisele?* He swept it aside. *Can't be.* But like tumbling dice, his thoughts came up snake eyes. *Is it Bratva*? He didn't know. He rationalized; thinking like this was caused by his meeting with the FBI. *Maybe this is General Franko's handiwork? No, no, can't be, impossible.*

The hour of flight time until the plane began its descent to Omaha seemed to stretch on forever. There was a dusting of snow on the checkerboard of land below. As soon as the wheels touched, Rich had his phone to his ear.

"Borodavka? It's Richard Rice."

People stood and pulled bags from the overhead bins.

"Welcome to Omaha ..." the pilot began.

"Did my wife come to see you yesterday?" Rich spoke over the pilot's announcement. He struggled up and waited in the aisle. "When was that?"

The cabin door opened, and people started filing off the aircraft.

"Yeah, she told me she got a subpoena. I told her to go see you." Rich gave the flight attendant a tilt of his head and stepped off the plane. "It was what?" He stopped. People flowed by him. "Fake? I don't understand." He leaned to the wall. "The subpoena was phony. Did you tell her to ignore it?" He pushed off the wall and walked up the jet way. "She's gone. No one's seen her since yesterday. I haven't heard from her since the afternoon. I've called, and I just get voicemail. I'm headed back to The Ordinary. Maybe she left a note. Yeah, thanks."

He accelerated his pace through the terminal, the parking lot and pay booth and was on 480 in little more than ten minutes. It occurred to Rich to call Bertoloni, but he stopped himself. He could hear Bertoloni laugh at him. "Got trouble at home, Rich?" He tried Gisele and angrily clicked off the phone when voicemail came on.

"Shit." He punched the accelerator pedal and pushed beyond the speed limit. When he pulled into the back parking lot of The Ordinary, Gisele's black Accord was not there.

"*Hola, jefe,*" Jorge, at the grill, shouted as Rich burst through the back door of The Ordinary.

"Yeah," Rich called back, crossing to Riku behind the bar.

A scattering of customers sat at tables and in booths. Daisy took drink orders for a trio of men in a booth. Roxy Music's "Out of the Blue" played over the speakers.

"Riku?" Rich leaned over the bar. "Riku?"

The young Asian looked up and grinned. "Mr. Rice."

"Have you seen my wife, Gisele?"

"No, not today."

Rich spun about. "Daisy."

"Hey, boss."

"Have you seen Gisele?"

"Yesterday, but not today."

"Has she called?"

Daisy put a round tray on the bar and tapped the touchscreen on the POS computer. "Nope. Did you check upstairs?"

Rich darted out the back and up the outside steps. He tried the back door. It was locked. He knocked loudly and fumbled with his keys.

"Gisele?" he called, entering the kitchen. A single coffee cup was in the stainless steel sink. Dried coffee rung its bottom.

Silence.

He went into the living room and then the bedroom. The bed was unmade.

"Gisele?" A white towel hung crooked off the rack in the bathroom.

Silence.

"Son of a bitch." Rich sunk into a chair in the living room. "Where are you?"

He heard the back door open. "Boss?"

Rich looked over to the kitchen doorway. Daisy cautiously entered the room.

"Where is she, Daisy?" His voice almost cracked.

"Mrs. Rice?" Daisy wrung her hands at her waist. "We haven't seen her since yesterday morning. She said she was going to see your lawyer." The young woman sounded on the verge of tears.

"Did anything different happen?"

"No, nothing I can think of," Daisy's voice shook. "Well, a guy dropped off a letter for her."

Rich went over to the young woman. "Tell me about the guy?"

Daisy shrugged. "Just some guy. I was across the bar. He held up an envelope and said 'for Missus.' Then he left it on the bar."

"Do you remember anything odd about him?"

"No."

"Long hair? Short hair? What color?" Rich probed.

"Short hair. Yeah, it was blond, I think."

"Young? Old? What was he wearing?"

"Hooded sweatshirt, gray, and blue jeans. He wasn't young, but wasn't old."

"You said he had short blond hair, but he wore a hooded sweatshirt?"

"He didn't have the hood up." Daisy glanced down.

"Was there a logo on the sweatshirt?"

"Not that I could see."

"Hard-looking face?"

"Hard to look at. He was really ugly in a scary sort of way. Boss, is everything all right?"

"Fine." Rich could see the fright in her eyes. "This is really uncharacteristic of Gisele." He stopped, not wanting to say too much. "She may be driving to her mother's or something." He took Daisy by the shoulders and gently turned her about. "She'll turn up. In the meantime, I need you, Jorge and Riku to keep The Ordinary running." He walked her to the door. "Can I count on you for that?"

"You know you can," Daisy smiled.

"Thanks." Rich opened the back door. "I've got to see some people this afternoon. I'll be back for tonight's shift."

"Okay." Daisy took a step out the door and stopped. "I don't know if it means anything, but when the guy called out, waving the envelope, I didn't understand him. Like he wasn't speaking English. Then he said, 'for Missus.'" She laughed slightly.

"Maybe you just didn't hear him at first." They shared a smile, and Daisy went down the stairs.

Rich closed the kitchen door. He went to the gun safe in the living room and dialed the combination. Jerking open the heavy door, he took out his short-barrel Smith and Wesson .32 and flipped open the cylinder. He reached into a cardboard box and filled the empty chambers with bullets. He snapped it closed and holstered the gun, clipping it on his belt.

CHAPTER 7

In his anxious state, the steep flight of stairs to the third floor over Prince Tong's Chinese restaurant to Borodavka's office presented no problem for Rich. He took the steps two at a time and reached the landing only slightly winded. Unwilling and almost unable to slow himself, Rich was down the hall and at Borodavka's door in seconds. The smell of boiled cabbage from the restaurant didn't bother him. He knocked and pushed open the door. He caught the large lawyer at his desk with half a jelly roll poised before his open mouth.

"I have to talk to you," Rich said, stepping over a pile of books, sitting and then standing.

"Certainly." Borodavka hastily swallowed and brushed crumbs from his hairy face. "Sit. Or stand. Or ..."

"Gisele's missing. You may have been the last person to see her."

"I saw her yesterday." Borodavka pretended to smooth down his tie, though he actually wiped sticky grape jelly off his fingertips. He carefully placed the half jelly roll on a napkin and took a slurp of coffee from a paper cup. "She came in with that phony subpoena."

Rich tried sitting again. "Tell me about the subpoena." He couldn't sit.

"I could tell right off it wasn't authentic."

"How?" Rich stood, fidgeting.

"How did you get served with your subpoena?"

Rich thought about it. "A deputy came up, asked my name, handed me an envelope."

"Someone left your wife's subpoena on the bar. That's not how it's done. Then there's spell check."

"Spell check?"

"Whoever filled in the form should've spell-checked Nebraska. It's not N-A-braska."

"Maybe English wasn't their first language?"

"That could well be." Borodavka cracked a hairy smile. "They also misspelled your wife's name. It's Gisele, with one *L*." The lawyer's eyes searched for the jelly roll.

"That could've been a secretarial error."

"Maybe." Borodavka swayed toward the pastry. "I thought of that." He half-lifted the roll and then took a snap at it. He tucked the bite into his cheek. "So, I called Nutkis' office."

Rich wrung his palms. "And?"

"Nutkis thought I was pulling his leg." The lawyer chewed.

Rich went to the window, looking to the street below. "So he didn't subpoena Gisele."

"No. It wasn't from his office." Borodavka washed down the jelly roll with coffee. "He wanted to see the fake subpoena. It's against the law to forge, fake or alter federal documents."

"Daisy says the subpoena was dropped off by an ugly blond guy in a hooded sweatshirt. She wasn't sure he spoke English."

"Blond? Like that Russian at the courthouse?"

"I don't know." Rich turned from the window. "Do you have the subpoena?"

"No. Your wife kept it. I suggested she take it to Nutkis. I don't know if she did."

Rich shuffled back to the chair, able now to sit. "I've called and called. All I get is her voicemail. No one has seen her since yesterday. She's not at The Ordinary. She's not at her mother's. You were the last person to see her."

Borodavka held and examined all angles of the last bite of jelly roll. He had sadness in his eyes. Then it was gone. "Maybe she's just taking some time for herself."

"That's not like her." Rich shook his head. "She'd have called." His voice rose. "She would have told someone at The Ordinary." His face tensed and he got louder. "She would've left a note," he yelled, pounding his thighs with his fists.

Rich's chin dropped to his chest. Borodavka gave him a minute to calm down.

"What're you going to do?"

"I'm going to go to the cops and report her missing."

"Hold on." Borodavka's hand went out, making a motion in the air like patting Rich's shoulder. "I don't think you want to do that."

"Why not?"

"You can do that, but they won't consider her a missing person if she's only been gone since yesterday. And then, all the suspicion falls on you."

"Me?"

"You. They're going to consider her murdered, not missing, and you will be the prime suspect."

Rich's whole body sagged as he exhaled. "You're right. I know you're right."

"Haven't you had enough crap lately?" Borodavka gazed at Rich through the tangled mass of eyebrow hair and cheek beard. The bald spot on the top of his head reminded Rich of a heliport in the middle of the jungle.

"You got that right." Rich agreed. "The grand jury is still out." He paused. "I assume."

"I asked Nutkis, and he said they were probably in deliberations today."

"It's nearly a month since the shootout at The Ordinary."

"You've been through the wringer. Are you reopened?"

"Yes, just this weekend. And yesterday, I was in Chicago at the FBI Office."

"Really?" Borodavka sat up. "Why didn't you tell me?"

"I didn't think it was a big deal."

"You've been up before a grand jury ... never mind." His tone shifted. "What was the meeting about?"

"They wanted to meet with me to clue me in on Suka Franko."

"That's Nikolai's mother?" Borodavka reached for his pipe. "What about?"

"She was wounded at the pier in Glencoe, taken away by a go-fast boat and somehow got back to Russia." Rich became reluctant to continue.

The lawyer appeared to note Rich's reticence. He lighted his pipe, thoughtfully puffing smoke clouds into the air, like a painter populating a barren sky. He waited.

"A year and a half ago, my life was shit," Rich began. "If Nicky Franko had pointed a gun at me right then, I would've thanked him for ending my miserable days."

Borodavka puffed and nodded.

"I was in a dead-end job, writing the cops beat and occasional features for a ho-hum suburban edition of Chicago's biggest newspaper. That's not where you should be at 44 years old. I had a novel half-finished in a bottom drawer. I wasn't hiding it from the world; I hid it from myself. I had nonfiction manuscripts started on the usual Chicago stuff: prohibition years, St. Valentine's Day Massacre. Boring."

They were quiet. The clang of dishes and muffled shouts in Chinese could be heard from the kitchen below.

Rich hung his left elbow over the chair back, turning aside and watching the undulating blue smoke drift across the room.

"It's called the velvet coffin," he confided. "Pay is good, but your career is dead. I will lie in state, hands on my chest, having been unable to achieve much beyond my frustration."

The lawyer took the pipe out of his mouth. "How was your marriage?"

"You my shrink now? Why do you want to know?"

"The cops are going to browbeat you on it."

"My marriage was..." Rich stopped himself. "...is good."

"The cops are going to want to know all of that. They'll pull records looking for any domestic violence or restraining orders, and they'll probably take your computer to check email and social media. They'll try and break your alibi."

"I think I have a good one. Like I told you, I was at the FBI headquarters in Chicago."

Borodavka pointed the stem of his pipe at Rich. "That's not a bad idea."

"My alibi?"

"No, the FBI. We should give Agent Bertoloni a call."

"Your pal, Paulie? What's that going to do?"

"Can't hurt." Borodavka thumbed through his phone and pressed the screen. He clicked the speaker on and propped the phone on his cluttered desk.

The phone rang twice and stopped. "FBI headquarters, Chicago."

Borodavka leaned his bulk toward the phone. "Agent Paul Bertoloni, please."

"Who's calling?"

The lawyer put a finger across his mouth to keep Rich quiet. "Molly Nutkis."

"Excuse me?"

"Molly ... Nutkis."

"Hold, please." The line went silent a few seconds.

"Hey, babe."

"Paulie? It's Coach Doug."

"Coach? I was told this was..."

"I didn't think you'd pick up."

"Funny guy. But you're right. I'm pretty busy, Coach."

"I understand." Borodavka said. "We're on speaker, and I'm here with Richard Rice."

"Rich? What's going on?"

Rich edged forward, speaking at the phone. "Paul, my wife, Gisele, has been missing since yesterday."

"Missing? Why do you say that?"

"No one has seen or heard from her."

"Huh." The agent paused. "Sure she didn't take off, a vacation for herself?"

"She would've told me."

"I was the last person to see her, Paulie," Borodavka added. "She came to me with a subpoena someone served her with."

"Is that the subpoena Rich told us about yesterday?"

"Yeah, and it was a fake."

"Fake, huh. Have you talked to the cops yet?"

"No. Borodavka says not to."

"He's right. Don't. They'll dick you around and try to tag you with it. I'll tell Jejune and—"

"Paul?" Rich interrupted. "Is Yuri Grimansky still in the hospital here in Omaha?"

"Yeah, far as we know. He's at Creighton Med. Why?"

"I want to talk to him."

"Why am I not surprised? I don't know if that is a good idea."

"I just want to ask him if he knows anything."

"Okay, I'll let the agents guarding him know. I really got to go, guys. Keep me posted. And Rich?"

"Yeah?"

"Strap that cannon down good."

"Thanks, Paulie."

"You bet, Coach. I mean, Molly." The agent clicked off.

Borodavka picked up his phone. “You think talking to Grimansky will get you any info?”

“I don’t know. Better than sitting around doing nothing but freak out.”

Rich stepped out of the stainless steel elevator and went to the nurse’s station. The third floor IC unit at Creighton Medical Hospital was abuzz with late afternoon activity. Nurses walked up and down the wide white corridor. A doctor with a flock of young students at his coat tails made rounds.

“I’m looking for Yuri Grimansky’s room.”

An older nurse with a weary expression gave Rich a dismissive glance. “I’m sorry, we don’t have a patient under that name.” A second nurse with a clipboard clutched to her chest asked, “Perhaps you have the wrong hospital?”

Rich stepped back and saw two men in dark suits at the end of the corridor. One agent sat, and the other stood, drinking from a white Styrofoam cup. “That’s his room down there.”

A nurse quickly came out from behind the counter. “That’s a No Info patient. Wait here.” She half ran down the corridor to the men.

Rich took a step away from the nurse’s station, toward the corridor.

“She said to stay here,” the other nurse snapped.

“They know I’m coming.”

“Stay here, or we’ll toss your backside down the stairwell.”

“Okay, relax.”

The nurse talked to the one of the men. He squinted down the corridor and saw Rich. He threw his cup in a waste can and returned alongside the nurse to the head of the corridor.

"Your name is?" He was young, tall and wide, like a football player.

"Richard Rice. Agent Bertoloni should've called and let you know I was coming."

"He did. I still need to see ID." He had coffee breath.

When Rich reached into his back pocket, the second agent at the far end of the corridor stood.

He checked Rich's driver's license picture. "Turn around. Raise your arms. What's that on your belt?"

"It's my carry."

"You can't go in there wearing that."

"Here. Hold it for me."

He took Rich's .32. "Follow me."

Rich trailed the agent.

"I don't know what this is all about, but an agent has to accompany you."

"Sure, no problem."

He handed Rich's gun to the seated agent. "What am I going to do with this?" the seated agent said.

The two entered the hospital room.

It was a big room. The large Russian lay propped up in bed, watching *Family Feud* on the wall-mounted television. His eyes shifted to Rich. "Is you?" Yuri mumbled. "What you do here?"

"How you doing, *boyevik*?" The room smelled of antiseptic and vaguely of turned milk. Rich went to the head of the bed and snatched the nurse's button from Yuri's hand. He hung it over the bed rail.

An IV tube was taped to the side of Yuri's neck. Wires from a cardiac monitor came out the neck of the Russian's blue hospital gown. A blood pressure unit on the wall showed a bouncing line. Both Yuri's shoulders were bandaged, and he had one heavily bandaged leg out from the covers.

"How I do? I don't want see you. You shoot me, and you kill Nicky."

Rich went to the foot of the bed. "That's right."

"Why you not in jail?"

"Because it was self-defense."

"Ahhhh, self-defense. I want self-defense too. Why you here?"

"I have questions for you."

"You waste time." Yuri turned his head away. "I no answer."

"Suit yourself." Rich reached out and latched onto Yuri's bare ankle. "How's the leg?"

The Russian's body tensed. "It fine," he said. But his face went white, and he glared warily at Rich.

"Good to hear," Rich said in a soothing tone. "Bet it would hurt like hell if someone pulled really hard."

"Hey, you no do." Yuri turned panicked eyes to the agent. "You no let him touch me."

The agent pointed to the television. "This is my favorite TV show." He went to the bedside table, taking the remote control and turning the volume up.

"You no touch me."

"Just a couple of questions, soldier."

"Okay, okay, what?" he breathlessly replied.

"My wife is missing."

"She the pretty girl?"

"Yes."

"Nicky want her when we stop her in gas station."

"After Dubuque?"

"Is that how you say?" His laugh was slight and shaky. "Nicky, he think it Da-boo-key."

Rich tightened his grip on Yuri's ankle. Sweat beads shone across the big man's broad forehead.

"If someone took her, where would they keep her?"

"I no know. You right. I just *boyevik*."

Anger twisted Rich's face as he threw back the blanket and grabbed Yuri's other bandaged leg. He snarled through clenched teeth. "I want an answer, or I'm going to pull on your legs so hard you'll scream in pain."

"No, no. I no know where they would take your woman."

"Who would know?"

"I think."

"Think fast."

Laughter came out of the television. The agent chuckled.

"The rat. The rat you put in jail. He know."

"Give me a name." Rich dug his fingernails into Yuri's flesh.

"It Yana. He rat. He talk to you." Yuri's face twisted.

"You mean Yana Volkov, in Cook County jail?'

"*Da*, he know. He know who take people."

Rich released Yuri's ankles and straightened. "You better be right, *boyo*, or I'm coming back, at night, while you sleep, with a hammer."

"I know nothing else."

"I'm done here," Rich said to the agent.

"Wait a second. I want to see if they get the right answer."

"Survey says," came out of the TV followed by a ding.

"Oh, I can't believe they got that wrong," he said, holding the door open for Rich.

Beneath a hovering sky of heavy gray clouds, the sprawling 96-acre Cook County Jail looked imposing and terrifying. High walls of rough concrete and old red brick stood like a gothic monument to the lost lives of the lawless. The architecture spanned more than a century as the jail had never stopped expanding. Brick towers and tall, round guard silos with walkways commanded views from this corner and that corner into the trapezoid hoosegow. A modern poly-hexagon tower with Plexiglas windows overlooked a wing and exercise yard. Something space-age and modern resembling a beige mushroom guarded the near corner next to a multistory blockhouse with row upon row of small, dark and dirty windows.

Rich pulled off South California Street into the maze of buildings. He parked in the lot across from Maximum Security Division 10. He emptied his pockets of change, his phone and his concealed carry, putting them all into a daypack on the floor of his truck. He had clothes in the backpack. Jorge and Daisy had known he might have to leave at a moment's notice, and they had assured him they'd take care of The Ordinary.

It was a chilly, damp morning, but that wasn't the reason Rich shivered. The walk into Division 10, between high walls strung with gleaming coils of razor wire and security cameras, unnerved him. This was the type of place you slunk into and scampered to get out.

A bank of Cook County Sheriffs went through the bags, bras and piled-up weaves of visiting wives and kids and sent them through metal detectors. A woman with three kids was turned back. "No phones." Rich waited his turn. Footsteps echoed in the hallway, but everyone remained quiet. Family visitors knew the drill. A black sheriff eyed him. A white sheriff motioned him forward. Rich went through fairly quickly. He joined a line shuffling along to a narrow, cloudy window of scarred plastic. The mother in front of him had too much of something floral but smelly in her glistening hair. It got up Rich's nose. A baby nearby needed changing.

"Name?" a female sheriff asked through a vented metal circle in the thick plastic.

"Richard Rice."

"Who ya here ta see?"

"Volkov. Yana Volkov."

The sheriff scanned a list on a clipboard. "Aw-ight. He ticked off he'd sees ya. Sign dis." She slipped the bottom half of the clipboard out a slit in the window.

There were small pencils in a blackened cardboard box. Rich signed.

She pulled the clipboard back. "Go ta da waiting room 'cross da hall. When y'hear da name of dah inmate, en number over da speaker, follow da arrow to da communication room. Next."

Rich sat on a bench in the corner. The air hung stale, thick. Babies cried. Two women talked or argued, he couldn't tell which. A sheriff opened a thick metal side door and stood. The speaker squawked out a series of names and numbers. People moved to the door. Rich listened for Yana Volkov.

Three days now since Gisele had vanished. The last time Rich had called her phone, all he got was silence.

The speaker scratched through a series of names. Rich heard "Yana Volkov five." He joined a group ushered across the hall to a wide room. "You get ten minutes," a sheriff loudly recited. "Ten minutes is all you get." Along three of the walls were stainless steel stools and dividers. Each station had a faded black number in white background above it. Rich stood in the middle of the room while the others found their stations. He located five and sat. A pair of sheriffs strolled around the room.

On the wall was a gray box with an LCD screen and a handset to talk through. Rich lifted the receiver. The rectangular screen flickered. A stocky middle-aged man in a khaki jumpsuit with *DOC* stenciled on the knee sat at the screen. He had tattooed and muscled arms that hung away from the yoke of his shoulders. His broad face resembled misshapen clay, and his full upper lip was split by a diagonal scar from a knuckle or a knife. The face was a map of a rough journey through life.

"Look at this," Yana said through the handset. "Look who comes to visit ... the scribbler."

"How you doing, Yana?"

"I do fine, fine, since you put me here," Yana snarled.

"You didn't have to talk to me. And you'd be in a fix if you hadn't talked. You'd probably be in a federal pen and alone."

"I have brothers here."

"I bet you do. They think you're a rat."

"Rat? Who tol' you this?"

Rich considered a moment. Did he want Yana and Yuri fighting? He didn't care. "Yuri Grimansky."

"That one? He muscle. No brain." Yana pointed to his temple and then laid back his head and laughed. "Hey, hey, scribbler. I hear you keel Nicky."

"Killed him before he killed me."

Yana chuckled, showing a crooked row of yellow teeth. "He want your blood very bad."

"He didn't get it." Rich hesitated. "Neither did Suka."

Yana's face opened, amazed. "You keel Suka?"

"No."

"Oh," Yana seemed relieved. "I no have to work for you then."

A woman yelled across the room. "I gets no money from you, you son-of-a-bitch." The sheriffs went over to the station to calm her.

"You been arraigned?" Rich asked.

"No, no, I no arraigned." Yana waggled his head. "They want deport me. But I am Ukrainian, and they don't know where to put me."

"Enjoy your stay."

"*Da*, I have roof. I have three cots and a hot, they tell me."

Rich took control of the conversation. "I want to ask you some questions."

"Yeah? Why I talk to you? What I get?"

"I know people in the FBI."

"Phfff. I know FBI too." He shrugged. "I know people here tougher than your FBI."

"I put fifty dollars in your inmate trust fund. I'll put in another fifty if I get some answers."

"That better. What we talk about?"

"I think you know."

A grin spread wide across Yana's broad face. "You put in more *fiddy* and maybe ...?"

"Depends." Rich stared at the Russian on the screen. "Where did they take my wife, Gisele?"

"Gisele her name? That nice name." Yana grinned. "She Deutsche girl?"

"Answer my question. I can pull that fifty back out just as fast."

Yana considered a moment. "Okay. What I hear ..." His voice dropped. "Do you know India?" He asked.

"India?" This can't be a coincidence, Rich thought.

"That what I say. Listen, scribbler."

"I traveled there when I was young."

"You want the woman, you be young again. But I tell you, it too late."

"She's in India?"

"Oh, you smart one." Yana put his hand out palm up and wiggled his fingers. "You want know where—'nother *fiddy*."

"You got it. Where?"

"General has villa. Hill Station, Ranikhet."

"Where?" Rich asked, anxious.

"Ranikhet. You figure it out, scribbler." Yana smiled an inscrutable split-lip smile.

"It doesn't make sense."

"Nothing make sense in world now. Why I here? You there?" Yana stood, his hands raised like he had given up. "I go."

"Wait."

"I no wait. I tell you what I hear. You think. You put money in trust."

Rich saw Yana hang up the handset, and the LCD screen went black. His head fell forward into his hand.

"If you're done, leave through the exit," a sheriff standing behind him said in a tired voice.

Rich got up slowly and walked out as if in a daze. *India*, he thought. *What the hell?*

CHAPTER 8

"Have you lost your freakin' mind?" Agent Bertoloni bellowed over the cell phone.

"Hold on, Paul," Rich countered, raising his voice. He sat in his truck in the parking lot of Cook County Jail.

"Rich—you hold on. Do you really believe Volkov gave you the straight dope?"

"Well, I ..." Rich stopped, realizing how stupid he would sound if he replied, 'I paid him money'.

"You put him inside. I bet, he was the main source for your stories in the paper." Bertoloni calmed down.

"He said the U.S. was going to deport him."

"That's a lie. He's fighting deportation."

"Being Ukrainian, he said they didn't know where to send him."

"You think we gave a shit where we send him? He doesn't want to be sent back. His *Bratva* buddies know he talked. He knows his life expectancy is zero from the moment he sets foot inside the Russian Federation."

Bertoloni went on. "They would like nothing more than to jerk you around and make you crazy." The agent let his voice fall, slowing the pace of his words.

"What if Yana is right? What if they grabbed Gisele and took her to India?"

"What if?" Bertoloni was silent a moment. "For one ... why should he help you?"

"He wants to stay on the right side?" Rich knew his argument was weak.

"And second, why the hell would they take her to India? Come on, Rich."

"He said the general had a villa. I'm just telling you what he said."

"Yeah, maybe. Listen, I'll run this India crap by Mr. Ogg and...."

"Who's Mr. Ogg?"

"You met him."

"I don't recall meeting anyone named Ogg."

"In Jejune's office. The silent guy—that was Mr. Ogg. Honesto Ogg."

"His name is Honesto Ogg?"

"Yup, and his beat is Russia and the subcontinent. Lately, it's been AQIS—al Qaeda in the Indian Subcontinent—and ISIL."

Rich regained his composure, listening.

"Look at it this way. Your wife, Gisele, may just have a gone off for some me-time after all the stuff you guys have been through."

The FBI agent made sense.

"It's been three days. I called her mother. She hasn't seen or heard from her."

"She have any other family?"

"Yeah. You're right." Rich slapped his palm on the steering wheel. "She has a brother in Michigan, Iron Mountain."

"Have you called him yet? Look, go back to Omaha. File a missing person report. Tell them Gisele is *Missing at Risk*, and give them my name as a contact. If you don't hear anything in a couple of days, or if someone contacts you, let me know. That's when we come into play."

"So how come I haven't heard anything?"

"They scattered like rats when the Chicago Police and the FBI came down on them. There are a couple of rats probably in hiding. They may think snatching your wife will let them bargain their way out of trouble. Or, like I said, they're messing with you."

"Thanks, man."

"No problem. Get back to Omaha; get some sleep. Don't let all this make you nuts. We'll get your wife back. They have others inside. If they want to trade, they'll let us know."

Rich clicked off his phone and tossed it onto the passenger seat. He wheeled the truck out of the parking lot and drove through city traffic toward the expressway entrance. Once headed west, he had a chance to thumb through his contacts and call Gisele's brother.

"Rudi? It's Richard. Yeah, I'm fine." Rich grimaced. "Well, no, I'm not fine, actually. Is Gisele at your place?" He waited. A car slid over into his lane without a signal, and Rich let off the accelerator. "Has she called you? No? Maybe within the last three days?" Rich let out a long breath. "She's..." He paused, realizing anything he said would be relayed to his mother-in-law. He called her already. He calls her again she'll start to worry. That wouldn't help the situation. "We had a small disagreement," he lied. "No, nothing big. I didn't do anything. After all the crap we went through, she needed some quiet time, I guess. But if she calls, or turns up on your doorstep, have her call me. Okay?" He let Rudi respond. "Thanks. Give my love to Marta."

A long and lonely drive back to Omaha followed. Rich missed Gisele. Mostly he worried.

Rich pulled into the Omaha Police Department on South Fifteenth Street. The building, located next to a pawn shop downtown, must've been designed by an architect who liked Sudoku, judging by the checked concrete exterior and raised lot. He parked and walked through the revolving door into the beige marble foyer, where a blue-uniformed officer sat behind a curving counter. An older couple stood talking to a middle-aged female officer. The gray-haired man looked around with a befuddled expression as his wife, a small woman, talked.

"Sometimes, he doesn't remember where he is."

"Have you consulted with your family doctor?"

"Yes," the woman replied. "The doctor thinks he has the onset of dementia." She fished out a tissue from her purse. "He's not bad. He just forgets."

"We understand," the officer reassured her. "But you have to keep an eye on him. He can't just walk into the neighbor's house and use their toilet."

The older woman promised it would never happen again.

"Uh huh," the officer said.

The couple shuffled off to the side, and Rich stepped up.

"Can I help you?"

"Yes, I'd like to report a missing person."

The officer sat at a computer and clicked through screens, pulling up a new incident report on the monitor. "You know, you can go online or call to report this."

"I know. I was coming back from Chicago."

"All right." The officer's head tilted back. She squinted down her nose at the computer. "Name of missing person."

"Gisele Rice."

"Relationship?"

"Wife."

The officer glanced up quick and then tried to disguise her reaction. "Can I have her full name?"

"Sure. Gisele Esslin Rice."

"Born?"

"Chicago, Illinois. Birthdate is November 30, 1974."

The officer asked Gisele's address, and Rich gave her The Ordinary. "I assume that is your address as well?"

"Yes."

"Can I see your driver's license?"

"Of course."

"And when did you last see her?"

"Three days ago." Rich thought a moment. "I saw her in the morning. Then I took a flight to Chicago. She called me when I landed."

"I can call upstairs, and a detective will come down and talk to you."

"I'm really tired. I haven't been sleeping. I just drove back from Chicago. I am beat and not making a lot of sense. Can we just fill this out? I'm going back to my flat. If someone wants to talk to me, they can come see me. And I am working with the FBI—Agent Paul Bertoloni, Chicago bureau. He told me to say my wife is Missing at Risk."

"Let's back up." The officer clicked around the screen. "Your wife's height and weight?"

"She's five-foot-eight, or nine. She weighs a 110 or 120 pounds."

"Eyes? Hair?"

"Hazel eyes." Rich's voice caught. He cleared his throat. "Kind of honey blonde, mid-length."

The officer and Rich went back and forth, rapid fire, with other data. "You can have a seat, and a detective will be down. They can help you way more than I can."

"I told you, I'm exhausted," he replied, irritated. "I'm not going anywhere."

"Standard procedure is to check out the home. I can get the detectives to come if you like."

"That works for me."

"Thanks for coming in."

Rich stood at the counter. "Can I have my driver's license back?"

"Oh, sorry." The officer gave a strained laugh and handed Rich his license. "That's an Illinois license. How long you lived here?"

"Not now, officer."

Entering The Ordinary, the first thing Rich saw was a mass of oily, curly hair and Borodavka's broad back seated at a middle table. The enchilada platter in front of him had been nearly slaughtered under the lawyer's knife and fork. Lettuce and Spanish rice lay strewn about the table.

Riku raised his head from mixing a drink behind the bar. "Mr. Rice."

A few people sat along the bar, spending an out-of-work afternoon nursing 12 ounces of liquid condolence. Those that cared glanced over with an 'Is that my wife?' expression on their faces.

"Boss," Daisy greeted him, coming out of the kitchen.

Rich nodded. He ducked behind the bar and bent to the computer, opening the music folder.

Daisy looked stricken.

Riku had a questioning expression. "What?" he whispered, leaning over the bar.

"He's going to put on those damn blues," she replied.

Rich came out from behind the bar just as the opening riff and rolling drums of Ministry's "Burning Inside" came over the speakers. He could hear Daisy and Riku's conversation but ignored it.

"Doesn't sound like blues," said Riku.

"Worse," she answered out of the side of her mouth. "It's industrial. He's not sad, he's angry. Get ready for Young Gods, KMFDM, Ministry, Killing Joke and some Sisters of Mercy."

"He's mad?"

"No, I said angry. If he was mad, it would be The Clash, Sex Pistols, X, Social Distortion and LA punk."

Rich pulled out a chair across from Borodavka. "She's still missing. She's just vanished."

"Did you file a missing person report?"

"Yeah, on my way back."

"Any luck with the Russian in Cook County Jail?"

"Not sure. Not sure he told me anything I can use." Rich massaged his temples. "Bertoloni ripped me a new one, saying I was being duped. Nobody seems to want to help me."

"Maybe I'll have better news." Borodavka washed down the last bite of enchilada, draining his beer. "Ahhh, damn. Your cook is *muy bueno*."

"Your news? What? Is it about Gisele?"

"No, sorry." The lawyer tore a paper napkin to shreds, wiping his fat hands up to his thick wrists. "The grand jury is coming in with its verdict this afternoon."

"What's it look like?"

"Can't totally tell. I called my contacts to see if your case had been put on the trial docket."

"And?"

"And." Borodavka raised his empty beer glass and wiggled it at Riku.

Riku's eyes went to Rich, who lifted his head, signaling okay.

"And nothing."

"Maybe they don't know."

Ministry's "Burning Inside" gave way to Sisters of Mercy's "Lucretia, My Reflection."

"They've known. The dockets are pretty crowded, so they would put the case on first thing."

"Do I need to be down there?

"No. I don't want you anywhere near there if it comes in a True Bill. They'll arrest you on the spot. In your frame of mind, I'm concerned you'll do something to compound the situation."

"Am I back on the run?"

"I can be there representing you. If you're indicted, I'll negotiate bail on own recognizance."

"How'd everything get so fucked up?"

Daisy came up with a fresh beer. She cleared the table. "You want something to drink, boss?" she asked, working a wet rag in front of Borodavka.

"Maybe a club soda."

"You got it."

"Thanks, Daisy."

"I think we're starting to unfuck the fucked-up stuff. I'll give you a call once they declare the verdict." Borodavka drank. "You've got to hang in there."

"Hang in there. Hang on there. I have been hanging in and on for months."

The Young Gods' "Longue Route" churned out of the speakers.

After Borodavka left for the courthouse, Jorge pled, "He no come, *no mas*."

"I can't not give him lunch."

"Lunch, *si*. *Tres platos enchiladas, jefe,* no."

"*Tres*?" Rich sighed.

"*Si*," Jorge said. "I not sure we cover dinner rush."

"We'll make due."

"*Jefe?*" Jorge tilted his head, looking apprehensively past Rich's shoulder.

Rich swiveled about. Two barrel-bellied men in cheap, off-the-rack suits entered The Ordinary.

"Mr. Richard Rice?" Both had their Omaha Police shields out. "I'm Forester, and this is Detective Lyons. You filed a missing person report?"

"I did. Have a seat, gentlemen."

Jorge retreated to the kitchen.

Both sat, with Lyons taking out a narrow notebook and snapping ready a pen.

"I have to be honest, Mr. Rice." Forester smiled and turned his head left and right, coming back with a small chuckle. "Everybody in the department knows this place."

"You here to sightsee or what?"

"No. Okay, so what kind of car does your wife drive?" The cops focused on Rich with intense looks.

"A black Honda." Rich glanced from Lyons to Forester.

"Accord?"

"Yes."

"Would you know the license number?"

"Ahhhh. The first three letters are R, A, F, I think." Rich struggled to remember Gisele's plate number, adding, "You found her car?"

"Illinois tags?"

"Y-yes," Rich slowly replied. "And my wife?"

"Early this morning, we got a report of an abandoned auto. A patrol unit investigated and found the car empty."

"Where?"

Lyons flipped back a page in his notebook. "Hummel Park."

Rich stood. "I want to go there."

Forester jumped up and put his hands out.

"No, no, you're not going anywhere."

"Why?"

"We still have questions. Where were you three days ago?"

Rich descended to his seat. "I was, was in Chicago, at the FBI office. Did you find my wife?"

"Are you all right, boss?" Daisy was at Rich's side.

"Miss, would you please leave us?"

Daisy drifted back, staying within earshot.

"We haven't found her. Searchers are combing the park."

"Combing the park? What are you saying?"

"We don't know anything yet." The cops exchanged strained expressions.

"Do you own a weapon, Mr. Rice?" Forester wanted to know.

"I own quite a few. You ought to know that."

"Do we need to get a warrant, or ..." Forester pinched his nostrils and checked his fingers.

"You already had them from the shootout investigation. I just got them back."

"We may need them." Forester pinched his nose again.

"Fine. I don't care. Take them. Just bring my wife back."

"We'll do our best, Mr. Rice." Forester pinched his nostrils, examined his fingers, and rolled something in his thumb and forefinger.

"You said you are searching for her." It dawned on Rich. "Are you looking for her body?"

"And might you know where her body is?"

"What's that supposed to mean?"

"Calm down."

Forester talked low to the other cop. "Go ahead and tell him, Lyons."

Lyons tensed his bottom lip into a big frown. "Mr. Rice, the interior of your wife's car...had quite a lot of blood spatter and indications of foul play. It was pretty messed up."

Rich sucked in a shuddering breath and held it a moment, knowing what the cop wouldn't say. He let it out slowly. He stared at the glass of club soda. Small bubbles clung to the inside, and a single drip zigged and zagged down the outside.

No one spoke. The slow version of KMFDM's "Virus" played throughout the bar.

"Mr. Rice?"

"Where did you say you found her car?" His voice came from a distant place.

"Hummel Park."

"I'm new here. Where's that?"

"It's off John J. Pershing, past Dodge Park."

Rich shook his head.

"North of Florence?"

"Okay. I know where that is." His words came out slowly.

"No. Mr. Rice, don't go there. I told you, we're searching the park."

"Cops don't like going up there," Lyons added. "It's got a strange vibe. Supposed to be haunted."

"If you guys are too scared, I'll go."

"No, Mr. Rice, you need to stay away."

"Are you going to arrest me?"

Lyons slapped closed his notebook.

"No, you're not getting arrested."

"Then I'm free to go wherever I want."

Forester's head cocked to one side. "I can tell you're pretty upset but I would advise you not to go out there. I can tell by talking to you that you're not the type who'll listen. If you do go out there, stay the hell out of our way. Deal?"

"We'll let you know immediately if something comes up." Lyons stuck out his hand.

Rich looked at the hand and then shook it.

The cops walked out.

"What'd they say, boss?" Daisy asked.

"They've found Gisele's car." Rich rose. "I'm going to Hummel Park."

"You scare me," she said, a deep wrinkle across her tan brow. "You go in and out of the shadows and think you got it all figured."

"You needn't worry about me."

"I can't help that I do."

The entrance to Hummel Park was cut into a copse of trees still dressed in fall foliage of red, orange and brown. Long limbs overhung the road as if burdened by strange fruit. The crumbling roadway rose before Rich's truck into heavily wooded hills. Potholes and cracks made driving hazardous. Rich picked his way up the road. Something small and white flitted among the trees. Rich glanced but saw nothing. After a couple of turns, he found the Nature Center parking lot. Closed in by yellow caution tape, police cars and white and red vans filled half the lot. Rich backed his truck into a vacant spot, turned off the engine and watched. Gisele's black Accord was chained on a flatbed car hauler. The passenger side windshield had a large jagged edge hole, with a reddish brown halo. A uniformed patrolman ran up a trail and disappeared into trees and heavy brush.

Rich's phone rang. "Yes."

"Rich?"

"Yes. Who is this?"

"It's Borodavka."

"Sorry."

"You sound distracted. Can you talk?"

"Yeah, what's up?"

"Thought you might want to celebrate."

"Celebrate?"

"Grand jury came in. They voted No Bill."

A group of police picked their way carefully down a steep dirt trail, precariously carrying a long sheet-bound bundle on a flat board.

Rich's heart all but stopped.

"The jury may have accepted your claim of qualified immunity or thought it justifiable homicide or unintentional manslaughter. You're off the meat hook. Rich?"

"No Bill? That means it's over?"

"Yeah. No indictment. You're free."

"Like hell I am," he whispered.

The police reached the parking lot. One jogged ahead to a van.

Rich said, "I'm probably going to need you again."

"What's going on?"

"I'll call you," Rich replied hurriedly, clicking off his phone. He jumped out of his truck and sprinted across the lot. The cops spotted him when he stepped under the caution tape.

"Hey. You can't cross that line."

"Is that my wife?

A trio of cops grabbed Rich. They grappled.

"Is that my wife?" he cried out.

"Settle down, pal."

Another cop came over, and they pinned Rich against a patrol car. He watched them put the stretcher into the van.

"No. No."

A man in a gray overcoat ambled over. He closed one eye, chewed his gum and studied Rich a moment.

"Please. No," Rich repeated.

"You wouldn't be able to tell anyway, bud."

Restrained in the burly arms of the cops, Rich looked at him.

"Somebody shot her face off."

A closed-casket ceremony. Rich stood between Gisele's mother and her brother, Rudi, and his wife, Marta. A stinging cold wind cut low to the ground and across Memorial Park Cemetery, Skokie. The white pall on the casket fluttered. Gisele's mother clutched Rich's arm, unsteady, openly weeping and murmuring. "Oh, Richard. Oh, Richard. *Mein baby puppe. Mein puppe*, Gisele."

Gisele's brother was silent and standoffish. He glared at Rich. He did not cry at the church. Rudi was a rustic millennial with long dreadlocks and a beard, piercings and earlobe plugs. He had tattoos peeking out the collar of his t-shirt under his short jacket. His wife, Marta, looked much the same, both in attire and attitude.

Supporting Gisele's mother and being uncomfortable near his brother-in-law kept Rich's pain in the background. He would never let anyone see how he hurt. They'd never know how he grieved for her. That was only for him, and her.

Many people attended the graveside service. High-school friends, college friends and clients who openly lamented the loss of Gisele handling their portfolios. The *Deutschamerikaner* relations stood off to the side.

With the pastor's last blessing, after the shovelful of dirt, people dropped flowers into the rectangular hole where Rich's beloved Gisele would lay forever. He hardly noticed the hugs, the handshakes, the expressions of deepest sympathy.

And then he stood, staring at the casket covered in dirt and flowers.

"*Arschloch*...you had to write those stories," Rudi hissed.

Rich turned. Rudi faced him, his back arched forward, his arms out and hands clenched into fists. His wide eyes blazed.

"What?"

"You had to write those stories on the Russians. The big shot journalist. *Du bastard.* This is all your fault."

Rich's mouth opened, but he could say nothing.

"Rudi, *nein*," Gisele's mother protested.

"I wish they'd killed you. I'd have my sister."

Marta came up behind Rudi. Her eyes pierced through Rich. "We should go."

"Not until I tell him how I hate him."

Marta tugged Rudi by his shoulders. "We go."

Rudi let Marta pull him away. He glowered and then spit at Rich's feet. He and Marta turned and walked to the line of black limos.

"I am sorry, Richard," Gisele's mother rubbed Rich's arm. "He is upset. He doesn't mean it."

"He does." Rich helped Mrs. Esslin to the limo. "It's all right." He aided her in getting into the back of the Cadillac.

"Are you coming?" She looked up at him. "Richard, I am concerned about you. What will you do?"

"I want to be alone for a minute. You go along. I'll see you at the house." He shut the limo door and watched the car pull out.

He returned to the grave site, where he sat among the empty chairs, brooding. Wind rippled sympathy banners and overturned bouquets.

A rusted and faded red pickup truck with squeaky leaf springs and bad shock absorbers bounced up the rutted road between headstones. Behind the pickup, spewing black smoke, chugged a backhoe, resembling a dirty yellow beast. The pickup parked past Gisele's grave, and a bald black man with silver stubble and over-packed eye bags climbed out with a rough-looking older white dude. The driver hiked up his faded jeans and looked around. A short stub of a cigar, tucked in the corner of his mouth, smoked. He pinched it from his mouth, leaned forward and spit. The shorter white man, also in denim, dropped the gate on the back of the pickup.

"Yo' gotta leave now, fellah." The driver squished out his cigar and pulled gloves from his back pocket. "We gotta pack up."

Rich stared blankly at him.

The back hoe idled with a throaty growl.

They started folding and stacking chairs in the back of the truck.

Rich sat as chairs, tables and decorations were removed around him.

The back hoe belched black smoke, maneuvering to a pile of dirt near Gisele's open grave.

He wouldn't let the back hoe fill in her grave.

"Ah'm gonna need dat chair."

Rich stepped over to the edge of Gisele's grave, between the back hoe and the hole.

"Man, you can't be standing there."

"Wan me tah go'n'git security, Earl?"

"Naw." The bald man cupped a match and lighted a skinny cigar. "You alright, fellah?"

"Member da time dat lady done dived herself into da ho'?" The rough dude cackled and hacked up something thick in his throat. "Dint id takes us fo'evah to pry da bitch hands from da lid'n'pull her out?" He spit.

"Ah seen wurz. Ah seens a guy takes a leek into da ho'. 'Dat fo' you, bitch.'"

They tried to stifle their laughter, turning into the chilly wind.

The back hoe driver sat in the cab. The two men leaned against the pickup, silently waiting, watching Rich.

The mess of dirt and flowers covered the shiny mahogany lid of Gisele's casket. He gave her dark grave a last look, and then he went away. He knew what he had to do.

CHAPTER 9

A solemn march of mourners in black—couples, families—entered at a slow pace into Gisele's mother's house. The house was a stately two-story Victorian with turret, gables, widow's walk and L-shaped veranda. Rich sat in the parlor, alone and all but hidden deep in a wingback chair. He didn't need to turn to see them to know they came offering sympathy and condolences between the coffee and the cake. He heard hushed voices in the hall. He stared out the bay window to the garden.

The garden showed the austere signs of autumn. Naked trees reached to a cold slate-gray sky. Color had vanished from the rows of rose bushes. Thorny stalks looked like bony fingers clawing out of the hard dirt.

The guttural sounds of German and the tinkle of china echoed from the dining room and kitchen. Gisele's father and mother had fled Germany a couple of years after the Berlin Wall went up. They never severed ties to their roots. Her parents were kind to Rich when Gisele first brought home her struggling young journalist. That first time, setting foot in the house, had impressed Rich. He remembered everything about that night. Reisling for the ladies and German beer for the gentleman.

Mostly he remembered Gisele, defiantly proud of her Rich. All he had to offer were dreams and potential. Her father pretended to be stern and the boss. After all, he was high up on the Chicago Mercantile Board of Trade. Obviously, he wanted much more than a fellow with potential and dreams for his only daughter. But Frau Esslin had looked at her husband, seated imperiously at the head of the table. She had a sparkle to her eyes and a teasing smile. Herr Esslin did his utmost to maintain decorum and ignore his wife, but his granite composure crumbled.

"My mother likes you," Gisele whispered. "She thinks you're just like Poppa when he was young."

Rich and Gisele were married in this house, in the garden between rows of brilliantly colored roses full in bloom and fragrance.

Tom Waller had come out from Oregon to be Rich's best man.

At the reception, Wilhelm Esslin took a deep breath and puffed out his chest. "Call me Villy," he said to Rich. But he was always Herr Esslin.

When Gisele's father died of a heart attack 10 years later, she and Rich had stayed in the house, helping *Mutti* through her grief. Over the years, Rich and Gisele would spend summer weekends at the house. Left alone, staring out the window, he remembered it all.

"Richard?" Gisele's mother came cautiously around to the bay window, bending, touching Rich's knee. "Richard?" Her voice was tentative.

Rich focused on her. Gisele had her mother's eyes.

"There are two men at the door. They wish to speak with you."

"Who?" He uttered as if coming out of a stupor.

"I don't know." She stood cautiously, watching Rich climb out of the wingback chair.

Two men stood on the veranda, their backs to the door. The taller of the two wore a navy-blue wool overcoat; the other, shorter and slight of frame, seemed to be swimming in an oversized tan London Fog belted trench coat.

"You wanted to see me?" Rich recognized FBI Agent Bertoloni when he turned.

"Rich." The young agent took a step toward him. "I am very sorry for what happened to your wife. You have my deepest sympathies."

The second man—the dark-complected man from the meeting at the FBI regional office—came up alongside Bertoloni.

Hearing Bertoloni express condolences struck a wrong note to Rich. Anger boiled up from his gut. But he would not make a scene on the veranda.

"Come on. Let's walk." Rich went down the steps and to the side of the house. The two followed.

"You recall Honesto Ogg?"

Rich stopped and half-turned. "Sure I do. You called me a Cowboy."

Ogg half bowed. "Forgive me for that remark, and let me convey my sincerest sadness for your loss."

Rich did not respond. Instead, he offered Ogg his back and walked on.

They passed the stalks of the rose bushes. In a tightly controlled voice, Rich asked, “Where were you, Agent? Where was the FBI?”

He heard Bertoloni take in a breath and start. “Well, Rich, we...”

“You blew it. You promised to protect us,” Rich snapped.

“Now hold on.”

“I won’t hold on. My wife was killed.”

Ogg anted into the pot. “We don’t know who did this terrible thing.”

“Like fuck we don’t know who did this.”

“It was already too late for her, Rich.”

“Too late? How do you know that?”

“It was,” Bertoloni paused. “A detective from Omaha PD called me to confirm that you were at the FBI headquarters in Chicago the day your wife was killed.”

“I figured they would.”

“The detective had a rough timeline. They believe Gisele was lured out with the fake subpoena. They were probably waiting near her car after she left your lawyer, Borodavka.”

Ogg listened, slightly nodding, as Bertoloni explained.

Rich steamed inside but stayed silent.

“I am sorry to say, the killers had already acted while we were meeting.”

Nothing could ease Rich’s anger. “The killers? They were Russians, and you know it.”

“More than likely.”

“What was Yano Volkov telling me then?”

“Try and remember exactly what he said.”

“He said, if I wanted Gisele, I had to go to India. He asked if I knew India. I said I went there when I was young." Rich thought. "He said I should be young, but it was too late." He paused. "Wait, he didn't say Gisele. He said if I wanted *the woman*."

"It's possible he wasn't telling you about your wife."

Ogg interrupted. "We've looked into it. He may have been telling you about Suka Franko."

"I don't follow."

"The Hill Station villa he told you about is an old KGB safe house in the foothills of the Kumaon Himalayas. The Soviets used it to entertain Indian ministers, the ones holding the purse strings. The Indian military buys most of its hardware from the Soviets. We have been trying to break this since the late sixties, when we sided with Pakistan in the India–Pakistan war. We picked the wrong side."

"What's that got to do with Gisele's killer?"

"Nothing and everything." Ogg locked his large dark eyes on Rich. "It's about the person that ordered Gisele's murder."

"Who?"

"Suka Franko."

"She's in India?"

"We believe so," Ogg waited, watching Rich as it sunk in. "We think she's at the villa. The Soviets abandoned it in the nineties, or possibly sold it to Odessa *Bratva*, Suka's bunch."

"I thought she was in St. Petersburg."

"We have surveillance information that she traveled to India to mend."

"Why would she travel all that way?"

"Suka's gang has taken a big money hit and been bounced out of this country. They've had key people killed, shot or in jail awaiting trial. Their stable of prostitutes and sex slaves has been deported back to their families. You can take credit for much of that." Ogg looked at Rich a moment, then went on. "More recently, the villa has been used for opium smuggling, arms cache, money storage, this and that criminal activity and as the collection point for Indian and Nepali children kidnapped or sold as prostitutes. We think she's recovering from her wounds and rebuilding her organization."

"Thought the Russians were mostly in Goa."

"That's true, and the villa could be a staging point for Yugoslavian, Romanian and Russian girls who're trafficked into Goa."

"So the agency plans to grab her and bring her back to this country to stand trial?"

Bertoloni and Ogg exchanged guilty glances.

"You are going to do something?"

Ogg squared up his shoulders to Rich. "This is not something we, um, the agency are currently focused on."

"What?"

"We leave the human trafficking to UN GIFT, the United Nations Global Initiative to Fight Human Trafficking. It's a branch of UNDOC, the UN Office on Drugs and Crime."

"Oh, Christ," Rich angrily responded. "You and I know UN GIFT was initiated off a grant from the United Arab Emirates. An amusing irony."

Ogg agreed. "Not the only bit of irony from the Middle East. I'm sure, from your research, you know what has been going on in the region."

Rich replied, "India's been active in anti-human trafficking—with the Criminal Act 2013 and regional task forces called ANTUs, Anti-Human Trafficking Units. All of that alphabet soup of concerned citizens amounts to a steaming pile of worthless shit."

"I am going to tell you straight, Mr. Rice. The agency is primarily focused on the war on terror. That's the way the world is now. Suka Franko and her gang's human trafficking is more an INTERPOL problem. It is a very low priority for us."

Bertoloni volunteered, "And we can't."

"You can if an American has been killed."

"On foreign soil," the agent countered. "We can send a team and assist the investigation. But I already know Jejune doesn't have the budget to send anyone halfway around the world."

"Your budget is my tax dollars."

"Rich," Bertoloni spoke earnestly, "it's complicated. We are actively assisting Omaha PD in the investigation. We will find out who killed your wife. More than likely, though, they are long gone."

Rich tensed, fighting an impulse to punch the agent in the jaw.

Ogg must've sensed Rich's tension. He stepped between them.

"We will keep track of Suka Franko, and if she sets foot in the United States, we'll nab her," Bertoloni assured Rich, talking over Ogg's head.

"Comforting."

"The agency will keep Suka Franko under routine surveillance, but more than that I cannot promise you. You have to admit, I can't think of a better place to hide than in a house full of Swallows."

"In plain sight." Rich sounded disgusted. "A little goose here, grease there, nobody sees nothing, and nobody says nothing."

The three stood in the yard, trapped in an uneasy silence.

A mobile phone rang.

"Your coat's calling," Rich said.

Bertoloni and Ogg went into the inside pockets of their coats. Bertoloni came up with the call.

Ogg eyed Rich in the same calculating manner as at the FBI office meeting. Rich answered with an unflinching stare.

"Mr. Rice," Ogg asked. "Do you have a valid passport?"

Rich thought a moment. "No, it's expired," he lied.

"Good. Good." Ogg, his head at an angle, regarding Rich. "Most people have no idea when their passport expires." Then he said as walked away. "We can't have you doing anything crazy—traipsing halfway around the world, fumbling about by guess or by God."

Rudi and his wife refused to stay in the house while Rich was there. They hugged Gisele's mother and stiffly walked past Rich, ignoring him.

"He will get over it, Richard," Mrs. Esslin assured him.

Rich pulled his lips tight over his teeth and nodded, giving his mother-in-law a mother-in-law hug. He went upstairs to his room. He lay on the bed, his eyes trained on the opposite wall for a long time.

He had run away from them. He had hidden, losing his name, falling off the grid. Constantly on guard, wary of everyone, paranoia was his mode of life. He waited for them, knowing they would find him. He prepared himself. And when they came, he matched them shot for shot. He wouldn't discount luck in his survival. They had paid a bloody price, as had he. Tom Waller, Rich's childhood friend, shot to death. Roommate, his dog, with his neck snapped. But he got the edge, wounding Yuri Grimansky and killing Nicky Franko with his own gun. He had wounded Suka Franko, freeing Gisele. Gisele, whose only sin was being Rich's wife, had been nabbed and killed. She was his rock, his well of strength. Moreover, she was his heart. They knew how it would hurt him. No one would ever see his pain. He would never be hurt again.

Rich flipped open his laptop and let the operating system boot up. He clicked on his browser. No internet connection. He knew at once that Gisele's mother had disconnected the router unit in the sewing room. Her old country ways made her think it would catch fire if left on. The house was quiet and dark as he padded barefoot down the hall. He reached the sewing room door and heard low sobbing coming from Gisele's mother's bedroom. Rich sagged against the door jamb, his head down, silently joining her misery. It took some effort to pull himself together, but he wiped his eyes and plugged in the router. The colored lights came to life. As quietly as he could, he went downstairs and grabbed two beers from the refrigerator. The cold beer cut through his dry throat. In the half-light of the open refrigerator door, he saw that even in her grief, Mrs. Esslin had cleaned and washed all the dishes from the funeral reception.

Back in his room, he rebooted his laptop. It automatically connected to the Wi-Fi. He typed in "travel visa to India." Search options came up.

He opened the Indian government website and clicked on electronic travel authorization. He read it, filled it out and submitted it. Four days hence, he would be permitted to enter India. The purpose of his visit? Pleasure.

He finished his first beer and opened the second. He searched nonstop flights out of Chicago to Delhi—O'Hare International to Indira Gandhi International—ORD to DEL. He chuckled sardonically at having to tick round-trip. US carriers averaged sixteen hundred dollars for a roundtrip flight. But Air India had a roundtrip priced nine hundred and eighteen dollars. The price was good until next week, Thanksgiving Week. He tugged his wallet from his back pocket and pinched out a credit card. He'd leave Chicago at 13:30 and arrive in Delhi at 14:35, plus a day.

The Indian government website had a warning for travelers regarding diseases. Rich had been economical, getting a round-trip ticket, so why not get malaria pills and dengue fever, diphtheria and tetanus shots? He didn't want to do anything that might prevent him from entering India. He logged onto the Health Department Travel Clinic in Omaha and made an appointment for the day after tomorrow.

With visa, air travel and meds all taken care of, Rich now booked a sleeper-class ticket on the Delhi-to-Kathgodam train, dubbed the Ranikhet Express. The four-hundred rupee ticket (about five dollars American) would be in will call at the South Delhi train station. Last, he searched for a hotel in the Ranikhet area. He searched long into the night, finally falling asleep with his laptop on.

He left at first light, placing a note to his mother-in-law on the kitchen counter.

When he returned to Omaha, he worked the night shift at The Ordinary. He didn't say much, and Jorge and Riku respected his silence. But Daisy had always been different.

"Looking a little scraggly, Boss." She tried to draw him out. "Growing a beard?"

"Not in a mood to shave."

At shift's end, Rich gathered Jorge, Riku and Daisy. "You guys have been great through all this," he started. "I assume there have been no problems while I was absent."

"Someone forgot to order hamburger and hot dog buns." Daisy said.

"*Ay, mi malo.*" Jorge put his arms out. "I send Carmelita to the *mercado.*"

"Liquor stocks, beer and carbonics all in good shape?"

"Yup."

"Vendors paid?"

"Yup. Yup."

"Got your paychecks on time?"

All nodded.

"I will be going out of town again. Daisy, are you having any trouble depositing the night's take?"

"No. I fill out the slip and drop it off. But ..." Daisy hesitated nervously.

"But? Daisy, I need to know everything."

"If I drop it off at night, I have Riku ride along. Mostly, I drop it off in the morning, just in case."

"That's good. Riku, put that down as time on the clock." Rich noticed Daisy fidgeting in her seat. "Anything else?"

"Well, I—I have papers due, and finals in a couple of weeks."

"You're telling me we need help?"

"Yeah, I guess so."

Rich looked around the table. "I won't have time to interview, so do any of you know someone we can bring in?"

Jorge raised his eyebrows and shrugged. Daisy glanced down to her hands. Riku screwed up his face thoughtfully.

"My sisters, maybe," he volunteered.

They all looked at him.

"Really? Yumi and Amy?" Daisy asked.

"Do they have restaurant and bar experience?"

"Yeah, same as mine, the family restaurant."

"Are they old enough to work a bar?" Daisy added.

"They're my older sisters. One could help wait tables, and the other could work the bar."

"Sounds good to me," Rich decided. "Here's the deal, though. I won't be here to put through their paperwork. So ..." Rich turned. "Daisy, pay them from the till each night. Make sure they record their hours, and I will fix the accounts..." Rich hesitated. "When I get back."

"What'll I pay them?"

"Same as Riku."

"Okay," Daisy murmured, studying Rich with narrow eyes.

"I'll be gone the day after tomorrow. Can they start then?"

"I think so, sure."

"I apologize for putting this on you guys, but I want to keep The Ordinary running."

"No problem."

"Good. Thanks for sticking around."

No one left the table.

"You guys can go."

"We, ah, we wanted to tell you how sad we are for what happened to..." Daisy started to choke up. "What happened to Gisele?"

"She was really a good person," Riku intoned.

Rich listened with bowed head, staring at his folded hands.

"*Mi tres* angels were crying. We all like *la patrona, mucho.*"

"When I lost Tom, she was there for me." Daisy sniffed and palmed away a tear.

"Thanks, guys. It means a lot to me. Just, please, bear with me while I work through this."

"You've done so much for us. It is the least we can do."

"And, *jefe,* I—I mean we—wonder where you be going?"

Rich looked earnestly into each of their questioning eyes. "It's for Gisele. I'll come back...soon."

Rich went to the travelers' clinic and got shots for dengue fever, diphtheria and tetanus, letting the clinician talk him into a polio booster. They filled his prescription for malaria prophylaxis and got his yellow immunization card filled out and stamped. He crossed off one less obstacle that might prevent his entry into India.

Lit by a single gooseneck lamp, the white-haired old man sat hunched over a desk at the back of the coin shop. He wore glasses with a magnifying monocle mounted on the silver frames. Glass display cases lined on either side showed off silver and golden coins, with some paper notes. There were no other customers in the shop. The dusty wood and plasterboard shop smelled of oatmeal and mildew. Rich walked briskly to the counter.

"Can I help you?" He had a frail, yet friendly voice and stood no higher than his chair back. Round bellied, he shuffled to the counter.

A fluorescent tube in the ceiling flickered.

"Do you buy coins?"

"Of course I do, this is a coin shop."

"Do you buy Krugerrands?"

"Pardon?"

Rich spoke slowly, deliberately. "Do you buy South African Krugerrands?"

"Ah." He scratched the tufts of white hair atop his head. "Not often. I have a few on display if you are interested." He gave off the scent of wet wool socks.

"I'm interested in selling, not buying. I would like to get 90 percent of the current value."

"Woof, ninety percent is a lot. It would depend." The dealer placed both hands on either side of a black felt mat on the counter. "What do you have to show me?"

Rich dug his hand into the pocket of his jeans and spilled out a pile of gleaming gold coins. Shock spread across the man's face.

"Whoa, how many do you have?"

"Should be twenty."

"Twenty?" He brought over a lamp and flipped down the monocle on his glasses. His short gnarled hand trembled as he picked a single coin from the heap and examined it under the light. "Any rare, special mint, old ones?"

"You tell me."

"Half ounce?"

"One ounce."

He lowered the coin and looked over the top of his glasses. "How do you know I won't cheat you?"

"I have a good idea what each is worth and what would be a fair offer."

"I figured that." The man replaced the coin on the felt and picked up another. "I have to tell you. I can't buy all of these. I don't have that much money available. Of course, if you would like to leave them with me on consignment ..." He picked through the pile of coins with a stubby, bent index finger.

"No, these are strictly for sale. And I will be visiting other coin dealers."

"Well." He flipped up the monocle. "I could handle ten. Maybe." The short man shuffled back to the desk and typed something into the computer. "If you don't mind me asking, where did you get all these Krugerrands?"

Rich pocketed the other ten gold coins. "Inheritance."

"Lucky you," the dealer said, looking under his glasses at the computer screen. He glanced from the computer to a small white pad at his right and jotted notes with a pencil. "Okay," he breathed out. He scrolled down the screen. Then he tore off the top sheet of the pad and scuffed back to the counter. He pushed his glasses up to the middle of his forehead and drew in a deep breath. "Each of these coins, weight one Troy ounce and minted from 1984, is worth…" He squinted, reading from the note. "… approximately thirteen hundred and ninety-nine dollars." His eyes shifted to Rich.

"All right." Rich offered little reaction.

"So, these, right here"—his hands shook slightly, hovering over the array of gold coins—"on the current exchange, are worth almost fourteen thousand dollars." Pausing, they stared at each other. "But you have to know, I'm not going to pay that much."

"What will you pay?"

He pursed his lips and removed his glasses, tapping his lips with the ear piece. "I'll give you nine thousand."

Rich maintained a stone face a couple of long seconds. "Well, thanks," he suddenly said. "I'll go someplace else." He began raking the coins into his open hand.

"Wait. Wait," the man loudly protested.

Rich stopped.

"Don't you know how this works? I say I'll buy ten for nine thousand. You say thirteen thousand. I throw up my hands and shout 'impossible' and counter with ten thousand."

Slowly, Rich picked one coin from his palm and replaced it on the black felt.

"You become irate and say, 'no deal' … you want twelve thousand."

Rich put another Krugerrand on the felt.

"I clutch my chest and pretend I'm having a heart attack. Out of breath, I say, 'Okay, okay … ten thousand five hundred."

Rich held the tenth coin just over the mat. "And I say eleven thousand five hundred."

The dealer slapped his hand on the top of his head. "No, you're supposed to say eleven thousand, and I say, 'done.' Then we shake hands."

"I want eleven five."

The old man exhaled. "I want these. But I have federal paperwork to fill out for any exchange over ten thousand dollars. I could turn these quickly and make decent money. What if I offered eleven thousand three hundred?"

Rich thought it over and then let the tenth Krugerrand clink on its fellows on the mat.

"Eleven thousand?"

"And three hundred."

"Of course."

They shook hands. "Now, we argue how I pay." The dealer stacked the coins and, with the sleight of hand of a magician, caused them to disappear from the black mat.

"What?" Rich growled.

"I hope that I have that much," he went to the desk and tugged the corner away from the wall. The leg of the desk made a loud scraping noise, revealing behind it the black door of a wall safe. "I have to ask if you are laundering money. Are you a terrorist? Are you a drug dealer?" He squatted and dialed the combination. "I will need you to fill out a form declaring these coins are not stolen."

"No. And no, I am not filling out any forms." Rich replied. "I tell you what, do you have foreign currency?"

"Yes, but I am not a currency exchange." The man twisted the handle and tugged open the safe. "Why?"

"Do you have any Indian rupees?"

The coin dealer looked over his shoulder. “I do. I think I have close to fifteen or twenty thousand rupees. You do know it is about sixty-five or seventy rupees to the dollar.”

“Eleven thousand U.S., twenty thousand rupees, then.”

The man’s face lit up. “Any other currencies you are looking for?”

“No.”

Rich knew he’d never be able to smuggle a gun through airport security in the U.S., much less slip one past customs entering India. He could use his concealed carry permit, but only in the US and that would get the kind of attention he did not want. He wracked his brain. What options did he have? He could not count on getting his hands on a weapon once in India. If he asked around, he might alert the authorities. He’d be picked up. If not a gun—what? Knives would be confiscated at the airport but could be readily acquired in Delhi. He didn’t trust knives or like using them. He could not repay Suka brandishing a cricket bat.

The night before his flight to the subcontinent, Rich worked behind the bar of The Ordinary. He was quiet. The regulars offered sympathy by leaving him be. Though they didn’t engage him in conversation, they still treated him as if nothing happened, as if no one had killed his wife. Rich pulled beers and mixed drinks in a detached manner, wrestling with the problem of landing in India with nothing but his bare hands. He put a couple of beers down, snapped up some bills and caught a snippet of conversation.

“The cops tased the guy, almost killed him.”

"No shit?"

"I shit you not. If you tase somebody long enough, they is dead. D-E-A-D, dead."

"Yeah, makes sense. If they got a bum ticker, they can go like that." The man snapped his fingers and reached for his beer.

"There was another guy a cop tased for ten or fifteen seconds. That guy's a total vegetable now."

The following morning, Rich went to The Exit Wound, a corner gun shop. People milled about, browsing rifles displayed along the walls or standing in a cluster watching a salesman break down a handgun. Rich casually walked the length of the shop, looking down at the weapons displayed in glass cases. The *pop-pop* of a basement gun range could be heard. The faint smell of cordite filled the store. Rich paused, seeing a couple of Tasers shaped like handguns and others that shot out electric wires. He knew the shape alone meant they would not get through airport security or customs. He spied a couple of Tasers shaped like flashlights.

"Anything I can help you with?" asked a salesman in red flannel. He had a closely cropped haircut that betrayed patterned baldness.

"I'm interested in a Taser."

"Okay. We have some nice ones here. Is this for your wife or girlfriend?" He stood tall and lanky, with an angular face and eyes that didn't shine very bright.

"No. Me." *Though*, Rich thought, *it is for my wife Gisele.*

The salesman gave him a sour face. “Don’t get me wrong, but why buy a Taser when you can buy a sweet Sig Sauer three-twenty?”

Rich tilted his head sideways, irritated.

“It’s only a hundred dollars more.” The salesman smiled.

“I’ve my reasons.”

“Suit yourself.” He pulled a handgun-style Taser from the display. “This bad boy right here shoots out wires that...”

“I don’t want one like that.” Rich tapped his finger on the display glass. “I want one like this.”

“Like a flashlight?” The salesman may as well have been saying, ‘It’s your funeral.’ He pulled it from the case. “This one is nine million volts—an 800-lumen stun flashlight.” He examined it critically. “Looks like a regular flashlight, but you aim that close up to the perp’s eyes, and it’ll blind ’em for five or ten seconds. You can get away. Or ...” He handed the round, black steel flashlight to Rich. “See those points, around the light? You touch those to somebody, even through their clothes, and then snap the red button. All those nine million volts shoot into their body. Let the dancin’ begin.” He smirked like he’d made a joke.

Rich pushed the flashlight at him. A crooked blue line snapped across the round front of the flashlight. The salesman threw his hands up and stepped back.

“Hey, careful. Ever seen somebody get tased? They crap their pants, go total spaz and are out for about 30 seconds.”

“Is it rechargeable?”

“Heck, yeah.” The man read, paraphrasing off the box. “It’s got a built-in lithium battery...I guess a full charge will last for two or three long zaps...then maybe one or two short ones. After that, I guess you use it as a club." The salesman watched Rich handle the Taser and work the buttons. "Listen, ah, if you're in the market for stealth weapons, take a look at this."

He brought out a black metal tube.

"What is it?"

"It's a collapsible baton, solid steel. This one is twenty-one inches when fully extended." The baton had a rubber handle and button at the end. In its current state, it was only six or seven inches long. "This is kind of slick. Some *brotha* comes at you—boogie, boogie, boogie." The man flicked his wrist, and two more sections snapped out of the baton. "A couple of slashes across that gangsta's face." The baton swished left and right. "And Milli is all Vanilli again." He let out a low, nasty giggle.

Rich glared at the salesman a second. "I'll take both. Exactly what I'm looking for."

"Okay. I'll ring you up down at the register." The salesman replaced the Taser flashlight and baton in the display case and took two white boxes from under the counter.

"Will I have to do any paperwork?" Rich asked, following him down the counter.

The salesman glanced over his shoulder and hesitated. "Not for these," he replied with a wink and a smile.

CHAPTER 10

Rich stuffed a pair of Levi's 505s in the bottom of the daypack. He packed a white, gray and black t-shirt with no logos. In separate plastic bags, he packed socks, underwear, a shaving kit with travel-size shaving cream, a plastic razor, a toothbrush, toothpaste, mouthwash and an electric outlet adapter. He had broken down the Taser flashlight into smaller parts in plastic bags, hoping that, mixed with toilet articles, it might pass TSA and airport customs. He slipped the baton into a side pocket of the daypack with a notebook and pens. His phone and identification, except for his passport, went in the safe in his flat.

Nicky Franko's beat-up blue pocket-sized address book lay between boxes of ammunition at the bottom of the gun safe. Not the most organized of hoodlums, Nicky had nonetheless kept an elaborate record of contacts and addresses. Entries were written in Cyrillic, English, French and what appeared to be Arabic. Rich thumbed through the yellowed, stained and ripped pages filled with Nicky's small block lettering. Flagged entries indicated US, RUS, MEX, SYR, IN and other country designations. Dropping the blue book into the front pocket of his daypack, Rich knew it would make interesting reading on the long flight.

He had transferred, to three pre-paid credit cards, nine of the eleven thousand dollars he had gotten for the Krugerrands. He put one thousand dollars of various denominations into his wallet, about three thousand Indian rupees, he tucked the rest into the daypack. One credit card in his wallet and the other two cards, along with the last 10 Krugerrands, into a small black bag, he slipped into a pocket in the daypack. He didn't like carrying that much money. He wouldn't check his daypack. It was a risk, but large sums of money often go missing in baggage handling and customs.

His passport, visa and immunization cards and Air India ticket he had in and outside pocket of his laptop bag.

Memories of Gisele swam through his thoughts as he took a last walk around the flat. A water bottle and half-sized white t-shirt hung on her exercise equipment in the corner. He could smell her. Some of her clothes lay on a chair, discarded, while the rest were in a neat row on hangers in the bedroom closet. The unmade bed still showed the last depression of her body. Strands of her honey-blonde hair were tangled in the bristles of her hair brush. An array of lotions and creams were cluttered on the bathroom shelf. The scent of coconut oil started him tearing up, nearly breaking down, but the anger pulled him back.

Wiping his eyes, Rich addressed a business envelope to his lawyer, Douglas Borodavka, with a note on the bottom: *Do Not Open until December 15—or If I Am Reported Missing or Dead.* Daisy, Riku and Jorge and his family would be taken care of. Rich wondered how Gisele's mother would cope if she had one more funeral to attend. He clipped a check for five hundred dollars to the letter and dropped both into an eight-by-ten manila envelope, also addressed to his lawyer. He didn't want it to come back, so he placed five stamps on the top right corner. Funny, how little things like immunization shots, round-trip air-fare and sufficient postage for an envelope had become so important.

Eppley would be the first test to see if he could slip the Taser through security. If caught, he'd play dumb, hoping TSA would confiscate the Taser and not prevent him from making his connection to O'Hare. He wouldn't get a slap on the wrist going through security at O'Hare, though. He'd get pulled from the line and taken to a room. "Oh, I didn't know" wouldn't fly, and neither would he. He'd rather arrive in India unarmed than be put on a No Fly list.

A pretty young woman worked the American Eagle ticketing counter. Two other agents helped a handful of people snaking along the cordoned line. Rich pretended to struggle with the computerized ticketing. The woman noticed his apparent dilemma and stepped over the luggage scale to his side.

"May I help you, sir?"

"Oh, yeah, thanks." Rich gave her a smile of relief. "I can't seem to get this darn thing to work. It's got to be something I'm doing. I'm so bad with computers. I swear, computers hate me."

"I can help you at the counter." She walked back.

Rich dropped his eyes to her round, shapely hips. He let his eyes linger on her backside as she went back over the luggage scale. She turned.

He raised his eyes slowly, approaching the counter. He had wanted her to see he'd been looking.

"Can I see your itinerary and identification?" A reddish glow shaded her cheeks.

Rich handed her his flight information and passport, and she keyed the data into a computer.

Her name tag read: *Maria.*

"I can check you through to Chicago, Mr. Rice." She typed loudly. "And check you in to your Air India flight."

"Maria, you're a genius. That would be great." He beamed, a little too wide, a little too sweet.

Maria worked the ticketing.

Rich made himself appear anxious, fidgety. "Those lines at TSA are long. My flight is pretty soon. Do you think I'll make my flight? I'd hate to miss my flight."

"I'm sure you'll be fine." Maria glanced up, almost smiling.

Rich caught her eyes and grinned.

Her cheeks visibly blushed. "Do you have any bags to check, Mr. Rice?"

"No, just my carry-ons. You can call me Richard." He knew he could check his daypack and not have to worry, but he didn't want to let it out of his sight.

Maria typed. "If you're worried about missing your flight, I can make your ticket Priority Screening."

Rich acted as if he didn't understand.

"It's a quicker TSA screening, shorter lines. There's a TSA prescreening service that you can enroll in. It's only sixty-five dollars."

He'd checked the TSA site and tried to get a pre-screening pass. There was a waiting period, and he had no time.

"You can get me through without all the hassle?" Rich's mouth opened. "You ARE a genius."

Maria tried hard but failed to suppress a smile. A printer sounded behind the counter. She put Rich's passport and papers on the counter and then leaned forward to explain. "You'll have to check in at Air India. So they are aware you arrived. Here are your tickets and boarding passes." She pointed to the top right of Rich's ticket. "This is prescreening with TSA. There's a lane to the side that you'll go through."

"That's great."

"I strongly suggest you sign up for prescreening."

"I'll do that."

"Your Air India flight leaves from the International Terminal. Terminal M. They will do some screening but not much. Just know that, if you check bags, you have to take them over yourself."

"Maria, you're the best." Rich gathered up his tickets and shouldered his daypack, clutching the handle of his laptop bag. "Now, which way do I go?"

Maria laughed. "Gate B3. Have a great trip."

"Oh, I will. Thanks, Maria."

Stepping onto the up escalator, Rich allowed himself a short sigh. "Okay," he muttered under his breath. "Here we go."

Rich scoped out TSA and the boarding area as he walked down the ramp. Long lines of travelers waited before two screening stations; meanwhile, an open lane along the wall to the right was unoccupied. A small sign indicated prescreened passengers. Rich took a pair of gray tubs and unzipped his laptop bag. A middle-aged woman in blue TSA uniform watched him with a bored expression. He unslung his daypack and put it in a separate tub along with his keys, change and wallet. Bending, Rich heard the TSA agent say: “You don’t need to take off your shoes or belt. Step forward, and let me see your ticket and ID.” She reached out with a blue rubber-gloved hand.

Rich handed her his ticket, boarding pass and passport. He pushed the tubs onto the conveyor belt that led into the stainless steel screening machine.

The agent looked over the tickets, made a check mark and handed them back.

A bickering couple, looking harried and upset, lined up behind Rich.

“Didn’t I ask you if you packed my sandals? Didn’t I?”

“Yeah, yeah,” the man guiltily replied.

“Now, you tell me you forgot. You forgot?”

“We don’t have time to go back home and get ’em.”

“Those were my favorite sandals.”

“I’ll get you another pair.”

“You think it’s that easy for me to find sandals that fit?”

Rich edged away from the couple and went through the screening. The agent’s eyes went from Rich to the couple and then to her screen. No beeps. Rich waited, and out slid the first tub. He put his laptop in the bag. The TSA agent squinted at the screen and reversed the belt.

The couple’s argument grew heated.

“Crap,” Rich softly hissed.

Then the second tub rolled off the conveyor belt.

"Hey. Hey," the TSA agent said. "You two are going to have to calm down."

Rich pocketed his keys, change and wallet, shouldered his daypack and double-timed it out of the TSA screening area. He slipped into the crowds milling about the boarding area.

"Made it."

The flight into Chicago was uneventful if not free of anxiety. Once down at O'Hare, he had three hours to kill. Instead of taking the tram, Rich walked across O'Hare to the international terminal.

The contrast between the domestic and international passengers was stark. It seemed that most of the world's population from Asia to Africa was crowding the large terminal waiting for flights. Armed Chicago police walked around, leading dogs.

Rich had been ticketed through in Omaha, but he had to check in at the Air India ticket counter.

People funneled into roped-off areas. Rich filled a spot leading to Air India and studied the security station. A short, round Indian woman wearing a saree, with tied back hair and a red *bindi* between her brows, pushed forward a suitcase and cardboard box bound by twine. Children played hide and seek around her wide hips. A group of young men and women and another family group stood in line. Rich realized that he was the only westerner. No one even stood close to clearing his shoulders. They surreptitiously checked him out.

Announcements called flights above the din of the world's languages.

Rich noticed the Air India ticket agent's well-oiled and precise haircut with its wide part. There was not a single black hair on the wrong side of his head. He had a cafe-latte complexion and roundish, puffy features, though he was quite thin. His clothing was stylish, a mixed bag of Indian cut and color in an American suit.

"May I help you, sir?" He spoke in the singsong way that some Indians do.

"I'm checking in for Flight 1501 to Delhi." Rich handed over his ticket.

"May I see your visa and passport, sir?"

He gave the agent the documents and folded his hands on the counter while the young man looked at his screen.

"You are checked in. Do you have any bags?"

"No. Do you have my seat assignment?"

"Yes."

"Aisle seat?"

"C-17." The agent handed back Rich's passport and documents. "Gate M-21. Have a pleasant flight, sir."

"Is there priority screening?"

"Pardon, sir?"

"I had priority screening boarding in Omaha."

"No, sir. Automated Passport Control is down. You go to the kiosk and show your passport. Then your bags are screened."

"Okay, thanks."

Bells rang. "*Attention, attention, mesdames et messieurs.* Air France flight ..."

Rich studied the security sector and the passengers and agents in it. He lined up at the customs kiosk, where one man checked tickets and passports. It moved quickly.

"Destination?" The guy looked like a certified public accountant, with glasses and a round, mousy face.

"Delhi, India."

"Ticket, visa, passport?"

Rich pushed his papers through the window slot. A Hispanic family, including a father, mother and a trio of energetic kids passed him in a chaotic swirl. The father grabbed for one child. The mother gave the other two a stare that could burn through steel. They clustered into the middle lane of security.

Worked in Omaha, Rich thought, taking his ticket, visa and passport from the man in the kiosk.

He stepped behind the family.

"Mobile phones and laptops separate," A TSA agents shouted above the heads of people in line.

A bell sounded. "Air Emirates Flight 7250 to Dubai now boarding gate M-18 ..."

The father attempted to corral the young ones and put their carry-ons into tubs. An agent with blue latex gloves pointed to a tub. "Mobile phone." Rich put his laptop and daypack in separate tubs, waiting. The littlest boy, laughing, squirmed out of his father's grasp and ran through the metal detector.

"Hey. You can't go through there."

"*Lo siento*," the mother said in a hopeless tone.

Rich casually dropped his keys and change in the second tub. He took out his wallet and held it in his hand.

The smallest girl fought the father's arm bar, wanting to run after her brother. Once they had everything in tubs, the kids went through security like a cyclone.

A sympathetic smile and knowing nod got a shrug from the TSA agent.

"That was something." Rich said, pushing his tubs forward.

"Mobile phone separate from laptop," the agent replied wearily.

"Don't have a mobile."

"Step through the metal detector."

"I have my wallet," Rich indicated to an agent on the other side of the metal detector.

"Arms up."

Rich grinned, casting a quick glance back to the screening machine. He beeped.

"Your sweatshirt. Either take it off or raise it."

Rich pulled off his sweatshirt. The man moved a metal detecting wand to Rich's belt.

"Belt." Rich shrugged.

The agent gave him an impatient wave and let him pass.

Both tubs rolled out as Rich approached. A group of agents stood on the other side of the conveyor.

"Just a minute, sir," one said.

Rich froze. "Yes? Is there a problem?"

"It was the little kid," another agent interrupted.

"Oh, sorry," the first agent said to Rich. "You're fine."

Dodging people getting through, Rich rounded up his laptop, daypack, keys and change. When he had enough terminal between him and security, he put his daypack on an empty seat and sorted himself out. It took him a moment to calm down. There were security stickers on this laptop bag and daypack.

With an hour to kill before boarding, Rich ambled through the crowded terminal to Gate M-21. He was relieved that he had gotten through security but reckoned that customs in Delhi might be tougher. His stomach growled. He hadn't eaten all day. *It's a seventeen-hour flight. They should feed us,* he thought, though he had no idea what food they would pass out. Near the gate, not surprisingly, was a McDonald's. Rich stood back from the bustling counter and tried to decipher the multinational menu. Looking past the Pizza McPuff, Poutine, Katsu Cheese Burger and Chicken Maharaja Mac, he settled on something universal—Chicken McNuggets, fries and a Coke. Rich took his tray to an outside table, sat, relaxed, ate and studied people.

As the time neared for boarding, Rich emptied the tray into a bin and stacked it. He walked to the boarding area and leaned on a pillar somewhat away from the gathering throng at Gate M-21. Though the crowd was primarily Indians, there was a smattering of Africans, Chinese and Western adventurers. People wore a variety of international dress, from traditional business attire to shirt and jeans (like Rich), but most had on track or sweat suits. Off to the side, an old man in a wheelchair was attended by a busy middle-aged woman. She was plain-looking yet attractive with an English structure to her face. Her resemblance to the invalid was so striking that she had to be either his daughter or, more likely, his granddaughter. She catered to his every need, from a drink to something to read. A trio of clean-shaven young men in white turbans, wearing white linen kurtas with black slacks, flanked a tall round-bellied man with a black beard and a blue turban. They had to be Sikhs. The three young men openly deferred to the tall one. He knew it, acting quite regal. Everything he said amused his listeners. Anything he wanted, they would fetch.

Announcements echoed above the heads of the travelers.

Eating had made Rich weary. He needed to stay awake long enough to board. After that, he hoped to sleep for the bulk of the hours-long flight.

The Air India counter personnel announced something that got the passengers restless. The door to the jet way opened, and families with small children and the man in the wheelchair made their way to the gate. The older woman struggled with the chair and their carry-ons as they passed through the door. General boarding began with first class. The Sikh in the blue binder left the young men and boarded with business class. Once he had disappeared down the jet-way, the trio laughed and talked animatedly. Then Group One of cattle class was announced. Rich glanced at his ticket—Group Four.

Not a full boat; Rich could see open seats as he shuffled down the narrow aisle of the Airbus 777. First class featured the diagonal seats that converted into sleepers. Business class offered wide seats. The old man had been moved from his wheelchair to a seat in the last row of business. His daughter bustled about, settling in.

Cattle class was configured ten seats across—three seats on once side, five seats in the middle and two on the opposite side of the cabin. Rich found row 17, seat C and noted that the other two seats were unoccupied. Other groups were still outside, preparing to board. He stowed his carry-on in the overhead bin and sat, waiting. The three young Sikhs passed him, heading to the back.

An overweight Indian woman squeezed by.

The flight attendant, a young woman with thick, striking black hair and deep black *bindi*, patiently walked behind her. She wore a modified, multi-colored saree.

"Excuse me."

"Yes?" She bent over the seatback in front of Rich.

"Are there open seats?" he asked.

"There may perhaps be a few." She had the trace of an English accent polished enough to be from London. "We are still boarding, but once we've boarded, you may move."

"Thanks."

In minutes, the aisle cleared, and over the speaker, the pilot asked the cabin crew to prepare for takeoff.

Rich had the row all to himself.

The cabin door closed, and sound became muted, except for the hissing of the overhead vents.

From business class, the tall man in the blue turban came down the aisle with a small black leather bag. He checked bins and found an open one in the row ahead of Rich. Leafing idly through a shopper magazine from the pocket on the seatback, Rich watched the man. He acted suspiciously, glancing left and right. He and Rich made eye contact. The man smiled. Rich nodded and went back to his magazine. He closed the bin and went back to business class. In the periphery of his sight, Rich saw the man stop and scan down the aisle before slipping into this seat.

A video came onscreen on the seatback. A woman demonstrated how to use the seat belt. Meanwhile, a flight attendant at the head of cattle class did the same.

The big airliner pushed away from the gate. The *ssssssss* of overhead air, the low rumble of turbines and odd squeaks, clunks and cracks filled the cabin as it swayed and rolled to the flight line.

The pilot made an announcement in English first.

"Good afternoon, ladies and gentleman. I am First Officer Singh, welcome aboard Air India Flight 1501 to

Delhi. Our estimated flight time is sixteen and a half hours, arriving at Indira Gandhi International Airport tomorrow afternoon."

Flight attendants went down the aisles checking seat belts.

"If you are interested in following the progress of our flight, a video is on channel 12 on your seatback monitors. You will be able to see the duration of flight and the plane's position. Thank you for flying Air India."

The announcement was repeated in Hindi as the airliner taxied to the runway.

"Flight attendants, prepare for takeoff."

The turbines roared, and the big Airbus lumbered down the runway. Then it pointed skyward and climbed and climbed and banked, leveling off in clear skies above the clouds.

A flat world map, with an outsized jetliner over Illinois, flashed on the screen. There wasn't enough screen to show both departure and destination; the right edge cut off everything east of Paris.

Fighting his weariness, Rich opened his laptop and worked on translating entries from Nicky Franko's address book. He logged the translations into an Excel spreadsheet.

A couple of hours into the flight, the cabin crew dragged the drinks and dinner carts up the aisle. Rich ordered a Coke.

"Vegetarian or chicken?" the good-looking attendant asked.

"Chicken, please."

Rich picked at the rice, vegetables and chicken vindaloo, which was a little too spicy. A flat, crispy bread and yogurt completed the meal. He noted that the knife and fork were plastic, while the spoon was metal.

The little airplane had just crossed the Hudson Bay. The other channels had reruns of *Friends* and *Seinfeld* in English and other languages.

He tried to listen to music, but happy songs irritated him and sad songs made him impatient.

The turbines droned. Fourteen hours to go.

He worked on memorizing some Hindi phrases from a conversational Hindi app on his laptop.

He paid four dollars for a glass of Chardonnay as the drinks cart made its second pass. The wine, combined with his sleepiness, made him woozy. He opened his pictures folder and slid through images of his stoic dad standing tall next to his shorter mother. The contrast of his dad's hard, unsmiling face and his mother's chubby bright eyes and impish grin made Rich realize that it was his mother who was the well of strength between the two. There were pictures of his friend Tom Waller, the pair of them looking like grunge rockers in Nirvana and Pearl Jam t-shirts. In contrast was a picture of the two crewcut and shaved, dressed in desert camo during their National Guard service. He remembered Tom was killed by the Russian Yuri Grimansky. The picture of Tom and Daisy became more poignant. A blurry picture of a young Gisele laughing made Rich pause. He then slowly leafed back through their life. The wedding pictures and those of their honeymoon in Lahaina hit him hard. It was like he fell into a deep black hole and a blue tarp was thrown over the top. He lay in damp, cold earth, lost in blackness and near silence. If he could just stop his heart, cease to breath—shut off his thoughts—the ache might go away. *She's gone.* He remembered her grave. He pulled his lips into his mouth and bit down. He deserved the pain. He hoped to control his quivering chin. Nothing helped. Wet filled the corner of his eyes.

"Are you all right, sir?" the young attendant asked.

"Yeah, fine, thanks." Rich sniffed and cleared his throat. "Just remembering something."

"Would you like a tissue?"

"No, I'm okay. Thanks."

Overhead lights started to go out in the cabin as people tried to sleep. Rich's knee ached from sitting for so long. He closed his laptop and set it aside. Walking to the lavatory eased the stiffness in the joint.

Back in his seat, he checked the 777 icon. It hadn't moved. He tapped the screen. "Come on, little airplane." He reached up, snapping off the light, thinking he'd try and get some sleep. The three seats, with armrests upraised, gave him room to lay but not to stretch out his six-foot frame. He punched the small pillow and tugged the thin blanket over his shoulder.

The turbines droned on. He dozed off.

Dad had a friend, a man he called E—just E. They would sit on the back patio, side by side on wire chairs, staring at the two towering oaks and drinking Olympia beer in white cans. They quietly traded terrifying tales of Vietnam with all the enthusiasm of a pair of accountants. Dad had stories from the early sixties, when he had advised the South Vietnamese military and did some wet work for the embassy. E pulled crazy tales from the full-blown insanity of the late sixties.

E was an All American and expert in long-range patrol. He was older and rounder, of average height, and young Rich had trouble picturing him as lethal. Yet, lethal he was. It showed in his eyes, blue as deep arctic ice. Some follow people with their eyes; E's eyes were there before you.

Like Dad, E had that innate stillness about him. Others possess noisy bodies, with boisterous movements boasting of potential danger. The two men, in their way, moved with economy, deliberate and certain. Neither ever needed to move into position to strike. They were ready.

They fell silent when young Rich brought out fresh cans of Oly. Whenever he was near, they said nothing. This made Rich even more curious. One time, he sat with them, hoping to catch some stories. They stared at the oaks, sipped beer casually, staying silent. After ten minutes, Rich took away the empties and went for more. As he entered from the patio, he heard his dad chuckle.

"There was this full bird colonel, chest of glory like chicken shit splattered all over his uniform. He was a holdover from the French and thought giving orders in French made him more important. Except none of his captains knew French. They entered this village with walking fire ..."

Rich stopped by the door.

E didn't need to turn around. "The boy can hear."

"Maybe he should."

E's accounts of combat were harrowing, though retold in a firm, yet bland voice.

"We lay in ambush at the top of the trail for three days. Those red ants were all up my crotch, but I couldn't move. I figured they would eat off half my dick before I could get out of there. Half my dick is a full dick to most guys. I set up two heavy weapons guys at the base of the trail. They were told to fire when the last man passed. Then we would pop up and have them in a cross fire. We expected a patrol or squad, but along came a company of North Vietnam regulars. We waited and waited, and they kept coming. Then the heavy weapons opened up. I swear to God, it looked like the running of the bulls coming at us. They did not stand a chance."

"Always get the high ground."

Rich woke with a start, hearing voices in the cabin above the turbines. He wiped sleep from his eyes and struggled upright. Why had he dreamed about Dad and E? The little airplane onscreen had passed Greenland and approached Iceland. Eleven hours left. He snapped on his overhead light and opened his laptop. He messed around on his computer for a couple of hours. A little work, Wikipedia, YouTube and reading news reports didn't make the flight go any faster.

He knew that he needed sleep or jet lag would screw him up for days. Shutting down his laptop and turning out the light, Rich settled back in his seat.

Throughout the dark cabin, the turbines droned.

He was just on the edge of sleep when a flight attendant rushed up the aisle. Rich opened his eyes to a commotion in business class. Blinking, he adjusted his sight to the cabin and saw four, perhaps five, cabin crew lugging something awkward. He thought it was a sack of potatoes. But as they struggled toward him, he noticed a blue swath of cloth hanging unwound from a turban. As they passed, a man's face, with mouth agape and eyes wide in surprise, nodded past him just inches away. The lips were as blue as the askew turban. He was dead, without a doubt.

"My god," Rich breathed.

His feet were bare and white.

Twisting in his seat, he watched the crew haul the cumbersome body to the rear of the plane, where three figures wearing white waited.

Poor bastard, he thought. He'll drift forever through the ambrosial hours with a face like a guy scared by a mouse.

The crew unloaded the body on the back row of seats. The three young men talked in hushed, excited tones.

"They're dying on this flight," Rich murmured. Then he remembered the man's bag in the overhead bin. Would they get it?

After the cabin crew moved up the aisle, Rich hopped out of his seat and went to the rear of the plane. The dead man lay on his back, a white sheet pulled up to his neck. He stared with that goofy startled expression. Blue tinged his brown complexion. Rich studied his face. A heart attack or maybe a stroke. There was no disfigurement to his face, though, so a heart attack seemed likely.

A flight attendant was at his elbow.

"Heart attack?" Rich asked.

"Are you a doctor?"

"No, just a guess."

"Good guess. Yes, heart attack, probably." She bent over and tugged the sheet over his face.

"How come we're not landing at the nearest airport?"

"Check your map. We are flying over Russia, then Afghanistan and Pakistan. The pilot decided it best to continue on to Delhi."

"Makes sense to me."

Rich went to the lavatory and splashed water on his face. When he came out, the attendant was gone. He returned to his seat.

Knees up, lying across the seats, as soon as he closed his eyes, he tumbled into the depth of sleep. He woke. The little plane had flown swiftly, violating Soviet airspace. He slept again while the turbines droned and the airliner flew toward the rising sun. Food carts lugged up the aisle woke him. He massaged his face with his hands, took a deep breath and sat up. The plane had almost traversed the LCD screen, banking left at Kabul. Over thirteen hours' flying time was behind them, and less than four lay before them. And still, the turbines droned.

"Tea? Coffee? Juice?" the attendant inquired.

"Coffee, please." Rich took down his tray table.

"Milk? Sugar?"

"Both, please, thanks." He opened the window shade a crack. Bright light invaded the dark cabin. Babies woke, crying.

Rich ate the food on the breakfast tray, which was tasteless but filling, and sipped a second cup of coffee, more to pass the time than for nourishment.

The small plane flew over Pakistan, approaching Kashmir.

People moved about the cabin. Rich clipped his tray table, stood and opened the overhead bin. He moved his daypack around and closed the bin. He opened the next bin and saw the dead man's black bag. Something metallic clinked. He quickly shifted the black bag to his bin and sat, listening. No one seemed to notice.

The pitch of the turbines changed as the big airliner started its approach to Delhi. They descended through clean white clouds and pure blue skies. The lower the plane dropped, the browner the clouds, until they were surrounded by a gritty haze. Rich peered through the window as, below, farm and green expanses gave way to dirt tracts and clusters of squat, square buildings. They flew over a motorway filled with vehicles.

"Please fasten your belt," a passing flight attendant reminded him.

Wheels cranked down and locked with a clunk. They bounced a little and reversed thrust.

"Ladies and gentlemen, this is your pilot speaking. Welcome to Delhi. The local time is 14:55 with an outside temperature of five Celsius. Thank you for flying Air India." The pilot followed this with an announcement in Hindi.

The plane taxied to the gate.

"Ladies and gentlemen, due to a medical situation that occurred during flight, we ask that you remain seated and the aisles clear for a medical examiner coming onboard."

A collective groan rippled through cattle class.

Once they linked to the gate and the engines shut down, the cabin door opened and a small Indian man in a tan suit stepped aboard. He was trailed by two brown-uniformed enlisted men with a folded stretcher. They moved quickly to the rear of the plane. The trio of young Sikhs waited there. People turned in their seats, watching. The large man's body was put on the stretcher, and the men grunted, raising it above the seats. They carried him up the aisle. A few gasped; others shrugged.

They passed. Rich grabbed his laptop and popped open the overhead bin. People looked at him. Someone said something sharp in Hindi. He ignored the comment and pulled his daypack and the dead man's black bag from the bin.

"Sir. Sir, please return to your seat."

"Sir?"

Rich reached the front of the plane just as they carried the stretcher out.

"Sir, return to your seat."

"This is his bag." He held it up.

A young Sikh took the bag and examined the tag. "Yes, it is Mr. Chaundry's. Thank you so much."

They continued up the jet way. Rich followed a few steps back. He hoped to tag along and be assumed as a member of the group. Maybe he could slip through customs. They exited the jet way, and the first thing Rich noticed was a trio of heavily armed Indian military stationed along the narrow corridor leading to customs. The second thing he noticed was one of the young Sikhs staring at him with a furious expression. Walking to a pair of chairs in a small alcove, Rich acted as if he didn't see.

The stretcher and party disappeared around a corner.

Passengers from Rich's flight and other incoming flights started spilling out of the jet way. Rich fell in among them, willing to take his chances with customs. If he'd tried to tag along with the young Sikhs they would've probably notified security.

The sound of a crash behind Rich made him turn. The middle-aged woman with the man in a wheelchair had lost her grip on her shoulder bag, spilling its contents across the marble floor. She scrambled on all fours, gathering things back into her bag.

"Sorry. Sorry," she said to the annoyed passengers flowing around her.

She had forgotten to put the brake on the chair, and the elderly fellow rolled slowly toward Rich.

"Grandpa. Someone, please."

Rich stopped the chair with his free hand. "Hey, old timer. Making your getaway?"

The man looked like he wore a curtain of thin, parchment-like flesh, freckled brown and draped over his skeleton. He smelled of diapers. "Where's Lucille?" he muttered.

"Thank you." The woman's hair was disheveled, her sweater askew, her face flushed.

"Need some help?" Rich smiled. Unslinging his daypack, he put it in the old man's chair, covering it with the blanket.

Her gray eyes greeted him like answered prayers. "That's so kind of you."

Rich went around to the rear and took the handles. "You've got quite a handful, Lucy."

She sighed. "You have no idea." Then it struck her. "How'd you know my name?"

The corridor ahead zigged left. The crowd of passengers started to bunch up.

"Your grandfather told me."

"How'd you know he's my grandpa?"

"You're too young."

"Grandpa served in the CBI in World War Two. He's wanted to come back to India for so long."

Rich nodded, listening.

Passengers began separating into lines.

"That's all he talked about for years. When grandma passed last year, he wouldn't stop talking about it."

They edged closer to a room filled with military men, sniffer dogs and tables with screeners.

"No one in the family wanted to take him. They said, 'Lucy, you're single. You never married and have no children.'" She smiled. "I said, 'Fine, I'll take him.'"

Rich feigned attention while checking out security as they inched nearer. Customs officials roughly opened bags and cases with little concern for the fragility of the contents.

"Are you traveling alone?"

"Yes," Rich replied, distracted.

The person in front loudly complained to the screeners about how roughly they were handling the bags.

"Where are you staying?"

"Lucy," Rich spoke softly, ignoring her question. "Perhaps I should go through first. I can be on the other side to help Grandpa through."

"That's a good idea." She took the chair.

Rich pulled his laptop out of its bag.

"Passport?" barked a small, tan-skinned Indian with black mustache, wearing Leon Trotsky glasses and dressed in a brown uniform.

Rich showed him his passport.

"That all?" The Indian said, checking the pockets of Rich's bag and opening the laptop. "Ah right. You go."

Rich stepped through the metal detector and waited on the other side.

"Come, come, come," the Indian impatiently said.

Lucy pushed Grandpa's chair forward. A small Indian woman went around the counter and poked through Grandpa's chair. She lifted the blanket and twisted up her nose. She leaned away, checked his chair and then pushed him into the metal detector. Lights and bells went off. A tall, well-built soldier wearing a maroon beret that matched the piping on his brown uniform used his AK-47 to motion the two through.

"I got you." Rich came up and took the wheelchair.

"They tore everything apart."

They rounded a corner, following signs to passport control.

Rich stopped. "You know, I think you have my daypack." He went to the front and lifted the blanket over grandpa's knees. It still smelled bad. The pack was gone. Rich quickly looked to the other side. It wasn't there.

Grandpa's forefinger slowly reached up and touched Rich's chin. Their eyes met. The old man winked and raised a leg. He'd sat on Rich's daypack.

"Why, you crafty old fox." Rich grinned and gave him a salute. "General Stilwell would be proud of you." He tugged his daypack out from under Grandpa.

"Merrill," the old man croaked.

"I should have known," Rich replied.

"Where do we get our luggage?" Lucy looked around.

"After passport control."

"You never said what hotel you're staying at."

"I'm at the Taj Mahal."

"Are you blowing me off? The Taj Mahal's not a hotel."

"Not in Agra. There's a Taj Mahal Hotel at India Gate."

"Ohhhhh. We're staying at the Hilton."

Lines snaked up the corridor, leading to three booths with men seated inside. Rich pushed Grandpa into line. A sniffer dog on a lead came up. Grandpa patted the dog on the top of its head. The military man jerked the dog away.

"Have passport, visa and other documents ready."

"How long are you staying?" Lucy asked as she got hers and Grandpa's visas and passports ready.

"Five days."

"Maybe we can ..."

"I have some traveling to do midweek. But if you're staying longer, when I get back."

She blushed a blotchy red on her cheeks. "Yes. I would like that."

Rich stepped to the booth. He slipped his passport, visa and yellow immunization card through the bottom slot. The puffy-faced Indian with slicked-back black hair pushed the immunization card back to Rich. "Mr. Rice. Purpose of visit?" He opened Rich's passport and swiped the number.

"Pleasure."

"How long are you staying?"

"Until I'm satisfied."

The government agent gave him a questioning look and then shrugged. He leafed to the last page and stamped it hard. "Enjoy your stay." He slid that passport and visa through the slot.

Rich slipped between the booths. *I'm in*, he thought. He could've gone at that moment, but he waited.

"I don't even know your name."

"It's Richard."

"And?"

"Just Richard, okay?"

"I'm Lucy. Oh, you know that," she giggled. "Lucy Starr. Grandpa and I are from Akron. Hey, how am I supposed to call you if I only know you as Richard?"

"Ask for Keeper."

They entered a large white-tiled room with an incline to street level.

"Oh my."

The top of the incline was a mass of brown-skinned people. Some held signs with names, others called out names of hotels or passengers. The crush, the noise of the street and the outside world started at the top.

"Welcome to India," said Rich.

"We're supposed to have a shuttle to the Hilton."

Rich pushed Grandpa's wheelchair up the incline.

"Thank you for helping." Lucy had to raise her voice to be heard.

"No problem." Rich reached the top and waved away people to give Grandpa's chair space. He clicked on the brakes. "If things work out, I'll stop by the Hilton. Tandori and drinks?"

Her head dipped with a faint smile. "That would be lovely."

"The baggage carousels are over there, and your Hilton shuttle is there." Rich pointed. "I'll be getting a car and driver."

"Bye."

"See you, old timer. Bye Lucy."

He waved and shouldered his way into the swarm of *desi*, *Dalits* and other *Varna*.

CHAPTER 11

Rich emerged, blinking and adjusting his eyes to the harsh light of mid-afternoon. It was hot but not uncomfortable. Outside the terminal, the sun burned off-yellow in a raw umber sky. Car horns honked while jockeying for position, edging forward. A grimy breeze chased after a gaily decorated lorry. Buses packed with people and hangers-on spewed black diesel. Donkey hooves clip-clopped on paved streets as they pulled odd wagon contraptions. Smells filled his nostrils: of sewage and sweat and urine and saffron cooking and petrol and, somewhere, burning tires. Flies in swirling dark masses roved head-high up and down the walkway. The chaos of the Third World.

And everywhere, people, people and more people. People in the colors of regional dress, women in bright sarees with clothbound bundles on their heads. Little children following short round mothers like ducklings crossing a street.

As if red meat had been thrown to hungry animals, a crowd of men surrounded Rich, all jabbering all at once.

"I take bag, a dollar."

"Five dollar. Delhi drive."

"Give me bags, 200 rupee."

"We go hotel, five dollar."

They rioted about him, no higher than his shoulders.

"*Nahain*," Rich shouted, using his arm to fend them off.

On the other side of the metal river of cars was a lot full of small vehicles parked bumper to bumper. A tall, lanky Indian leaned against the hood of a silver Maruti. He had his ankles crossed and was casually smoking a cigarette. He looked off into the distance, oblivious to the tumult of life around him.

Rich stiff-armed an aggressive driver grabbing for his daypack. "*Nahain.*" He stepped off the curb and dodged his way through slow-moving traffic.

The man turned to Rich as he approached. He had a look of why-are-you-bothering-me.

"*Angrejee bolate hain*?"

He snorted and dropped his smoke, crushing it on the pavement. "Enough." His hair was a home dye job of shiny reddish brown, combed back and needing the attention of a barber's scissors around the ears. Taller than most Indians, his face was long and bony with a shade of tan less deep than brown. Rich noticed that the whites of his eyes were veiny, cloudy and yellow, the color of mustard. He'd have brown eyes had they not been dilated into large black holes.

"You drive?"

His hands and shoulders pulled up, and his head waggled. Rich recalled right away. Westerners nod for yes; Indians sort of bobble their heads side to side.

"I don't want just a ride. I want a driver I can count on."

He spit. "Whatever you want, sir."

"This your car?" Rich bent low and looked in. A brass statue of elephant-headed Ganesh waved to him from the dashboard. Colorful red and yellow streamers hung off the rearview mirror. *I don't care if it rains or freezes as long as I got my brass Ganesha*, Rich thought.

"Yes. I will open the boot for your luggage."

"I don't have any." Rich tossed in his daypack and took off his laptop, sitting in the back. The car was clean but smelled musty, like cigarettes.

"Where to, sir?" the driver asked, getting in and buckling his seat belt.

"Taj Mahal Hotel." Rich settled. "What's your name?"

The tall man started the car and gave a short beep to the car in front to get it out of the way. "My name? My name is Vicky."

"I'm sorry. What was that?"

"Vicky, sir." The driver of the other car didn't respond. Vicky sucked his teeth and growled low in his throat.

"In honor of the queen?"

"Pardon, sir?" Vicky inched the car forward, very close to the front car's bumper. He leaned his head out the window and shouted something in angry Hindi. The other driver held his hands out, replying loudly, and then got into his car. He moved off to the side, allowing Vicky room to ease out of the parking spot and merge with the stream of traffic.

Cars, lorries, scooters, three-wheelers, rickshaws and pedestrians crowded all four of the lanes, moving at just above a walker's pace. Horns beeped short, or twice, or long, in a language of the road. Rich quickly understood: a short beep let another car go ahead or move into the lane. Two short beeps meant Vicky was passing. A long beep was what-are-you-doing-moron, which Rich considered international.

"First time visiting India, sir?" Vicky asked, glancing up to the rearview mirror. His dark eyes were curious.

"No. I've been here before."

"When, sir?"

"Maybe twenty years ago."

Vicky sucked his teeth and looked to the road.

"I need a driver I can call. And I will pay well."

Vicky picked something from his shirt pocket and handed it back. It was a dog-eared brown stained business card. Vicky Dixit, with a mobile number. "This is my card, sir. You call anytime."

Rich took the card. Dixit was a Brahmin surname. "I need some things before we get to the hotel."

They passed a sandbagged machine-gun nest manned by the Indian Army. With a couple of beeps, Vicky merged onto M.G. Road headed to Delhi.

"I can get you anything you need." Vicky's eyes were steady in the mirror.

"First, I need a disposal mobile phone, something Americans call a burner phone."

"I know just where, sir."

They drove through crowded streets of little enclaves with shops and food stands. Cement poles were topped with tangles of wire like electric spaghetti. A man turned to the street and urinated. A family of four mounted on a small engine motorbike whizzed by.

Vicky pulled into a vacant dirt lot littered with garbage. Dogs with ribs on display hungrily nosed a trash pile. A skinny man in a loincloth bathed out of a rusty bucket. There was a bamboo-framed blue tarp and cardboard shack with colorful signs and numbers advertising SMS and mobile phones. Rich started to get out.

"Sir? You'll be cheated. Let me." Vicky led the way to the open side of the shack. A small, barefoot, dark brown black-haired boy sat on a stool. Behind him were plastic cases hanging on strings strung between bamboo struts.

Vicky gave the boy a head up and rapped off instructions in Hindi. The boy's eyes were locked on Rich the whole time.

"*Ek ha zaar, ek ha zaar, ek ha zaar,*" the boy said, still not taking his eyes off Rich.

Vicky made a sucking noise and grumbled low: "*Nahain.*" He held up five fingers.

The boy nodded vigorously, showing seven fingers. "Service *do.*"

Now Vicky took a step forward and drew back his left hand. He growled: "*Nahain. Do* and *Paanch.*"

The boy flinched, and his head wiggled back and forth, answering *yes.* He reached and took down a plastic case with a Chinese knockoff iPhone. Rich took it and looked at it. He gave Vicky a single nod okay for the deal. He pulled out his pocket cash, a mix of Indian rupees and greenbacks. The boy's eyes opened big.

"Seven hundred, sir."

Rich peeled off seven 100 rupee notes.

Back in the car, Rich inspected the phone, turning it every which way, deciphering the pictures because he couldn't read the Chinese characters. The number was printed on the back, and it would activate the phone with a call.

"Sir, need anything else?" Vicky smoothly inquired, maneuvering the Maruti into a space between a bus and a lorry.

"Just drive."

"Alcohol?"

"No."

"*Bhaang*?"

"That what I think it is?"

"Drugs."

"No."

"*Bhosada*?"

"That is?"

"Girls."

"No."

"Boys?"

"No."

"If sir needs ..."

"I will not need any of that." Rich paused, mulling it over a moment. "I need a gun."

"Pardon, sir?" Vicky jerked, and fright showed in his eyes as they peered back from the mirror.

"A gun. Can you get me a gun?"

Vicky made a low rolling sound in his throat. "This is difficult in my country."

"Look around."

They turned off onto 48 at the outskirts of Delhi and drove along the tree-lined streets of the Cantonment. They stopped at a red light. Down the lanes ran ragged dirty-faced children. Rich stared straight ahead. *Didn't matter*; they spotted his white face in the back of the car. They clustered on either side, tapping coins on the windows.

"Lo. Lo. Lo. Lo. Lo."

"Sir, you cannot ..."

"I know. It's against the law." Rich said. "I also know they are exploited and used by adults."

Vicky waggled his head slowly.

The light changed, but the traffic rolled slowly forward. A military checkpoint lay ahead. Vicky stopped and rolled down his window. He and a machine-gun-toting soldier spoke quietly while another soldier went around the car with a mirror on wheels, checking underneath. They were waved on.

"A lot of terrorist activity?"

Vicky just sucked his teeth.

The walled villas on either side of the street gave way to a line of shops and a swarm of people on the sidewalks. Rich spotted a bazaar.

"Can you stop here and wait for me?"

"Certainly, sir." Vicky double parked. "I will be here when you come out."

"Thanks." Rich jumped out and then reached back in, grabbing his daypack. He went into the Mehruali Bazaar.

Something sounding like uptempo sitar rock music played over speakers, mingling with announcements and loud conversations. Rich walked up one aisle of women's clothing and down another aisle of electronics. People looked at him as he passed. He found an aisle of men's clothes and wandered around some racks. Amongst the long shirts and square-toed shoes, he found a rack of sweatshirts and outerwear. He went around and saw a group of saffron-colored medium-weight hooded cassocks like those worn by monks. *Perfect*, he thought. He found a large one and pulled it from the hanger. In an adjacent aisle, he found a cosmetics display. Searching among the tubes, bottles and boxes, he found mostly women's goods.

"Excuse me?"

A chunky woman turned an attentive face. "Yes?" Her eye shadow was too thick and too green.

"Do you have any *mehndi*?"

"Dye?"

"Yeah."

She took a small tube from a display and handed it to him.

Rich examined the tube of golden dye. "Do you have something a shade darker, but not real dark?"

"Ah, yes." Her chubby fingers took back the *mehndi* and brought down a squat bottle of brown foundation. "This is makeup, not dye."

On the label, an exotic-looking young woman with a clear, almost perfect caramel complexion held the bottle of foundation on her finger tips. She had big dark eyes, thick black hair and wore a gold necklace, earrings and green bangles. Rich opened the bottle and spread some of the makeup on the back of his hand. It gave a good, deep-brown skin tone. "Is this waterproof?

"Yes."

Rich read the English on the label. "It'll work. Thanks. And is there a place with food?"

She smiled and pointed.

"Ah," Rich replied with a grin. "*Dhanyavaad.*"

It took a little bit of hunting, but he found bottled water and power bars. He grabbed a handful and went to the checkout lane.

Vicky waited outside, engine running. He got out, rounding to the back, but Rich held his hand up and opened the back door.

"Sir find what he needs?"

"I think so, Vicky."

They traveled up Prithviraj Road by India Gate. The sky had gone from umber to rusted red, with the sun a yellow hole on the horizon. Light shone through the high arch of the monument, reminding Rich of the Arc de Triomphe. Vicky turned into the circular drive of the opulent, multistoried Taj Mahal Hotel, parking behind taxis and luxury sedans beneath an overhang. Valets in short white jackets bustled about. Vicky shut off the engine and quickly got out, pulling open the door for Rich. Standing at attention by the door, he looked straight ahead as Rich climbed out the back.

"At ease, soldier," Rich said. "What do I owe you for the ride?"

"Eight hundred, sir."

"Fair enough. You want rupees or greenbacks?"

Vicky's eyes lit up. "Greenbacks, sir."

Rich pulled out a twenty dollar bill and a five. Hesitating, he added another five. This would actually be 1200 rupees.

Vicky took and pocketed the notes swiftly and, with a head bow, said, "Most kind, sir."

"I want you back here," Rich pointed, "at nine tomorrow morning. I will be waiting. Okay?"

"Yes, sir." Vicky smiled, closing the door.

Rich slung his daypack over his shoulder, hefted his laptop and plastic bag from the bazaar and then started toward the glass door of the Taj Mahal Hotel. Weariness from the long flight came over him. For a moment, he wondered where he was. Gisele's face came to mind. She would be so excited to be here. He imagined her skipping and hopping about in delight.

Doormen dressed in long coats and wearing gold lame turbans from the days of the Raj pulled back the doors as Rich approached. "Sir," they said, bending in unison.

"Thanks."

The cavernous marble lobby was lit in a warm golden light, with dark wood accents throughout. A deep-pile hand-woven red Indian rug with a mandala design spread across the lobby. Tapestries hung from one wall while the other wall had a large painting of a tiger hunt, with a sultan in a basket on an elephant's back as gun bearers scurried alongside. In the tall grass lurked a majestic tiger. Portraits of various Indian dignitaries flanked the hunt. Much like the caste system, low-level staff were all dressed in the antique costumes of turbans and long white linen shirts while upper-tier desk staff wore modern black suits.

"May I help you, sir?" said a young man with a touch of an English accent. The desk clerk's hair seemed cemented by Gatsby Wax.

"You have a reservation for Keeper." Rich plucked one of the credit cards from his wallet.

The desk man input the information into a computer terminal. "Yes, sir. Mister Keeper. Five nights, single, deluxe room." He swiped the credit card.

'Mister Keeper' amused Rich. He half-smiled.

"I will need to see your passport as well, sir." The young man took the passport and began to type information into the computer. His face clouded over. He stopped and looked from the passport to Rich.

"Is there a problem?"

"Sir, ah, the name here is not the same as the reservation."

"I would prefer if you used Keeper. I am traveling *in cognito*."

"I'm not sure I can ..."

Rich cut him off. "Oh, come now. You must have many people who use a false name so they won't be bothered by..." He paused, tilting his head and raising his eyebrows. "By the press."

"Oh," he smiled. "I understand, sir. Certainly, we can accommodate your wishes."

He finished registering Rich and handed him back his passport, key card and form to sign. "Do you have luggage to take up?"

"No."

"Very good, sir. The elevators are in the center aisle. Breakfast is from six to nine in the dining room. Dinner is served from five to seven. There is room service until midnight. Enjoy your stay." He smiled.

Rich side-stepped out of the elevator on the sixth floor. The room numbers went up toward 649. A young staffer wearing the olden-day livery opened a double door. "Sir," he said. Rich nodded, passing through, and murmured, "*Dhanyavaad*."

His room was laid out like any hotel room in any city in any country in the world: closet on the left, bath on the right of the entry. Two double beds with a desk and armoire. A television was in the armoire at the foot of the first bed. He unloaded his daypack and laptop on one double bed and opened the curtains on the large window. Darkness approached the vast city. Minarets, like needles, poked at a reddish sky. In the distance, three plumes of dense smoke rose and swayed left across the flat horizon. His immediate view, just beyond the tree tops, was of Connaught Place and India Gate. Lights were starting to dot the cityscape.

The room was close and warm. He located the chiller unit. It came on loud and blasted cold air.

He pulled the Taser from his daypack and, using the DC adapter, charged it. He opened the Chinese iPhone and plugged it in to charge.

The marble bath filled quickly, and he eased into the steaming hot water, sighing. Soaking took the stiffness out of his joints from the long flight. The warmth lulled him nearly to sleep. His belly was empty, hungry. He climbed out as the water started to cool, toweled off and found the room service menu on the bedside table. There wasn't much he thought might appease his hunger. The Indian entrees looked too spicy. He picked up the phone and punched room service.

"This is Room 649. Can I get a chicken sandwich?" He listened. "Yes ... with a packet of chips. Okay, I mean crisps then. Do you have Tiger Ale? Then I'll have a bottle of Kingfisher. How long will that be? Okay. Thanks."

Lying on the bed, wearing the thick hotel-provided white terry cloth robe, he surfed the television channels. He found CNN in English with Hindi subtitles, Al Jazeera, a movie with singing and dancing, more singing and dancing, field hockey from Hong Kong, some sort of news panel, dancing and singing and fashion shows, a western movie in Urdu and cricket.

A knock on the door. Rich let in an attendant carrying a tray. The middle-aged man's turban went askew as he bent to set the meal on the dresser. Rich fished a ten rupee note from his pants and handed it over. The man bowed and backed out. Rich ate the first half and downed nearly the full liter of lager. Not the best tasting, yet it still satisfied his thirst. Sleepiness came over him again. He dozed off with the television going and the plate of food on his lap. He woke with the room lights on and nearly frozen by the chiller. People were still dancing on the television. Local time was eleven thirty, but Rich's body clock was still on yesterday and western hours. He shut off the television, put the plate on the other bed, dialed back the chiller, turned off the lights and climbed under the blankets.

Rich slept fitfully, having violent dreams all through the night. Waking at seven local time, he went down to the hotel lounge and had juice, a croissant and a malaria pill with coffee. He ate, reading a copy of the *Times of India* and idly watching people check out in the adjacent lobby. Vicky would meet him at nine, and Rich needed time to get ready.

Back in his room, he went into the bathroom and he daubed the dark makeup on the backs of both hands to the elbow. He got a consistent brown tone to his skin. Dressing in a t-shirt, he rolled up the cuffs of his Levis. With a flourish, he took out the saffron cassock, pulled off the tags and shook it. He ducked his head into the cassock and slipped his arms through the sleeves. In the bath mirror, he wondered if he would fool anyone. Closing and locking his room, he walked down the hall to the elevator. The staff at the door ignored him, making Rich open it himself. "That's good," he murmured. As the elevator doors opened to the lobby, Rich went into character. He stooped and staggered, with a slow, halting gait. Two staff spotted him and crossed quickly. One pushed Rich toward the door, while the other hissed at him in fast Hindi with an unmistakable nasty tone.

"*Door ho jeo*!"

I got 'em fooled, Rich thought.

They snarled and shoved Rich through the lobby and out the glass doors. Standing, arms akimbo, they watched as he shambled down the circular drive. He wore the hood low, halfway over his face. Vicky was not waiting for him. He shuffled to the side and squatted. The two staff went back inside but stayed at the window, keeping an eye on him. On his haunches, Rich cupped his hands and held them upward to couples passing by. They ignored him.

Vicky's gray Maruti eased up the drive. He parked and got out. He scanned the outside while sparking a cigarette with a lighter.

Rich half rose and staggered toward Vicky. His hands out, he said: "*Krpya a. Krpya a. Dhanyavaad.*"

The slick-haired driver blew a thin plume of blue smoke from his pursed lips. He gave Rich a quick glance and raised his left arm. "*Narak mujh se door ho jeo.*"

Rich pushed his hands toward Vicky's impatient face. "*Krpya a.*"

As if enraged, Vicky wheeled. He cocked his left arm, preparing to back hand Rich.

Begging no more, Rich stood upright and caught Vicky's arm.

The driver looked startled.

Rich pushed back the cowl. "What's the matter, Vicky? Don't you recognize me?"

Vicky's eyes bulged out. "Sir? I ... almost ..."

The two hotel attendants came out the glass doors.

Rich gently chuckled and let loose of Vicky's arm. "Fooled you." Crawling out of the long cassock, Rich opened the back door of Vicky's car. "Come on. Show me the Red Fort and a couple of sites." He tossed the cassock in the back and rolled down his pant legs. "I need to find a paint store also."

The two staff stopped and glanced at each other.

Vicky dropped his half-smoked cigarette, imploring. "Sir. I am sorry. I did not know it was you."

They both got in.

The attendants turned and went back into the hotel.

"That was the point, Vicky."

"Why is sir wearing beggar's clothes?"

"Long story. I'll tell you in a couple of days." Rich eased back in his seat.

Vicky started the engine and slowly drove out of the Taj Mahal Hotel's circular driveway. He let traffic clear and turned toward Connaught Place.

"Did you find what I asked for?"

The driver's black eyes flicked to the mirror. He sucked his teeth.

"I'll take that as a no."

"Sir, the laws of my country ... they are very strict."

"Why do you think I'm asking you? I know your law on possession of firearms is very strict. Otherwise, I'd ask you to take me to the nearest gun shop."

"Even air guns require a license, sir." Vicky stopped sucking his teeth. "I will continue."

Rich stared out the window at the passing India Gate. "If you don't find a gun for me by tonight, forget it."

The lanky driver's shoulders eased as if a burden had been raised. "To Red Fort, sir?"

"Yeah," Rich replied, distracted. "And the embassy, Shantipath Chanakyapuri. Don't forget, find me a paint store."

"Certainly, sir. Perhaps Agra tomorrow?"

"I've seen the Taj Mahal."

"And Jaipur?"

"Not interested in the pink city."

"Dilli Haat?"

"Don't need arts nor crafts."

They toured Delhi, stopping at the Red Fort, Qutb Minar, Jama Masjid and the Lotus Temple. Rich, his shoes off in accordance with custom, walked around the temple. At the other sights, however, he stood and looked from the car park. The couples walking around Buddha Garden disturbed him. He was too preoccupied. Vicky waited an hour outside the iron-gated, Stalinesque Russian Federation embassy. They found a catchall hardware store. Vicky followed Rich throughout the store with a very puzzled expression on his face. Rich bought zip ties, a ten-power monocular, a four-by-eight meter sheet of black plastic and two pint-size cans of paint, black and red. Vicky's brows knitted above his narrow eyes as he quietly sucked his teeth. He didn't ask aloud, but his expression wondered, *Why the paint?*

At a HSBC Bank, Rich changed five hundred dollars to twenty thousand rupees.

Vicky sniffed and seemed somewhat dazed when Rich returned and opened the door of the Maruti. A faint medicine scent filled the car.

"Hungry?" Rich asked.

"Me, sir? No."

"I'm buying."

"None for me. But you ..."

"Forget it. Just take me back to the hotel."

With an exaggerated waggle of his head, Vicky pulled into the heavy flow of traffic. They rode in silence, through a confusion of cars, trucks and pedestrians along wide unclean streets and narrow cut-offs in upscale and dirt-poor areas of Delhi. Between the debris and squalor of two crowded apartment complexes, a grinning young Indian fellow with impeccable grooming advertised *Schwarzkopf Professional Taft Power All Weather Hair Lacquer Spray*. A white bull lay beneath the large sign, chewing, with not a care in this world.

It gnawed at Rich. Something was missing from his preparation. He couldn't pin it down. He stared out the car window, looking past his reflection in the glass. Then he focused on his face: his sandy brown hair and steel-blue eyes.

"Vicky?"

"Sir?"

"Is there an optometrist near here?"

"I do not know what that means, sir."

"Eyes, an eye doctor, eye glasses, contact lenses."

"Ah, yes. There is a shop in Shehnai Shopping Mall."

"Take me there."

Vicky parked in the lot. Rich walked into the sprawling multistory white stone mall. People browsed, children raced about. Lilting sitar music played low. The mall was laid out with a central rotunda that went all the way up, four stories, to a glass roof. He wandered until he located a directory, finding a listing in English for an eye glass emporium. Up an escalator and to the left was a small shop with a wall of eye-glass frames and mirrors left, right and center. A young woman stood behind a glass display.

"Hello. Do you speak English?"

"Yes, how can I help you?" Dressed in a tight black frock, she had a red *bindi* with a golden nose ring, large brown eyes and a smile as white and bright as the keys of a brand new piano.

Rich replied with a smile of his own, leaning forward, over the display. "I am looking for clear contact lenses."

A thin thread of smoke rose off the end of a smoldering stick in a cup by the register. The scent of sandlewood filled the shop. *Posh*, thought Rich.

Her small face turned quizzical. "I'm sorry. Clear?"

"I mean contacts to change the color of my eyes."

"Oh," she nodded. "Opaque. We have an array of fashion lenses." Turning, bending, pulling out a tray from a cabinet, she continued to talk. "Everything from vampire red to cat's-eye yellow."

"I just want something brown or black."

She squinted, studying Rich's eyes. "But you have ... um, nice blue eyes. Why would you want plain brown?"

Rich shrugged.

The woman handed Rich a circular plastic case. "These are hazel, soft contacts, no prescription." She squirted a solution on the lenses and handed Rich the case.

Rich picked up a lens on the tip of his finger. "I hate this part."

She pushed a large circular magnifying mirror close to him.

Rich stooped close to the mirror and held open his eyelid, placing the lens on his blue pupil. Blinking, he stood back.

"How does that feel?"

"Fine. Fine." Rich, opening and shutting his eye, looked around. He checked in the mirror. His pupil was a light brown. "And I can wear these for a couple of days?"

"Shouldn't be a problem."

"Yes. These'll do fine Thank you."

Vicky pulled up as Rich waited outside the front entrance to the mall. "Sir get his eye lenses?"

"Yup, now you can take me back to the hotel."

They maneuvered through traffic, and soon, Vicky beeped and crossed two lanes, turning right into the Taj Mahal Hotel drive.

"Vicky, I'm taking a train out of Delhi Junction at eight o'clock tonight. I need to be there maybe an hour early."

"Yes, sir." Vicky eased to a stop. "Traffic in Chandni Chowk is quite heavy in the evening. I will pick you up at six o'clock. How long will sir be gone?"

"Three days." Rich fished out a thousand rupees, handing it over the seatback to Vicky.

"Sir is much too generous."

"I told you I would take care of you." He gathered up his cassock and bag from the seat.

"Certainly, sir."

"See you at six." Rich opened the passenger door.

"Will sir be in disguise?"

Rich laughed lightly, climbing out. "No, Vicky, not this time."

A faint smile spread across the Indian's bronze face. "Very good, sir."

The valet bowed his head while the doorman opened the heavy glass door to the lobby. Rich wasn't sure, but the doorman may have been one of the two that ran him out of the hotel in the morning.

Rich nodded thanks. The dinner buffet was an hour from opening, so he went up to his room and packed his daypack. He swallowed an Imodium and chewed a couple of pink pills. He'd been drinking only bottled water. But, even the most careful should expect the dreaded Delhi-belly.

Sipping from a bottle of Sandpiper, he moved through the buffet, filling his plate with rice, butter chicken, some vegetables and a spoon of yogurt to stop the burn of spicy food. He didn't want to overeat, so he stopped at one plate. With a second Sandpiper in his pocket, he went back upstairs. Lying on the bed, he tried to keep calm and not let his mind race to what lay ahead. When it was time to meet Vicky, Rich asked the desk clerk to put his laptop, two other credit cards, his cash including Krugerrands and his return tickets in the hotel safe. "An embassy will be contacting you about a visa for me. Please print it out."

"Certainly, Mr. Keeper."

Standing outside, the night pollution started to smudge up the gray blue sky. In the distance, over the traffic noise, he could hear a call to prayers. Vicky arrived exactly on time.

"Delhi Junction, sir?" he asked—as if Rich might have changed his mind.

"Yes." Rich climbed in with his daypack.

"Sir is traveling north?" Vicky knew that Delhi Junction served the Northern rail line.

"Yes."

"Where, sir?"

"Best you don't know."

Through unlighted, chaotic and noisy streets, they drove. Old neighborhoods, gated enclaves and slums passed by in a blur. Rich sat enveloped in the shadows of the back seat, detached from the noise and turmoil of the living world around him.

Gisele would have been enthralled by Delhi, marveling at everything: the lavish estates next door to lots filled with poor people in makeshift cardboard and blue tarp shelters. She would have wandered the bazaars and picked through the peddlers' carts, haggling with glee over strings of pearls or folds of silk.

He missed her and experienced no thrill in this ancient, exotic land, where strange people spoke an old language and wore different clothes and venerated reincarnated gods who wandered the streets and countryside in the guise of white steers. It offered little fascination for him. He existed apart, separate.

They stopped at an intersection, and Rich noticed a one-legged man hopping from car to car. No one paid any attention to him, nor filled his outstretched hand with help. His bony face was scarred, perhaps by fire, and his open mouth was missing teeth. Rags hung off his skinny shoulders.

Rich pulled out a hundred rupee note. “Give this to him, Vicky.”

“Sir?” Vicky resisted.

“He’s got one leg. He’s not scamming anybody.”

“But, sir?”

“If the cops come, I’ll take the rap.”

As the man hobbled over, Vicky rolled down the driver’s window just a crack. He stuck the note out, keeping his eyes forward. The man plucked the bill and awkwardly hopped away, saying, “May the gods bless you.”

I hope so, Rich thought. I will need Shiva’s heart and Kali’s fire.

Delhi Junction rail station was a lasting monument to the British Indian government. The oldest functioning station in Delhi, it had opened in the late 1800s, becoming fully operational in 1903. Dark masses of people moved under drooping strings of electric lights. Carts selling food, clothes and bolts of fabrics lined the streets. Built in a classic Indo-Islamic style, the station very much resembled the Red Fort, with towers, guard walks and Arabesque arches. Crowds wandered in and around chain-link entrances and exits. Vicky fell in with a line of three-wheel taxis, buses and cars snaking into the station. Delhi Junction showed its age in its peeling paint and disrepair. A jungle of scaffolding fronted the station.

A small Bajaj scooter swooped in front of the Maruti. Sucking his teeth, Vicky hit the brakes and grumbled, “*Chootia.*”

People flowed about and between the slow-moving vehicles at Kashmere Gate. Vicky honked. He reached a drop-off point and stopped. The car behind beeped and maneuvered around.

Vichy opened the back door. Rich stepped out and faced him.

"Meet me here at four in the morning, three days from now." Rich pulled out a Taj Mahal Hotel envelope. "This is for today and picking me up. But … if I am not here on that morning, don't wait."

"Sir?" Vicky looked down on the thick envelope, his expression troubled.

"I have the phone and will call if I am late or arriving the following day. If I am not here and do not call, I won't be coming back."

"Yes, sir." Vicky said slowly, his voice thick.

"Now go."

Vicky, glancing back, slipped into the car and disappeared in traffic. Rich got his bearings and walked into the noisy, bustling railway station. A mix of odors assailed him, from paint and plaster to body odor, frying food, cheap perfume and cologne, tires, petrol and urine.

At a blue ticketing window, Rich stooped low and spoke through a cracked hole in the glass. "I have a ticket for Train 15013 in will call."

"Pardon, sir?" an older man in shabby silver-patterned polyester shirt replied. "Will call?"

"There is a ticket being held for me."

"Oh, yes. You may collect the ticket at the Questions Desk."

"*Dhanyavaad.*" Rich walked through the teeming station. He dodged people. A sound very like an old computer operating system error message was followed by a woman's voice announced trains arriving from destinations and departing to other destinations. He spotted the Questions Desk.

"I'm here to collect a ticket."

A motherly woman with streaks of gray shot through her thick hair, dressed in a red and yellow satin saree, gazed up. Creases of brown wrinkled skin nearly obscured her red dot. She didn't seem to hear or understand.

"Tic ... ket?" she replied.

"Yes, a ticket. You're holding a ticket for me."

"Ah, *tik tik.*" She waved her hands and looked around the desk. Paper and pen were put before Rich. She made a writing gesture. Rich understood and wrote, *Train 15013. Destination Kathgodam, Richard Rice.* He turned it about and tapped his written name and pointed to his chest.

The woman acknowledged this by moving her head side to side. She pulled out a cardboard box. Her age-worn brown fingers walked up the envelopes. She pulled one from the box and, glancing at the scrap of paper, handed it up to Rich.

The writing was tiny, faint and hard to decipher. He opened the envelope. It held a sleeper car ticket to Kathgodam, Train 15013, with a return ticket. "Yes. *Dhanyavaad.*"

The woman smiled.

"What track?" he asked.

Her smile sank in confusion.

"*Alavida,*" he said, walking off to find the platform.

Overhead, a man on a rickety ladder was placing black letters and arranged times on a white board by hand. Rich studied the board, finding Kathgodam. The train was leaving at 20:15, on time and on North Track 4.

An oily and stained walkway led up to Track 4. Rich emerged into the crowded platform. Crates and canvas sacks and barrels and wood carts lined the wall. People stood facing the empty tracks and railyard. Rich ambled along the dimly lit platform. A kiosk sold drinks, snacks, the *Hindustani Times* and *Times of India*, magazines and comic books.

"*Gora*," someone growled, passing him.

"Butter man," his companion added.

Rich half-turned. A long time since he'd been called that. He found a spot between piles of mail sacks. He leaned back, waiting and watching.

Gurus sat with a circle of disciples while crowds of rambunctious youngsters in school uniforms played tag in and out and between disdainful upscale youths staring at their mobile phones, wearing last year's western fashions. A radio played eastern-flavored guitar rock. Rich saw a pair of oversized black cats scuttle between the rails, nosing the small tips of garbage. The cats' long thin tails and pointed noses betrayed that they weren't cats at all.

Rich checked the time on his burner phone. Half an hour yet. He relaxed.

A mother in white saree, holding her baby's bare bottom, raced across the platform. She stopped at the edge and, clutching the babe under its chubby shoulders, let him shit a soft brown ribbon of feces followed by a bent yellow stream of urine into the rail bed below.

With upraised eyebrows, Rich watched it all. Then he could smell it. It didn't smell earthy; human shit never does. Those on the platform seemed nonplussed.

When the toddler appeared empty, the mother gave him a shake, then cooed and cuddled the babe as she carried him back across the platform.

Down the line, a train's air horn trumpeted two short blasts. A single bright white light approached, shaking.

Reeking of old diesel, the big and blue rectangular engine rumbled slowly into the station. As it passed the platform, Rich scanned the blue and beige striped cars, searching for Sleeper Car 21. People scrambled forward, packing the edge of the platform. Some jumped on the train before it had fully stopped; passengers stepping off the train did the same. With a loud hiss and quick horn, the train came to a halt. Crowds funneled toward car doors. Rich pushed against the tide of people, wading down the platform. He found his car and climbed in. He worked his way along the narrow, crowded corridor, checking the metal plates above the sleeper areas, until he located 13. Sleepers consisted of triple tiers of bunks on three sides. The bunks were covered in brown leatherette, much like a dentist's waiting room couch. Bottom bunks were already occupied by couples and kids huddled like bundles of cloth and hair. The middle tiers on either side were also occupied. The top tier at the back was empty. Rich tossed his daypack on the bunk and climbed up the side railing. The bunk was wide and long, with a small dirty window. No pillow. No blanket. The sleeper area had no door, only heavy vinyl hung like a shower curtain. A plastic smell from the curtain mixed with something like wet wool. People crossed back and forth. Loud and excited Hindi sounded along the corridor and from other cabins.

Two blasts from the engine, one short and one long, echoed throughout the old station. Car doors started to close.

Rich looked at his cabin mates. They were all Indian.

Babies cried outside.

Two quick notes from the air horn, and the cars shuddered as the train started forward.

He wiped dirt from the window but only saw blurry light and shadows go by.

People settled themselves.

Shivering from the cold, Rich used the cassock as a blanket and his daypack as a pillow. He hugged himself for warmth.

The ticket taker appeared, punched the passenger's tickets, then drew the vinyl curtain closed.

The train shook and bumped its way out of Delhi, trucking down the old track and lulling Rich into a half-sleep.

Someone—a woman—exclaimed. A child screamed. Rich's eyes opened. A figure stood in the white light beside the open curtain. A second, shadowy figure, moved swiftly from bunk to bunk. A man shouted. The shadow barked back. Flesh slapped flesh.

Rich did not move. His heart raced.

A hand came over the railing, feeling around. The hand touched him. Rich lashed out with his left grabbing a thin wrist. He bent the arm violently to the side. He heard a yelp.

A dark head came up.

Rich's right fist jabbed into the brown face. The head jerked back. He drew back and punched through, and the body went limp. A crack sounded in the shoulder of the arm Rich held. He let go of the arm, and the body clumped onto the floor. The shadow in white light fled. Rich jumped down and grabbed the thief on the ground by the collar of his shirt. The train swayed and bumped as he dragged the body out of the cabin, into the corridor light.

He called back into the sleeper cabin. "Anyone understand English?"

"I do," a woman's voice answered from the dark.

"Ask if he stole anything from them."

There was a quick exchange of Hindi.

"A gentleman's wallet."

Rich rifled through the unconscious thief's pockets, pulling a couple of wallets out. "Which one?"

"*Theek hai*," someone said.

"The black one."

Rich tossed it to the woman. He pocketed the other wallets.

"Thank you."

"Anything else?"

No one spoke.

Rich hauled up the thief by the belt and collar and carried him through the doors between cars. He dumped him in the jouncing platform. He stepped into the narrow cabinet lavatory and pissed into the tall shit-smeared white porcelain toilet. Then he went back to sleeper cabin.

"Thank you, sir."

"Not a problem. Listen, when a ticket agent comes by, will you give him these wallets and tell him what happened?" Rich said to the English speaker as he climbed back to his bunk. In a minute, his heart had slowed to normal. He sighed, pulling the cassock up, and heard nothing until a scratchy speaker squawked in the corridor: "Kathgodam. Station Kathgodam."

Yawning, stiff and still weary, Rich swung his legs over the edge of the bunk and leapt down. He slung his daypack over his shoulder. Those of his fellow passengers who were not asleep in their bunks smiled and nodded to him.

Sleepy people lined the dimly lit corridor, swaying with the slowing train. Out the window, it was still dark. Rich shivered in the chilly air.

Metal screamed against metal.

A loud hiss came from the front of the train as a bumping rolled down the cars. With a lurch that nearly tumbled some passengers, the train stopped.

"Kathgodam. Station Kathgodam."

Doors opened, and passengers stepped down into the predawn darkness.

Rich stood on the platform as people scattered. There wasn't much to Kathgodam, a small, old station that resembled a Swiss chalet. He walked around to the front, where people were climbing into buses and cars. At the end was a cab stand. Two men dressed in multi-colored sweater vests and shabby overcoats stood talking.

"How much rupee to Ranikhet?"

"Seven thousand," one quickly replied.

"*Nahain,*" Rich shot back.

"Five thousand, you come," the second said, waving Rich to his old sedan.

"Forty-five hundred," the first man interrupted, with a pained look on his face.

Rich looked at the two cars. The first driver's car appeared newer and capable of the drive up the mountain.

"Done." Rich opened the back door.

Right off, he realized he'd made a mistake. The driver started his car. It needed a muffler.

They roared away from the lights of the train station, down unlighted roads with hillside houses, veering left toward dark mountain shapes and the villages of Nainitol and Ranikhet.

Carbon monoxide filled the backseat, and Rich rolled down both windows, letting cold air blow in.

"You come from Delhi?" the happy-faced driver asked above the noise of wind. He wore a yellow and red knitted cap with flaps and strings. It was too small for his bushy brown hair and round head.

It was a silly question; he had just got off the train from Delhi. But being tired, Rich responded simply, "Yes."

The road started to climb and switchback left, right and left again. The driver beeped at each turn as the tires squealed.

Within half an hour, they had reached a plateau. A large, flat lake spread out for acres before them under a wispy tule fog in the dawn twilight. The half-light caught Nainitol on the far shore, its white buildings stacked up and climbing each crook of the mountain.

"Nainitol," the diver murmured, limply pointing.

They passed a green sign with white lettering reading *Nainitol* in English and Hindi.

Steep roads passed the town, and they climbed through terraced hills and sheer upswept peaks.

"Ranikhet, sir? Where?" The driver slowed, sounding his horn and approaching a blind curve.

Rich pulled his face from the open window. "West View Inn, Mall Road." He got a snootful of carbon monoxide and was nearly sickened. He leaned back to the open window. "Do you know where that is?" he shouted over the wind.

The driver waggled his head. "Near regiment, Kumaon Hills."

Forests of pine bordered the narrow roadway. Breaks in the trees offered Rich a vista of hundreds of kilometers. They rattled through the clouds, reaching the snow line. The rising sun burned bright but cold on the eastern horizon. Guard rails and shoulders ended, with the road edge bordering deep cliffs.

Rich started to feel headachy and nauseous. "Stop. Please. Stop."

"Sir?" The driver slowed and stopped. The car backfired. "We be there nearly."

Rich climbed out and breathed deeply the cold air. The sick feeling cleared. "Okay." He got back in. "I'll be all right. I just needed some fresh air."

The noisy car got back up to speed. After a hard left and then a nearly full-circle right turn, the driver dipped into a narrow, rutted road between sheltering pines. The car bumped along, entering a grassy clearing. A two-story, stucco and timber turn-of-the-century house dominated the open area. It was trimmed in black with a tall peaked slate roof. Outbuildings and a wire cage with chickens lay off to the side of the clearing. The car braked. Rich could not get out fast enough. A large white-chested Bernese mountain dog stirred before the building's heavy wooden doors. Lazily, the dog roused itself and, yawning, lumbered slowly toward Rich.

"Here." Rich handed the driver five thousand rupees. "Keep it."

"*Dhanyavaad*, sir."

"I'll need a ride back to the train in a couple of days."

"They know me," the driver said, grinning. "They call Gupta."

The car loudly backed up and turned. Heard but unseen, it traveled through the pines.

Rich let the large dog sniff the back of his hand. The animal breathed through its mouth as its wide, flat, pink tongue wagged. It had droopy, sleepy eyes. As the noisy car drove down the mountain, its sound was replaced by the sound of a gentle breeze that bent the pointed tops of the pine trees. Birds, chickens in the pen and the soft huffing of the Bernese filled the entire world. The air was scented of pine and wood smoke. Rich scratched the thick fur of the dog's neck. A couple came out a side door of the inn. They were deeply absorbed in each other and walked across the clearing to a tree swing.

Bone weary from his journey, Rich trudged to the heavy timber door and tugged an iron ring. It creaked as it opened and clanked as he let it go. He stepped up a couple of stairs into a tiled foyer. Made of the same stucco and timber as the exterior, the foyer had an odd combination of colorful woven mandalas and blotchy old black-and-white photos of hiking parties and a military tattoo.

"Hello?" he called. He glanced back to see that the Bernese had reassumed its position before the door.

Rich pulled the door closed. "Hello?" He peered carefully into open doorways.

"Yes?" a very British voice said from a side room. "Who's there?"

"I'm Richard Rice. I have a room reserved."

A tall, aged woman with gray curly hair and wearing a long-sleeved cotton shirt, fleece vest, woolen pants and hiking boots came striding out into the foyer. She held, for drinking or for warmth, a steaming mug in her hands. “Indeed, the American. Mr. Rice. We’ve been expecting you.” Her narrow face had a mature beauty, albeit showing age in wrinkles that were not unflattering. “I am Evelyn, though everyone calls me Evie. Did you have a pleasant trip up?” She had a fresh, soapy scent about her.

“It was ... interesting. It’s very nice to meet you, Evie.”

The woman sipped from the mug and walked into a back room.

Rich followed. “Do I need to fill out a registration?”

They crossed a banquet room with rows of linen-dressed tables and a fireplace sooty around its brick edges. Above the mantle were crossed spears, sabers, an Indian flag and the Union Jack.

“Oh, nothing like that here. We’re very casual. You are set for today and two days forward. That was all taken care of over the internet. And your Wi-Fi password is in your room.”

“Okay.”

“Your room is around the corner.” She worked a weighty, tarnished brass key from her vest pocket and handed it to Rich. “It’s number six, to the left of the side door. Do be careful of Slingsby when you go out. He’s not as agile as once upon a time.”

“The guard dog?”

“After a fashion. Oh, breakfast is within the hour. We have fresh eggs.”

Rich paused at the heavy door. "I'm pretty tired from the trip. And I'll be going out hiking later. Don't worry if you don't see me for meals."

"Rightie-oh." Evie disappeared into a side room.

Walking back outside, Rich stepped over Slingsby and turned to the side of the inn.

Before going in, he crossed the clearing to a break in the pines and a concrete abutment at the stark drop-off. This was the Chaubattia Ridge, and he could see east for hundreds of kilometers into the valley. Breaks in the clouds showed the four-cornered lake at Nainitol and the little village of Ranikhet. Tall, conical hills, terraced to the top, loomed in the south. North, he saw the snow-tipped gray serrated peaks of the lower Himalayas.

"Gisele would've loved it here," he whispered with a heaviness in the pit of his stomach.

His room was quite spacious, almost cavernous, and cold. The door showed light underneath and at the top and did not seal the room from the breeze outside. An electric baseboard heater ran along one wall. The bath had an antique western-style commode and walk-in shower. The bed was wrought iron with red rust at the seams. The bed clothes were a thick pile of mismatched wool blankets and a down comforter. It squeaked, as it looked like it might, and sagged in the middle. Rich unslung his daypack, untied his shoes, pulled himself out of his hooded sweatshirt and turned back the heavy comforter.

"Shit." He recalled that he had to charge his electronics. Plugging in the DC adapter, he charged the Taser and portable charger.

His head still ached from the ride up. He collapsed on the bouncy, squeaky bed and drew the comforter to his shoulders. The bed clothes smelled in need of a wash, but he was too soon asleep to care.

CHAPTER 12

A shaft of quicksilver light burned through the parted curtains, falling across Rich's face. He opened his eyes, shielding the bright with his hand. For just a moment, he didn't recognize the room.

The time had come.

He sat up, fully awake. Dressed, he packed a drawstring bag with water, power bars, plastic sheet, zip ties, spray paint, monocular, Taser and extra charger, steel baton and—was he forgetting anything?

In the bathroom, he studied his face. More than a couple of weeks without shaving had left an unruly beard sprinkled with gray bristles from his long jaw to his high cheekbones. Not having had a haircut in weeks gave his hair a wildness. It just touched the top of his ears. Vigorously, Rich wiped his face and neck with the brown foundation. After a second application, he got the deep complexion he wanted. His steel-blue eyes shone bright against his tan mask. After washing his hands, he carefully put the hazel contact lenses in his eyes. Blinking, he checked his face in the mirror. Face and hands made-up, he thought he could pass—though not on close inspection.

Looping the drawstring bag over his head, Rich slipped on a sweatshirt and pulled his head through the hooded cassock.

If this fucking works, he thought.

Without hesitating or listening to his second mind, Rich quit the room. Slingsby lifted his giant furry head as Rich passed. The dog cocked an eye to one side, yawned and lay back down, guarding the door.

Rich darted across the clearing. Reaching the pines, he glanced back at the inn. A thin silhouette moved away from an upstairs window.

It was neither dusk nor afternoon; the round red sun sat low in the west.

He broke out of the pines at the Mall Road. Having studied the map many times, he knew the way. The Mall Road climbed for a quarter kilometer. Rich walked slowly on the dirt and gravel shoulder. Pine trees bordered the road, with a break here and there showing dizzying vistas of the valley below. Patches of old snow lay off the road on the edges of the wood. The air turned brisk. Black eagles glided above, searching. A chattering in the trees seemed to follow Rich. Maybe it was the altitude, but he verged of breathlessness.

A car honked and swerved around him.

The intersection of Khari Bazaar Road and Sarna Gardenrdad lay ahead.

A brown sign at the crossroads read *Kumaon Regiment* with an arrow to the right. Down the road, he saw a machine gun emplacement, gun house and three white flagpoles with the regiment, state and India flags. This was the main gate. Rich picked up a long stick to use as a staff and turned left up Khari Bazaar Road.

The buckled and potholed roadbed had been patched with asphalt here and there. The forest grew denser the higher he climbed. He sweat though the air was cold. Rich was in good physical condition, but he could tell the altitude affected him. He labored up the rising road.

Occasionally, through trees, he saw a chain link fence, topped with barbed wire. This marked the regiment's grounds.

Then ahead, to the right of the road, the trees broke on a small open area. The front of a car could be seen. Rich was fairly certain this was the old KGB villa, now Suka's villa. He crossed to the left side of the road.

Shambling up the gravel shoulder, he saw the villa grounds appearing cut out of the trees.

Two men sat in a black Mercedes parked at the open gate of a stucco wall. Fragments of glass topped the wall. A courtyard and two white vans with Kozmos Corp in faded letters on the side were parked before a square two-story structure of Moorish design. This was the villa, and it was smaller than Rich had imagined it. The front had a wooden deck with chairs and overhang. The front door was in the middle of the deck. An outbuilding like a carriage house was on one side of the villa while on the other side was a large propane tank. Red barrels were piled along the wall next to the propane tank.

As Rich neared the villa entry, both doors of the Mercedes opened. One man stepped out. A tall, heavyset man in mismatched black and gray tracksuit stood on the passenger side. He had a bulbous nose, oversized head and a wrestler's snarling expression. The AK-47 in his hands caught Rich's attention.

Coming slowly out the driver's side, smoking a cigarette, was a short man with dark roots to his bottle-blond hair. He had a hard face. Rich recognized him at once. He flushed, fighting an impulse to go after him right then.

Rich dropped his staff, made motions toward his mouth and then cupped his hands toward the men. "Ah ah ... *rupee, dhanyavaad ... rupee, dhanyavaad.*" He kept the cowl low, not giving the men a good look at his face.

They laughed.

"*Dhanyavaad ... dhanyavaad,*" he said.

"*Nyet, ty kusok der'ma.*" The blond shouted.

The heavy one leveled his Kalashnikov and made a menacing motion toward Rich. "*Bakh, bakh, bakh.*"

Rich brought his hands up, feigning fright with a strained cry.

Again, they laughed.

The blond pulled out an automatic and waved it up the road.

"*Idti mudak.*"

Rich didn't need to understand the words to comprehend the tone. He retrieved his staff and struggled up the road.

"*Bakh,*" the blond said, aiming his automatic at Rich.

The villa had metal pipes with mounted cameras sticking up at each corner. He saw the top curve of a satellite dish behind the building. Power came from a thick black cable, with transformer and UPS (uninterrupted power supply) on a tower in the back corner where the propane tank was located. Rich looked but didn't see a camera at that corner.

He could hear the guards talking and joking behind him. When he had walked past the villa, he stopped, squatting at the road side.

The Russians shouted and waved at Rich to keep moving. He didn't. Eventually, they just stared back, finally giving up and getting back into the car.

Rich let out a breath. The blond with the dark roots was definitely the same Russian that Rich had seen at the courthouse in Omaha. He would be the man Daisy described who had brought the fake subpoena for Gisele. Where was his greasy-haired pal?

With the monocular hidden in his fist, Rich surveyed the villa in more detail.

The parked vans had dirty windows, yet he could see rows of seats.

He scanned the windows on both floors of the house, discerning movement and shapes but nothing distinct.

"Are you home, Suka?"

Darkness came quick and deep on the mountain. Yellow lights lit windows in the villa. Spotlights cast white, shadow-less light on all three corners of the courtyard. A single spot hung over the eave and threw a round circle of light on the front door.

"Dammit," Rich murmured. He couldn't see a way in.

The gate wasn't well lit, but the guards were there.

There were no animals that he could see. If they had dogs, they would've come out barking when he passed.

He noticed how, at the far corner behind the propane tank, shadows from the wall fell across the tank. He checked; the three corner cameras appeared stationary. It might be possible to scale the wall and drop down between the wall, tank and red barrels.

A rumbling at the top of the mountain road startled Rich. He dropped the monocular into his pocket, kept in a squat and lowered his head. The headlights of a Maruti Gypsy leading a deuce and half truck lit up the trees and road. The Indian Army insignia was painted on the sides of the vehicles. The canvas cover of the truck was rolled up. There were soldiers seated on either side. As the convoy closed in, Rich cupped his hands and motioned toward the lead vehicle. The mustached rider and young driver in the Gypsy ignored him. Then the truck sped by. A couple of soldiers looked over their shoulders.

A tinkling sound on the asphalt, and something hitting Rich's shoulder, made him look. He picked up ten rupee coins from the gravel road.

The hillside behind Rich's position was wooded with dense brush. Almost blindly, he scrambled through the undergrowth and up the hill. Thick shrubs thinned the higher he trudged. "Always get the high ground," he remembered. He located a tall pine tree and cleared the debris, needles and soft dirt under the low branches. Out of the drawstring bag, he retrieved the black plastic sheet. He folded it lengthwise and covered it using short boughs. Realizing that he'd had nothing to eat all day, he took out a bottle of water and power bar from the bag. He devoured the power bar.

Night air turned misty and crisp. A deep breath refreshed Rich. The bright half-moon lay just above the rough shapes of the eastern horizon. Between the trees,

Rich noted that the moon light cast silver on the mountainside.

Disturbing the woods silence, a car started.

Rich recapped the water, wrapped the bar and put them in the bag. Reaching into the bag, he pulled out the steel baton. Quietly, he went down the hillside to the road. Low and behind a tree, he saw the headlights on the Mercedes at the gate. The sedan edged forward, did a three-point turn and drove into the courtyard, coming to a stop by the front deck. The white overhead light caught the blond guy and large guy getting out, stretching and climbing to the deck. Two other men met them at the front door.

"Changing of the guard."

The big man and the blond passed the two and went into the house. The other two got into the Mercedes.

Through the monocular, Rich focused on the driver. He was of medium height, slight at the shoulders, with oily hair. Rich was certain this was the blond's Omaha cohort.

The Mercedes drove through the gate and then backed at an angle, blocking the entrance. They shut off the headlights but left the car running.

Rich made his way back up the hillside to the pine tree. He urinated around the area. He finished his power bar and washed it down with a couple of swallows of water. Wind rushed through the trees, rustling the pine limbs. Just a riffle of cold air moved down the hillside. Night blue skies showed between tree limbs, with gray clouds roving past. A moisture in the air worried Rich.

He held up the plastic, rolled himself between the sheets and lay out on the soft dirt. Keeping a small opening to peer and breathe from, he settled for the night.

The opening piano notes of The Pretenders' *I Go to Sleep* crossed his thoughts. He imagined Gisele. Loneliness and a wave of sorrow swept over him. He missed her terribly. In the back of his mind, he knew they might soon be together again. And that was okay with him.

He teetered between sleep and wakefulness. The night was quiet, save for occasional wind and noise in the trees. Sometime in the middle of the night, a low panting outside in the dark brought him alert. Something was out there. A soft tread on pine needles. He convulsed up his spine. Breath caught in his windpipe. Something stepped toward him. A cloud slipped by the half moon and Rich saw a pair of glowing yellow eyes, low to the ground, staring at him. Sniffing, a large dark shadow crouched, slowly approaching.

His mind raced. Startle it, and it might pounce. Let it get too close, he was dinner. Easing his hand into the pocket of the cassock, Rich brought out the Taser. He clicked it on, and the shadowy animal drew back. A low growl rumbled in the animal's throat.

Closer it came.

As a cat would, it tentatively reached out with a massive clawed paw.

Rich pushed the Taser toward the pad of the paw, pressing the red button.

Blue light lit the sides of the trees as the Taser crackled.

The animal gave out a high-pitched cry as it tumbled sideways.

Rich threw off the plastic and jumped up, ready for the cat to recover and attack.

The long black leopard struggled to its feet, shaking its paw like it was wet, and glowered at him. Then it slunk silently away, disappearing into the trees.

Rich exhaled and dropped to a knee. He turned off the Taser. There would be no sleep tonight. After a while, watching, he became confident the leopard would not return.

"Thieves on the train, man-eating leopards in the woods... this is a damn dangerous country."

The moon had fallen from its peak and slid off to the west. Cold penetrated his sweatshirt and made him shiver. His teeth chattered. He got up and picked his way down to the road. Behind the cover of a bush, he saw the black Mercedes still parked at the gate. Two shadows showed in the sedan.

Rich ran at a crouch across the road. He took cover behind the corner of the wall. The shadows inside the car didn't stir. All the spotlights were aimed to the inside of the walled villa, providing shadowy cover on the outside. Staying low, Rich felt his way to the back corner. Keeping to the base of the wall, he hoped he wouldn't show up on the cameras. A good thing there was no camera on the back pole. Shards of glass on the top of the stucco wall gleamed in stray light.

Surveying the area, Rich noticed a pine near the wall. He quickly climbed and edged out onto a thick limb overhanging the wall. He eased himself down, carefully placing his feet between jagged edges of glass. Pieces broke off. Glass stung his palms as he felt around for a place to set his hand. Below him, the propane tank was visible in partial shadow.

He jumped, landing with a ringing noise on the top of the tank. He slid quickly off and hid in the dark between the wall and tank. In a squat, he waited. His pulse thumped in his ears. In a minute, he thought it safe. Coming out from behind the tank, he crept to the satellite dish behind the villa. There were two dishes. The larger white one was old with a faded parabolic; the smaller gray dish was newly installed and suited more for phone and internet. Cables ran from the dishes to an electric panel on the wall. Disabling the satellites would be relatively easy.

The panel had lines running to the surveillance cameras on the corners. There were but three inputs. Perhaps that was why the back corner did not have a camera.

Rich stayed down and hugged the foundation of the villa as he prowled around the back. He listened below an iron-barred window, hearing nothing. At the front corner, he looked into the courtyard. He saw the two silhouettes in the Mercedes. They still hadn't moved.

Bright spotlights flooded the courtyard. He had tripped the motion sensor.

The front door rattled open.

Rich went flat and rolled into the dark under the deck.

The blond walked out onto the deck, a lit cigarette in his hands. He walked to one end and looked. Then he slowly came over to Rich's side. He stood above Rich, taking a slow drag.

Rich held his breath.

The blond flicked his cigarette into the courtyard. "*Is obez'yana*. Monkey. Monkey," he said, going back inside.

Crawling back and then getting on his feet, Rich reconnoitered the other side of the villa. He scuttled between the vans, each of which would hold nine or twelve passengers. Examining a pile of garbage in a can yielded nothing more than empty Maggi noodles bags, Britannia biscuit boxes, candy wrappers, greasy papers, brown beer bottles and the grounds of Good News.

The courtyard lights tripped off.

Back on the other side, Rich tipped and rolled a red barrel to the propane tank. Some liquid sloshed inside. It smelled of petrol. He stopped. From an upper window, he heard crying, like a young girl sobbing. He stepped from the barrel to the tank and pulled himself up the wall. The limb was just out of reach, so he leapt and rolled in the soft dirt. He couldn't resist sneaking to the Mercedes and checking the guards. They snored, sound asleep.

A light snapped on in an upstairs room. Rich backed away from the car to the far corner. He dashed across the road and took concealment behind a bush.

Shadows crossed the lighted windows. The moonless sky left a blue dome with white dots of morning stars scattered above. A band of light stretched across the eastern horizon. Weary, fighting sleep, Rich watched the villa.

Interior light moved along the second level and down to the first floor. Smoke came out the chimney. The dome light went on inside the Mercedes. The engine turned over. The two figures inside moved. One man got out from the passenger side. He stretched, hacking up phlegm from his throat. He spat on the wall and then stood, pissing at it.

A pair of stout men in heavy coats came out the front door. They waited on the deck with white mugs in their hands.

Dawn washed the sky with gray. Fog drifted from the valley.

Rich observed for a while but couldn't keep his eyes open. He needed sleep, and he staggered up the wooded hill. Halfway to his encampment, shouts and slamming doors made him wheel about and return to the road.

The men from the porch were in the well-lit courtyard. Armed guards were at the gate. Herded out the front door were a group of young girls. Rich could hear their fearful crying. They pleaded in panicked voices in a language he did not recognize. They were dark haired and dressed in an odd assortment of shifts, pants and ethnic clothing. Studying the girls' faces, Rich realized that they weren't all girls. They had olive complexions, distinctive noses and large dark eyes. Some appeared no older than eight or ten years. Other men came out and went to the vans. They got in and warmed up the engines.

The girls and boys clustered in the courtyard. There must've been almost twenty huddled, clutching each other. Rich watched through the monocular. He figured out what was going on, and there was nothing he could do about it.

He shifted the spyglass to the front door. An orange-haired woman stepped out. Her left arm was in a sling, and her shoulder sagged. Rich recognized Suka Franko. His chest tightened. His teeth clenched. All the thousands of miles; all that burned in his gut, and he had found her. Suka had a young girl under her good arm. She fondled and stroked the girl's black hair. The girl tried to lean away from Suka's hand.

From behind Suka came a trio of thick-bearded, black-haired men wearing white tunics, woolen vests and black linen hats. They stood alongside her.

Suka pushed her girl off the front deck.

The four casually watched from the deck as the men divided the girls and boys and yelled, slapped or kicked to get them into the vans. Some screamed. Others collapsed and had to be forcibly picked up and pitched into the van. Most, with heads bowed, stepped up and disappeared inside—resigned.

A guard with an AK-47 balanced on his shoulder stood off to the side of the gate. The Mercedes drove out and then stopped, idling on the road.

One of the bearded men shook hands with Suka while the other two climbed in the van. The vans slowly drove out of the gate and turned toward Ranikhet.

Rich watched Suka. She talked to someone in the house and then went back inside. The blond and the tall one came out. They stepped off the deck, walking toward the gate. The Mercedes backed into place. The driver got out, and all four met at the gate. The tall man caught the AK-47 tossed to him. Both guards crossed the courtyard to the villa. The blond sat behind the steering wheel, leaving the door open.

If Rich had counted correctly, there were only Suka and the four men left at the villa.

Rich moved through brush up the hill to his encampment. He scanned the area and lifted pine boughs to see if he had any unwanted visitors. His mouth was parched, and his stomach gnawed. He emptied a bottle of water and ate a power bar.

The sun broke out between layers of high clouds. It appeared to be warm, but the air was chilly and smelled like snow approaching.

His tiredness returned. He stowed the empty bottle and wrapper in the drawstring bag and backed around the tree with a branch, sweeping away footprints in the patches of dirt. Rich rolled under the plastic and pine branches. In a moment, he was out.

Hissing, like steam, startled Rich awake. He raised the plastic slightly and saw sleet falling through the trees. White patches spotted the ground around the pines. Assured that the noise had not been a predator, Rich closed his eyes and caught another hour or two of sleep.

When he awoke, as far as he could tell, it was late afternoon. He emerged from under the boughs and immediately shook from the cold. He'd been warm under the plastic, but outside, the damp had given the air a bite. He dug a hole, relieved himself and kicked dirt over it. He ate a power bar for a meal. With no mirror, he couldn't check his brown face makeup, but hoped it still concealed his light skin. Ducking into the cassock, he dropped the steel baton and zip ties in one pocket and put the Taser in the right, handy pocket. Picking his way down the hillside to the road, he knelt behind a bush. There was no activity at the villa. The Mercedes was still parked at the gate. A black plume of smoke curled out of a rusted stovepipe chimney.

A car drove cautiously down the wet road with lines of slush on either side.

Rich edged out from behind the bush and squatted by the road. Military vehicles and some cars drove up and down the mountain road. Afternoon whiled away to evening. Drizzle pissed from the cloudy sky and then stopped altogether. The villa was quiet. The only activity seemed to be lights going on and the guards starting up the car to warm themselves.

The sound of a crack on the roadway caught Rich's attention. The guards were out of the sedan. One was throwing rocks at him. Another rock bounced past him, skipping into the brush. The blond guard gestured, either encouraging or mocking his comrade.

The tall guard threw sidearm. Rich saw him fling another. Stray light caught the rock at the top of its arc. He knew it would bend away from him, but when it hit the pavement, Rich loudly cried and cringed. The guards laughed. A barrage followed, with both guards taking sport.

None of the missiles hit Rich, though one or two came close. He played out the charade as if he was being pelted. Then a bottle crashed near Rich. He ducked and was showered by sharp pieces of glass. Another followed, but soon, the guard's arms and interest were spent. They threw a couple more rocks and gave up. A light shower began, and the two went back into the Mercedes. The cassock was wet but not soaked.

A waiting game now. Rich watched until it looked like another guard change. The greasy-haired guard and his companion strolled through the courtyard.

He slipped back, hidden by the bush. The four guards talked, with the tall one pointing up the road. Rich surmised that he was telling them about trying to chase Rich away.

Hours passed, and Rich's anxiety grew. Lights went on and off across the villa. The lights showed a light sleet coming down.

It seemed the right moment. Rich stepped out, shambling down the road.

"*Dhanyavaad* ... *dhanyavaad*," he repeated, gesturing toward his mouth.

The passenger-side door opened. The interior light showed the greasy-haired driver pointing at Rich. The passenger-side guard left his AK-47 in the car and started toward Rich.

Rich stopped. "*Dhanyavaad* ..."

"*Otoydi mudak.*"

Mudak translated to asshole. The snarl and loudness of the other word needed no translation.

As the man closed in on him, Rich cried out and staggered backward. This seemed to enrage the guard. Rich kept him just beyond his reach, going back up the road.

"*Vernis' ty kakashka.*"

Kakashka. Rich knew that word. He was calling him a shit. He dived back into the brush with the guard close on his heels. In his pocket, he clicked the Taser on. Slipping and swearing on the wet dirt, the guard barged up the overgrowth.

Near the top, Rich stopped and wheeled. He watched the large shadowy figure of the guard fighting through bushes and tripping on roots, breathing heavily with the effort but still in pursuit. Rich gripped the steel baton in his other pocket.

The guard stopped, panting.

"*Nahain*," Rich cowered.

"*Ya ub'yu tebya.*" The big man advanced.

His face was flat, flushed and sweaty. He had raised his fists, which looked the size of Christmas hams. He stepped forward, readying to take off Rich's head with one swing.

Fear made the end of Rich's nerves spark and nearly paralyzed him. But he pulled himself out of it. Quickly, Rich flicked the baton open and slashed it across the bridge of the guard's nose.

"Ahhhh," the man shrieked in surprise. Both hands went to his eyes.

Steady with anger and purpose, Rich thrust the Taser into the fleshy wet flab of the big man's neck. He gritted his teeth and held the red button down. The Taser crackled, and blue lightning connected with skin. Immediately, the man seized, and his face went white. His eyes looked bloody and full of fear. He jerked and jiggled and went to his knees. Rich held the Taser firmly on his neck, careful not to touch him. Tiny curls of smoke came upward. The smell of frying bacon filled Rich's nose. The guard's eyes rolled back until all Rich could see were the veiny whites.

"Three Mississippi ... four Mississippi ..."

He smelled gas, urine and feces as the guard filled his pants.

"*Kakashka* ... seven *kakashka* ... eight *kakashka* ..."

The guard pitched forward, his face falling into sleet, dirt and pine needles.

"Ten *kakashka* ... eleven ..."

He lay motionless.

Rich let off the Taser and pulled it off the guard's neck. He took a half-step back. Two burn marks with blisters showed on the white flesh. Rich rolled the big guard over and dragged him by the shoulders to a tree. He didn't know if the man was alive or dead. He didn't care. Zip ties secured the man's ankles. Pushing him up, Rich brought both arms behind and jerked a zip tie over his thick wrists. The guard wore track pants with a drawstring. He reeked of shit. Rich pulled the drawstring string out and wound it tightly around the man's throat. He tied the end of the string to a low-hanging tree limb.

The guard had a shoulder holster under his puffy down coat. Rich pocketed the Makarov 9mm automatic, along with the man's wallet, a Gerber fighting knife and set of keys. He had papers and half a pack of gum but nothing else useful to Rich.

Rich took a moment to gather himself and mentally go over how to play the next part.

The greasy-haired guard leaned on the Mercedes, smoking, hands in pockets, idly looking up the road.

Rich broke out of the brush and hobbled out into the roadway. He waved wildly and made *come here* gestures with his arms.

The guard flicked away his smoke and started up the road.

Rich pointed into the underbrush. "Ah, ah, ah, ah, ah."

"*Chto sluchilos?*" The man's long greasy hair flew as he jogged toward Rich.

Frantically, Rich motioned up the hill. He kept the cowl low over his face as the Russian neared. His narrow eyes looked Rich up and down. Then he started up the hillside.

"*Dimitri? Vy s uma ublyudok.*" He sounded annoyed.

Rich followed.

The greasy-haired guard stopped and turned, his face a mobile mask of bewilderment. "*Botinki.* You boots." He pointed at Rich's Hoka One One hiking boots. "I never see beggar man with such boots. American boots." His face burst wide as if to say *aha*. He fumbled, reaching inside his coat.

Taser out, Rich pushed back the cowl. "Remember me, you son of a bitch?"

The guard's mouth fell open.

Rich jammed the Taser under the man's ear and pressed the button. The Taser sparked as blue light flickered around the man's face. He twitched wildly, making rattling noises in the back of his throat while his teeth chattered. Slowly, he collapsed. Rich followed him down. Again it smelled of frying. After a while, the man stopped jerking. The Taser crackles were becoming longer between. Rich let go of the button and sat back, breathless.

With a spasm, the body went limp.

He had to work fast. He zip-tied the man's hands and feet and then went through his pockets. He also had a 9mm automatic. Rich realized that, if the guard become conscious and started yelling, he'd be discovered. He took a zip tie and threaded it around the man's neck.

"You killed Gisele," he growled. It made a sharp zzzz sound as he cinched the plastic tie tight.

Rich stowed the wallets in his drawstring bag. He hoisted the greasy-haired guard's body across his shoulders and carried him down the hillside to the road. Seeing no cars, Rich walked across the road and lay the man's body at the corner of the villa wall. Keeping to the shadows, he listened.

"Two down. Two more. Then the prize," he whispered to himself.

Stealing along the villa wall, Rich made his way to the back. He was up easily and over silently. He crept to the front and froze. Through the window, he saw someone seated on a couch in the living room, watching television. Through another window, he saw the blond Russian in the kitchen, pouring Black Tower into a tumbler. Yellow light lit an upstairs window.

He jerked the surveillance camera cables from the electric panel. The lines came away with a snap and flash. At the satellites, he grabbed the feeder horn on the large dish. Unable to twist the horn, he pushed up and wrenched the metal tripod to the side. The smaller dish was easier as it was mostly plastic. He broke off the single strut feeder horn.

It didn't take long. A yell sounded from an upstairs room.

Rich slipped away from the satellite dishes and hid in a dark corner.

Shouts in Russian were exchanged throughout the villa.

Heavy steps sounded on the front deck, down the steps and on the soft dirt. The motion sensors flooded the courtyard with light. A man dressed in a sweater and pants tread around the corner, not noticing Rich hidden. It wasn't the blond. He went to the panel and bent forward. He checked connections and traced cables to the dishes. As he leaned over the parabolic, Rich came up and put the Taser to his neck. The Taser crackled. The man jigged for a few seconds and then fell over into the big dish. He breathed heavily.

Rich turned the Taser off, saving it. He went for the Gerber knife and quickly pulled the blade across the man's neck, ear to ear. The carotid artery spurt a foot out, into the satellite bowl, pooling blood and slush.

The man was unarmed.

Rich realized he had but a few seconds and needed to get ready. He ran from the back of the villa to the carriage house. He couldn't use the automatic. If he started shooting, they would come out firing. He was fairly sure only the hard-faced blond and Suka remained. Yet, he wasn't certain.

Rich stabbed the knife into the ground, within reach.

A woman upstairs and a man downstairs yelled back and forth in Russian.

Someone barged loudly out the front door and started to go to the Mercedes. It was the blond.

"Shit." Rich's mind spun. He'd have to slip into the house if the blond got to the Mercedes and saw the guards gone. The man would figure out quickly that something was wrong. And Suka was upstairs. Rich would be between them. The whole purpose was to kill Suka. The blond might kill him, but he would get Suka first.

The blond stopped and turned for the back of the villa. As he walked toward the corner, his tall shadow slid along the walls. His arm was out, an automatic clearly outlined.

Rich's mind all but seized. He had to focus. Breathe. Let him come. Just get the automatic. Everything else will fall into place. Focus. Get the automatic. He clicked on the Taser.

"Monkey...monkey...monkey," the blond said as his shadow neared.

Rich broke from hiding and got the blond's wrist, pushing it away. He thrust the heel of his right hand upward into the man's chin. The automatic banged against the wall.

The blond fought back. He pivoted and went for Rich.

They grappled, but Rich managed to parry the blond's moves, punching and keeping him back. They grunted and grabbed, close enough that Rich could smell the whiskey on the blond's breath. Both fought hard. The man lowered his shoulder and drove Rich into the wall. He pushed, grimacing.

"You're going to die," Rich snarled through clenched teeth.

"*Amerikanskaya*?" the blond sputtered. He squinted, trying to recognize.

"You killed my wife."

"Is you. And now I keel you, monkey." He muscled Rich to the side, breaking his hold.

Rich tumbled. He scrambled to his feet, the Taser ready.

The blond leapt at him, throwing a right fist.

Rich leaned back and left, letting the fist slip over his right shoulder. He latched onto the man's thick arm and pulled him forward. It threw the blond off balance. Rich thrust the Taser into the man's under arm. Blue light lit up the back of the villa as the Taser cracked.

The blond danced, losing his footing and falling on his side.

The Taser went dead. Silence. The man lay stunned, shaking. Rich reached back, feeling around. He found the Gerber knife and stabbed it into the man's chest. The blade stuck at the sternum. Gripping the handle with both hands and using the weight of his upper body, he plunged the blade to the hilt. Blood bubbles sputtered around gleaming metal in the wound.

Dead almost immediately, the blond lay in a heap.

A car rushed by on the road.

A woman's shrill voice sounded upstairs.

"*Da.*" Rich yelled back, gasping, withdrawing the knife.

"It's just me and you now," he muttered between breaths. He retrieved the 9mm and checked the magazine, pulling back and releasing the receiver. Slipping through the front door, he scanned the room. The large flat-screen television hissed and showed gray snow. Cigarette smoke curled up from an ashtray on the table, which fronted a short red velour-covered couch. A couple of crushed and bent beer cans with newspapers littered the table top. A glass of whiskey with ice sat on the armrest of the couch.

"*Idioty, vy idioty,*" Suka bellowed at the top of the stairs.

Rich snapped off the kitchen light and stood sideways to the doorway, gun up. He heard her coming down the stairs, a step at a time.

"*Vy idioty.*"

His heart pounded in his chest. There was no spit in his mouth, just cotton. His belly shook. A deep breath, let out slowly and quietly, eased his fear.

She entered the living room, orange hair and angry face. Moving slowly, she opened the front door with her free arm.

Rich stepped out of the shadows with both hands aiming the automatic. "*Zamerzat'* Suka."

Suka froze at the door. "*Kto ty*?" Her back to Rich.

"You know who I am." Rich came into the light of the living room.

In a flash, she crouched and pivoted.

He fired, splintering the door jamb.

"Yaaaaa," she screamed, running for the stairs.

Rich was after her.

Suka struggled up the stairs.

He grabbed her leg, bringing her down.

She kicked and slapped at him with her good arm.

"Look at me," he yelled.

Suka pulled loose and jumped up and climbed the stairs.

Rich got a cuff of her pant and pulled her leg out from under her.

"Yaaaa." A heel to Rich's face knocked him sideways. He took a shot, but missed.

She made the landing and darted right.

Rich was a step behind her. He knew it would be a mistake to follow her into the room, so he ran to the left, down the hallway.

A red dot searched the hallway. A shot rang out behind as he dived into a dark room. He returned fire just to keep her back.

The room was a mess: unmade bed, clothes all over. Rich took the second automatic from his cassock pocket. He wrestled the cassock over his head and stuffed it under the bed, leaving a corner out.

"You're dead, Rice."

She shot again.

He went into the closet, kneeling in the dark, leaving the door ajar.

Rich heard her slowly coming down the hall.

"You keel my Nicky, my *malchik*."

He wanted to shout, *you killed Gisele*, but he kept silent.

She was at the door. He could see her shadow on the opposite wall.

He held his breath.

At once, Suka was in the room. The laser dot jumped across the walls and corners. She must've spotted the cassock under the bed.

Bam, bam, bam. Bam. She shot through the mattress.

Rich's ears rang. "That's six," he thought.

"You're dead. You bastard. *Mertvyy*." She went down to a knee, looking under the bed.

He took the chance, breaking out the closet, shooting.

Suka tumbled to the side with the bullet's impact. She lay half in the room, half in the hallway on her good arm.

Rich stood over her. Her cheek and jaw was splashed with blood. She squirmed, trying to get her arm and gun free. Rich stomped his left foot on the automatic.

Bam.

The bottom of his left foot burned like fire from ball to heel.

"You bitch." He aimed. "This is for my wife."

Bam.

It seemed the loudest shot, deafening Rich. Warm drops splattered his face. A red hole showed on Suka's temple. A messy, round hole with deep black center. Her head lay in a spreading pool of blood, surrounded by bits of orange hair and tissue. Her eyes stared at nothing, mouth slack. Her face empty.

This should've been satisfying; yet, it wasn't.

Rich kicked the gun away, and something like an electric shock went from his heel up the back of his leg. His hearing slowly returned. His mind spun with what he needed to do. He picked up Suka's automatic, dropped the magazine and cleared the chamber.

Limping down the hall, he checked the other rooms. Two had mattresses and clothing all over the floors. Another was clear. In a daze, he grabbed Suka's shoulder and dragged her down the hall. She seemed amazingly light. A trail of blood followed. Half her head remained at the end of the hall. Coming to his senses, he dropped her by the bed. A computer on a desk showed a blank blue screen. There was a Roverbook laptop next to it. Rich found a yellow plastic bag with a Marks & Spencer logo and raked in a mobile phone, thumb drives and the Roverbook.

At the top of the stairs, he listened. Nothing. Each step made him wince. He surveyed the living room and kitchen. Rich pulled open a sealed, insulated door. Cold air blew out. Cautiously, he stepped down wooden steps to a basement.

Low watt bulbs glowed on wires dangling from a ceiling of exposed floor joists. Rich glanced around and noted stainless steel tables, sinks and electric burners with large pots. A chiller unit blasted on high. White tubs were stacked on the wall. The basement smelled of pickles. He flipped on a light switch near the tables. A bank of florescent lights lit the basement. He read the English label on the tubs: *Acetic Anhydribe. Do Not Store Above 120 F.* On the opposite wall were stacks of plastic-wrapped bundles containing greenish black bricks. Ripping a corner, Rich pinched and smelled. Raw opium. He dug into the package, wrapped a golf-ball size wad in plastic and stuffed it in his pocket. His fingers were sticky with opium. He licked them, tasting the bitter drug. It might ease the pain of his left foot, he hoped.

He jerked the thick electric cord of the chiller unit out of the socket. The basement became quiet, except for the hum of florescent lights.

Dawn would break within hours. Rich knew he had to get a move on.

He remembered the cassock.

Hopping on his good foot, he went up the stairs and retrieved the cassock from under the bed. It was nearly in tatters, torn and bullet-holed. He hobbled down the stairs and out the front, up the road to his encampment. The guard's face had swelled and discolored, his tongue out and eyes bulging. An animal scampered off into the dark brush. Rich threw back the plastic and packed his drawstring bag. He untied the dead man and dragged him to the plastic sheet. He covered him with the plastic and boughs. The body wouldn't be found quickly.

Rich's mouth was numb, his stomach queasy; but his foot didn't bother him half as much as before. Fetching the dead man from the corner of the wall, Rich carried him to the Mercedes and put him into the passenger seat. He backed the sedan into the courtyard, parking it next to the villa. Sweat ran down his face as he rolled a red barrel of petrol under the propane tank. He punctured the sides with the knife and let gas spill out. He piled wood boards and garbage around the barrel. He mounded petrol-soaked paper and wood between the tank and the house.

Taking the second barrel, he tilted and muscled it across the deck into the living room. He stabbed holes in the middle of the barrel and let the petrol soak the carpet. When the barrel seemed half empty, Rich wrestled it into the kitchen and lay it inside the doorway to the basement. He made holes in the top, and petrol drained down the wooden steps, splashing on the basement floor.

He became dizzy. *From the gas fumes*, he told himself. On the table was a pack of Winston cigarettes and a book of paper matches. He could use these. Outside, he took deep breaths until his wits returned.

"Like taking a ride with Gupta," he said.

At the wall of the villa, he opened the drawstring bag and took out the cans of spray paint. He thought a moment while he shook the rattling can. In large black letters, he sprayed, *Allahu Akbar Insha' Allah.* He used the red paint for the front side of the wall, spraying a symbol with a crescent and star.

On the deck by the front door, he fished out a cigarette from the pack. His hand shook as he lighted it and puffed. He spit on the match instead of throwing it. Smoke caught in the back of his throat. He hacked, choking.

"Damn," he sputtered, coughing. "Killing Russians, eating opium and now smoking. I am picking up some bad habits."

He blew out the pilot light on the propane stove and turned the knobs on full. By the open front door, he wadded a pile of papers with the spray cans in the middle. He tucked the filter end of the burning cigarette under the rows of matches in the book. Carefully, he laid the cigarette and matches on the spray cans. Once the cigarette burned down to the match-heads, they would flare up, catching the papers. This should heat up the spray cans, making them explode and igniting the propane and petrol throughout the house.

Softly, Rich closed the front door. He jumped off the deck and ran as fast as a man with one good foot could run. Out the gate, down the mountain road, he flung the knife as far as he could into the woods. His hiking boot made squishy noises. He didn't look, knowing it must be filled with blood and petrol. There was no stopping as he went past the regiment gate intersection.

With a clap, yellow light lit up the road behind him.

As he turned on Mall Road, a loud whump sounded, and a mushroom of fire climbed to the sky, casting a golden glow on the tree tops. He stayed in the shadows, knowing there was a machine gun emplacement and regiment's main gate down the road. Was that explosion the acetic or the propane tank? The answer came a moment later when night turned to day, white light flashed and a low boom shook the air. Fire rained on the mountain.

In minutes, sirens sounded back in the hills, somewhere inside the regiment. Flames flickered up the road. Smoke boiled into the sky.

Breathless, he made it to the pine-tree lined drive. The fire was so bright that the yellow light flickered on the gables of the Inn. Rich dug around his drawstring bag and found the key. He unlocked the door to his room and, leaving the light off, collapsed across the bed.

He drifted in and out of consciousness. Sirens screamed in the distance. People gathered outside his window, talking excitedly. Big trucks roared up the mountain road. A helicopter chopped up the sky. There was a banging on his door. Someone rattled the knob. "Mr. Rice?" A woman called. "There's been an explosion and fire on the mountaintop. If the fire spreads, we have to evacuate."

Rich grunted, falling back unconscious.

Hours later, he woke. He winced, stepping out of bed on his left foot. Blood had seeped out the tip of his hiking boot, creating a dark wet spot on the carpet. Fingering the window curtain aside, he saw it was quiet. There was smoke visible above the pine tops, high up on the mountain.

Sitting on the toilet lid, he carefully rolled down his tattered, bloody sock. He raised his ankle and gently laid it on his right knee. There were burns and blisters at the ball of his foot. A deep red gash ran down his instep to the heel. Blood seeped from the exposed wound. He reached into his hiking boot, and something sharp pricked his finger. He pulled back the tongue and saw jagged metal sticking up along the inner sole. Using a wash flannel, he wrenched the metal from the inside of his boot. Had a piece of the bullet splintered off when Suka's automatic shot under his boot? Or, perhaps, had the shank split? The outer sole was ruined but wearable.

He couldn't look himself in the mirror. His hands were cut up, dirty and red. His face was streaked brown and bloody, with clumps of dried blood and pine needles in his beard. Purple bruising was evident on the thenar space of his right hand. He had an inexplicable burn along the inside of his left index finger. His ribs ached with each deep breath.

Walking on his left toes, he stepped into the shower. He lathered with soap and angrily scrubbed his face, hands and whole body. The water and soap stung the bottom of his foot. He knew it was good. He dried himself. In the mirror, the flesh of his face was pink and raw. The soap hadn't washed off all the dark foundation. A brownish-yellow stain could be seen around the edge of his face. He took out the brown-tinted contacts and replaced them in the case.

For a long minute, he stared down at the sink. *What have I done?*

Then he roused himself to dress. His clothes reeked of petrol. He changed into a fresh pair of jeans and a t-shirt. He tried to shake the stink out of his sweatshirt.

With halting steps, Rich went around to the main entrance. A layer of black haze rung the mountain peak. Slingsby moved cautiously toward Rich, sniffing.

"Mr. Rice," Evie exclaimed, looking up from a computer. "We tried to wake you."

"Yes, I heard." Rich leaned against the door frame, keeping weight off his foot. "I was exhausted, though. What happened?"

Her eyes disbelieved him. "We're not quite sure. The reports are a terrorist attack on the old Russian villa."

"Really?" He grimaced, shifting his footing. "Would you happen to have a First Aid kit?"

Evie got up. "Certainly. Are you hurt?" She opened a closet and brought out a large white metal case. "Sit over there."

Rich wobbled over, sat, and started to remove his stained shoe. A chunk was missing from the middle of the rubber sole and the back of the heel. Burns were visible, and some of the tread appeared melted. As he eased off the shoe, the smell of cordite and petrol filled the room. The sock was not as clean as when he put it on; now the bottom was soggy with blood.

Evie took one look at the long laceration and said: "You need to see a doctor. That has to be stitched."

"Can't happen. I have a train to catch tonight."

She tugged a latex glove onto her right hand and then daubed at the wound with gauze soaked in antiseptic. "You might have severe damage to the muscles, and perhaps a fracture."

Rich flinched with each touch.

"Are you going to tell me what happened, Mr. Rice?"

He let out a breath. "I was hiking on the mountain and stepped on a sharp piece of metal."

She stopped, lifting her eyes. "Near where the fire started?"

"No, near Almora. South of the regiment."

She put the bloody gauze on the table and fished around the kit. "Did you see the fire?"

"I was sleeping. I got back before it started."

Evie said nothing for a few seconds, holding gauze pads and tape in one hand and a tube of Himalaya Wellness in the other. She let a sharp breath out both nostrils. "Okay. I can dress this wound and tape it, but you really need to see a doctor. I can have one here in an hour."

"Thanks, no thanks. Call Gupta. I need to catch the train to Delhi."

"Put your finger on that."

Rich held the gauze in place while Evie wound the tape around his left foot. "Have it your way, Mr. Rice. I'll call Gupta. And if you're hungry, the buffet is out."

"Very." Rich paused. "You have a, um, maxi pad?"

Evie looked horrified. "Mr. Rice, I'm 57 years old. What use would I have for a ..."

"For a dressing?"

"Ah, I see. Let me check for a Whisper." She got up and left the room.

Whisper?

"I do have a Whisper." Evie sat again and ripped open a single Whisper-brand sanitary napkin package. She taped the napkin in place. "There." She slapped her thighs with both hands and regarded Rich with her lips tight. "That'll hold you for now," she finally said. "When you get back to Delhi ... do see a doctor."

"You bet." Rich half-smiled. "Got an extra roll of tape and gauze?"

"Yeah." She put tape, gauze and wrinkled tube of disinfectant next to Rich. "Here's a Tylenol. Sorry, that's all I've got."

"It'll do. Thanks." Rich gingerly rolled his bloody wet sock over the dressing.

Evie pushed back and stood, hands on hips. "Sure." She watched him guide his toes into the shoe. "Is that just your blood on the shoe?"

"Who else's would it be?"

"I'll call Gupta."

The gauze pad and tape let Rich put some weight on his foot. He went to the buffet. A few people watched him enter and followed him with their eyes. He piled on rice, topping it with chicken in a curry sauce, bread and cheese. He pulled two cans of iced tea from a bucket of water. He went to an open table in the corner and devoured his food. People shied away from his eyes.

Back in his room, Rich dumped out the Marks & Spencer bag onto the bed. He sorted through the wallets, taking credit cards and a variety of currencies from rupees to rubles. The shot-up cassock he stuffed back into the bag with the Roverbook laptop, automatics, phones and thumb drives.

He could hear Gupta's car in the distance, climbing the mountain road. His eyes swept the room. The bottom of his foot alternated between soreness and stinging pain. He pinched raw opium off the wad and rewrapped the plastic package. He let it dissolve partly in his mouth and then choked it down with water.

Evie stood out front, arms folded across her chest. She was talking to two men wearing Indian military uniforms next to a Maruti Gypsy painted in brown camo. The men, a tall young-faced adjutant and short, pudgy older man with thick, wavy black hair and waxed mustache, turned as Rich limped over. The short one was an officer, showing badges and ribbons on his round chest and a gold insignia on his collar.

Both wore sidearms. The adjutant had his hands clasped behind his back. The major's thumbs were hooked in his belt, the pudgy fingers fanned out on either side of the buckle.

"No one on the mountain liked it when the Russians returned," Evie was saying.

Rich, room key in hand, came up. "Excuse me, gentlemen. Thank you, Evie. I had a wonderful stay."

Evie looked at the key. "I am sure you did, though I am not sure why." She added, "Mr. Rice ... Major Babbar would like to speak with you."

The major had a broad face. He smiled, his teeth filling his face.

Rich took a long time to respond. He peered from all of his six-foot height down on the major. "Yes?"

"Mr. Rice, may I see your passport? Missus Evelyn says you were hiking on the ridge early this morning."

"I was." Rich replied. The major's collar was tight, and sweat wet the crease. Odd, considering the chill in the air. He handed the major his passport.

"We're investigating the attack on the villa this morning." The major opened Rich's passport.

"Villa? What does that have to do with me?"

Gupta's car neared.

"Did you see anything suspicious? Anyone suspicious?"

"No, can't say that I did. I was back here, in my room, when all that happened." Rich turned to Evie. "Isn't that right?"

"Well...I, suppose."

"There were reports of a beggar near the villa."

"A beggar? In India? How extraordinary," Rich deadpanned.

The young officer snorted and covered it with a cough.

"And what is the purpose of your visit to Kumaon?"

Rich noticed Evie eying the yellow Marks & Spencer bag. When her eyes lifted, she caught Rich's hard gaze. Fright crossed her eyes, and she took a small step to the side.

The muffler-less auto wheeled into the drive.

Rich raised his voice to be heard above the noise of Gupta's car. He put up a strong front. "I'm here because I'm a hiking enthusiast."

"Missus Evelyn says you have a wound on your left foot."

"It's just a scratch."

"And how did you get that *scratch*?"

"Stepped on something sharp on the trail."

"Mr. Rice," the major started. "We have many questions and may have grounds to keep you...for further questioning."

Gupta parked, and bluish smoke billowed upward. He got out, still wearing the goofy knit hat.

"Am I being detained?" Rich sensed he needed to be careful with the major. He could try and overpower him, but wasn't sure how the man would react. And, Rich had no idea what the adjutant might do to protect the major.

"Just for questioning."

"You have no authority over me."

"But..."

Rich plucked his passport from the major's grasp. "Like fuck you will." He smiled. His tone soft, almost joking. "If you detain me, I can guarantee the U.S. embassy will have someone here in a half an hour's time. They will crawl so far up your ass, you'll be busted back to riding camels, playing the tuba with the regimental band parading down Connaught Place on Independence Day."

The adjutant's eyes blinked and blinked, and his face contorted. He shook in what appeared an effort to not burst out laughing.

"Neither one of us wants that. Right?" Rich left the major empty handed.

"Come on, Gupta. Take me to Kathgodam train station." Rich tossed his daypack and plastic bag into the back seat. He climbed in and slammed the door.

"You got it, Batman." Gupta slipped behind the wheel.

Rich slowly slid his hand into the Marks & Spencer bag. His long fingers grasped the cold metal butt of one of the automatics, and he thumbed off the safety. The major was gutless and looked anything but fit. If he was angered by Rich's response, he knew he'd order the young adjutant to pull him from the car. He wouldn't wait for the kid to open the door. He'd meet him with the automatic. He'd disarm him and the major. The choice was either to getaway in Gupta's car or steal the Gypsy. The major's Gypsy was the better bet.

Gupta started the loud car and backed up.

The major, facing away from Rich, wildly gestured to his adjutant. Evie had edged to the front door, and Slingsby crouched by her side, barking.

Gupta dropped the gear lever to D, and they were off with a roar and a cloud of oily smoke.

The major didn't follow.

Windows down, beeping at the blind corners, Gupta got Rich to the small train station just at dark.

Alone on a bench, in the orange glow of a single overhead light, Rich gazed far into the inky blue night, to where land touched sky and streaks of clouds hung motionless across a purple heaven. He waited on a southbound train.

Lumbering iron approached slowly out of the darkness from the north. People appeared on the platform. Metal shrieked and air brakes hissed as the train came to a shuddering stop. Few got out. Tiny, dark human shapes hopped about on the top like fleas on the back of a beast. Shards of glass in his shoe—that's what it felt like to Rich as he took a step at a time, rising into the innards of the smoking, noisy, oily, smelly monster. He found a berth in the sleeper car, chasing away a young boy with no ticket.

The train shook, rattled, creaked and leaned. Every piece of metal complained loudly about being pulled along.

Rich lay his head against the vibrating bulkhead. A yellow curl of glowing filament inside the foggy glass of a small bulb in the ceiling lit the compartment in murky light. He stared, mesmerized. People whispered, slept and snored. The throbbing ache of his left foot seemed little nuisance compared to the pain in his heart. This was not the life he thought he'd lead. Everything had gone seriously astray. The events of the past year were out of his control. He knew all that he'd lost and who he would never see alive again. Thinking that, he saw Gisele. He had one more promise to keep, though he might die trying.

Code of the Bushido, he thought. *Death before defeat.*

A few hours into the journey quiet descended on the train. The iron beast drove through the night and its own black, acrid smoke. It snaked south, satiated, with innards gorged by sleepers. On the outside, people hung on desperately to its metal skin, clinging against a ruthless gale, a lurch to the left, the right, and a sudden shudder down the length of the cars. Rich grabbed his daypack and the Marks & Spencer bag and carried them to the bouncing platform between cars. He worked down a window, letting in wind stinking of diesel. The wallets went first. Then he took out one automatic and unlocked the magazine. By thumb, he slowly unloaded bullet after bullet, letting them drop toward the fast-moving land. With each disappearing bit of brass, he remembered the face of the man he'd killed. When all that remained was an empty magazine, he flipped it into the passing dark. That was for Suka Franko. Rich pulled the receiver loose and chucked it. The trigger and butt assembly he heaved far into a gorge. He broke down the second automatic and did the same.

The train slowly chugged up a rise. He waited, hanging the ripped cassock out, letting the breeze embrace and spirit it away.

Favoring his left foot, his teeth grit and grimacing, Rich returned to his berth and lay down. He had fought with monsters, but did that not make him a monster as well. He tried to sleep.

CHAPTER 13

Drowsy people stumbled and stepped down from the hissing train into the cold predawn gray of Delhi Junction. Rich came down sideways, easing his left foot. He shuffled through the busy station.

Coming out of the station into the teeming streets, he didn't see Vicky. He wasn't surprised. He stood on the curb as traffic streamed by him. Small children ran up to him, tiny hands out, begging. He took out his phone to call Vicky, but thought better of it. If the driver had figured Rich wasn't returning, and bailed out on him, he couldn't blame him.

"No. *Nahain,*" he said in a tired voice, pushing through the children surrounding him, looking for a cab or three-wheeler.

A horn sounded. Vicky's gray car pulled up. He double parked and jumped out.

"I am sorry, sir. The traffic."

"That's all right." Rich walked between cars with some difficulty.

"Sir, I am pleased to see you." The tall man had a relieved expression on his narrow face. That relief melted into deep concern as Vicky noticed Rich's faltering stride.

"Sir, are you all right?"

"Doesn't matter."

"Do you need to go to the hospital?" Vicky opened the back passenger door and took Rich's daypack.

"No. Can't." Rich lowered himself into the sedan.

"A doctor?" Vicky shut the door and got in behind the wheel. "Is your foot broken?" He started the engine.

"No, nothing like that. Just cut it up pretty bad."

The driver checked right and left, beeped and slipped into the flow of metal. "No doctor?"

"No. I said I can't. Take me to the hotel."

Vicky pulled his mobile phone from his pocket, pressed a number. "Certainly." He listened. "I just need to make one stop."

"Fine, Vicky. I'm totally beat." Rich replied impatiently. "I just want to get back to the hotel."

The driver nodded while speaking Hindi softly into the phone.

They turned off D.B. Gupta Road and drove by the small Moorish Ajmeri Gate, through half-lit neighborhoods, on paved and dirt roads, into Paharganj. The sun came up, staining the sky mustard yellow. Rows of buildings piled upon buildings passed by, with signs and awnings all dirty and strung together by sprung hay-wire atop power poles. The poorer the area, the more lines to the poles stealing electricity. Noisy, crowded and squalid. The Shiela Cinema was playing *X: Past is Present.*

"I was worried about you, sir."

"You'd be the only one."

"There was a report of a terrorist attack in the north." A large colorful poster of blue-faced Lord Shiva watched them pass.

"Really? Hadn't heard."

Vicky handed back a quarter-folded section of the *Times of India.* In the dawn light, Rich focused on a black-and-white photo of a burned-out building with an inset photo of a spray-painted Islamic slogan. He read: *Four persons are dead as suspected Pakistani terrorists attacked a former Soviet Union compound north of Ranikhet, Uttarakhand.* Rich scanned down. *The victims were Ukrainian nationals and employees of the Kozmos Corporation.*

He looked up and around. They were in an unfamiliar neighborhood. "Where are we going, Vicky?"

"I know a place." They passed Gali Number 1 and Number 3, heading toward Number 8.

They slowed before a shop with the blue-cross-and-single-serpent caduceus sign. Down the steps of a brightly lit shop, a long line of ragged Indians snaked.

"Is this a drug store?"

"Pharma, sir." Vicky pulled into a dirt alley between buildings and slowly drove to the back. He parked in a walled yard. There were rusted hulks of bicycles, broken pottery, a curious goat staked in the corner and a pen with rabbits. Rich and the goat stared at each other.

Vicky surprised Rich, jerking open the passenger door. "What's going on, Vicky?"

"I'm getting help, sir."

"I told you I don't need any." Yet Rich used Vicky's shoulder to steady himself as the two entered the back of the pharmacy.

The smell of hot cooking oil and medicinal alcohol filled the room. Rich carefully eased down into a chair at a table in the back room piled high with pharmacy supplies. In a side kitchen, a short round woman cooked while humming along to the bouncy Bollywood music on the radio. Through a break in a curtain, Rich could see the pharmacy counter. Two men took money in the left hand and with the right hand, passed packages over the counter to the next man, the next man and the next man.

"Stay here, sir." Vicky went through the curtain.

The room was decorated with a diploma and colorful portraits of Indian gods. A white stone statue of elephant-headed Ganesha lay on its side on the table. A crooked chiller unit buzzed.

Across the top part of the concrete wall, a long brown cockroach scuttled. Right behind it stalked a small albino lizard. Two young ones ran into the room, pointing at the lizard and laughing. They were half dressed and excitedly followed the lizard's hunt. The roach darted right, only to be countered by the lizard. Rich raised his foot and propped it on a chair. The roach was trying to make its escape through a crack in the wall. The lizard seemed to sense this. When the roach made its move, the lizard's short tongue tagged and sucked in the roach. The little ones jumped up and down, clapping and happily squealing.

Vicky came through the curtain speaking Hindi to a man wearing a stained off-white lab coat. The man shooed away the kids and took a long drag on a cigarette.

"Sir, this is my cousin, Samar."

"*Angrejee bolate hain*?" Rich wearily mumbled.

"Fuck, yeah. What happened to you?" Samar's face was oddly formed; he had a large head with bronze hair and a broad forehead. But nature had been cruel, putting his features too close together. His eyes were set, except for the ridge of his nose, all but side by side. The large-lipped mouth had a short slit for hole. His ears had retreated to either side of his skull.

"I've a bad cut on the bottom of my left foot."

"Let's have a look." Samar pulled up a stool and started unlacing Rich's hiking boot.

The woman came in with two plates. She smiled small discolored teeth like a row of winter corn kernels. Samar barked in Hindi, and she went into the room where the children had fled.

Vicky sucked his teeth and paced behind his cousin.

Samar laid the cigarette on the table edge, gently easing off Rich's boot. The bottom of the Whisper maxi-pad had fresh wet blood bordered by dried brown blood.

"Looks like your foot's on the rag."

"Funny."

"Vicky?" Samar said, placing the boot on the table. "Hand me that canvas bag."

He rummaged inside the bag and came up with scissors and a small bottle of alcohol. "So tell me, how'd you do this?"

"Stepped on a nail in the dark. You know how that is."

Samar arched his eyebrows, studying Rich. He doused and washed his hands with alcohol and started cutting away the bandage. "Good thing it's not a gunshot wound. All gunshot wounds have to be reported to the police." He took a quick drag and tamped out his cigarette in a bowl of dried food.

"By a real doctor."

Smoke seeped out his nose as Samar laughed soundlessly, carefully pulling away the bloody gauze. "Woo. That's nasty. Hurt?" He poked Rich's foot.

Rich jumped. "Just stitch it up, dammit."

Samar leaned back, regarding Rich with half-lidded eyes. "How much money you got?"

"*Nahain*," Vicky begged his cousin.

"I got enough."

"I want ten thousand."

Rich's eyes narrowed on Samar. "I only have seven. Take it or leave it."

The two stared at each other a few seconds. Samar broke into a smile, shrugged and put his hand out.

Rich dug into his pocket, pulling out a fat fold of rupees, greenbacks and UAH bills.

"What kind of money is that?" Samar wanted to know.

"Nepali."

The pharmacist's face screwed up in doubt.

Paid, Samar shot Novocain around the deep laceration. He said something out of the side of his mouth in Hindi to Vicky, who fetched a plastic bag and took away the bloody dressing. Samar irrigated the wound, letting red tinged water drain into a dirty bowl. He wiped down the wounded area with a paper towel; then rummaged around the bag, coming up with a curved needle, fishing line, tweezers and forceps. "Don't fucking faint on me, tough guy." He threaded the needle, clamped it in the forceps and did his first throw in the center of the laceration. He drew the needle through with the tweezers, pulled the nylon line out and knotted it after each throw.

Rich only felt a tug with each stitch.

Working out from the center, Samar closed the laceration in short order. He talked while dressing the wound. "Keep it as dry as you can. Leave the stitches in for ten to seventeen days. A doctor...or you...can remove them." He spoke to Vicky again. Vicky went into the pharmacy and came back with a small paper bag.

"Stay off that foot for a while." He handed Rich the contents of the bag.

"What's this?"

"Vicodin," Samar replied, standing. "Those are the speckled ones. And tetracycline to head off any gangrene until you get to a hospital." He spoke to Vicky. They shook hands. "And get to a fucking hospital." Samar disappeared behind the curtain.

Rich laced and loosely tied his hiking boot. "Ready?" He carefully took his foot off the chair and got up.

"Easy, sir."

"Find someplace I can get socks and new boots. Then get me back to the hotel."

They stopped at a bazaar, and Rich ditched his Hora One Ones and bought a pair of hiking boots and thick wool socks. Coupled with the Novocain and the new kicks, Rich was able to walk with less pain. Arriving at the hotel, he told Vicky he was flying out of Delhi that night. Vicky slowly waggled his head, understanding.

"Mr. Keeper," the Taj Mahal Hotel desk attendant said. "You have a fax and messages under your real name." He handed Rich a stack of papers.

The fax was from the Russian embassy, denying his request for a visa to the disputed state of Ukraine. A second fax was from the US Embassy, urging Rich to appear at the embassy yesterday. Rich wadded up both faxes and passed them to the attendant. “You can toss these.”

“Toss, sir?”

“Throw ’em away.”

Three messages were from Lucy, asking Rich to call her at the Hilton. A last message from late yesterday evening was from the *charge d’affaires* at the U.S. Embassy, strongly requesting that Rich appear there. He ripped up all the notes except for one message from Lucy.

“Can you arrange a FedEx pick up?”

“Certainly. What size?”

“A box, large enough for a laptop.”

The attendant brought out a flat, white and blue FedEx box from under the counter. He put the box together and placed it before Rich along with an address form and pen. Examining the Marks & Spencer bag, which contained Suka’s Roverbook laptop, thumb drives, phone and papers, he slipped the bag into the box. The pack of Winstons was in the bag. *Souvenir*, he thought, putting it into his daypack. He sealed the box and addressed the form to Agent Paul Bertoloni, FBI Headquarters, Roosevelt Rd., Chicago, IL. He wrote the return address as Keeper, The Ordinary, 16th & Vinton, Omaha, NE.

“Put the charge on my bill. And you have my laptop and other items in your safe.”

“Certainly, Mr. Keeper.”

On the way to his room, Rich stopped in the lounge and got a Sandpiper. When the door was closed and locked behind him, he unloaded everything. He took a long pull on the cold beer and dialed the number at the Hilton.

“Room 1066, please.” He waited.

"Hi, Lucy? Yeah...Richard. I'm good...good. And you?" He listened. "It happens to everyone. Here's a tip. Take an Imodium every morning." Rich waited. "How's the old soldier? Glad to hear it. Me? Oh, I was hiking up north. You too? Oh yeah, the Burma Road. That's way east from where I was. Hey Lucy, can you hang on?"

Rich drank more beer and began to feel at ease.

"I'm back," he said, taking up the phone. "Lucy, I know I said we could get together for dinner...but, I have to tell you, I am really bad company. No no, it's not you. I didn't tell you that I lost my wife a couple of weeks ago. I'm still in shock. You didn't know. It's okay. Tell Gramps he's my hero. If you're ever in Omaha...No, I don't think I'll be in Akron any time soon. Safe travels." He hung up and let out a long breath.

The phone rang as Rich settled back on the bed. He lay his bandaged foot on a pillow. As the television churned, he let the phone ring and ring. Lucy calling back? He doubted it.

The Novocain started to wear off. He picked up the packet of raw opium and the handful of Vicodin from the bed. He decided to keep the Vicodin for later. Pinching off some black tarry opium, he tucked it under his tongue.

After a room-service sandwich and a liter of Kingfisher, Rich packed and went down to the lobby to check out and wait for Vicky.

The gray Maruti eased under the alcove and stopped at the hotel entrance. The bottom of Rich's left foot was very tender, but he was able to put some weight on it and walk.

Rich waved Vicky away as he jumped out to open the back door. They rode in silence as night drew a dark curtain over the city and hazy skies. Vicky's eyes flicked from the road to the mirror and back. Rich knew he wanted to talk.

"Your foot, sir? Is it better?"

"Fine," he said, fixed on the window. "Thanks for asking."

Vicky sucked his teeth, moving along with the speed and flow of traffic. They exited off the highway, toward IGI Airport. "Terminal 4, International?"

"Yes. Air India."

The driver maneuvered by shuttle buses, cars and military vehicles.

"Pull over at the end."

"Yes, sir." Vicky braked, starting to get out.

"Hold on, Vicky."

"Sir?"

Rich pulled out the plastic wrapped ball of opium. He handed it over the seat. "Be careful. It's raw."

Vicky smelled the black wad. His eyes opened.

"Yes. Sell it, or use it. I don't care." Rich took out an envelope. "And this is for you. I told you I would pay well for a driver I could depend on."

Vicky opened the envelope and thumbed through greenbacks and rupees. His mouth dropped. "Sir?"

Rich gingerly stepped out, reaching back for his laptop and daypack. When he straightened up, Vicky stood before him. There were tears glistening in the corners of the driver's yellow eyes. "God bless you, sir."

"God is not going to bless me." His hand went out to shake Vicky's hand. Vicky grabbed Rich's hand, bent and kissed the back of it, repeating: "Bless you."

Embarrassed, Rich tried to pull his hand away. "No, Vicky. You're welcome. Don't do that."

Vicky let Rich pull his hand away. He sniffed and dried his eyes with the inside of his sleeve. "Will sir be returning to India?"

Rich wanted to wipe his hand down his pants but thought it would offend Vicky. "I don't know. If I do, I know a good driver." He patted Vicky on the shoulder and turned toward the terminal.

"*Surakshit yaatra.*"

Rich held his hand up and went through the heavy glass doors into the well-lit, busy terminal. Even with his bad foot, he pressed to get away. Once inside, he let out a breath and shook off the awkward feeling. "God bless babies, drunks and killers."

He checked in for his flight and, with boarding pass, got through security and stood at the gate. After Group Two, Rich's group got the call. He held back, waiting on the last group. An attendant in an Air India saree took the boarding passes and scanned each. The passengers filed down the jet way.

"Thank you ... thank you ...thank you," she said.

Rich handed her his boarding pass, palm out for its return. The red light crossed the pixel code and beeped. "Thank you." She gave him the boarding pass. Rich went down the jet way, then swung about. He feigned reading his ticket and boarding pass, but his eyes were on the jet way entrance and the passengers filing in. He could see the attendant's hand taking the boarding pass and passing it under the red light. A group of late passengers filed past Rich. He cautiously looked out. The Air India attendant had gone back to the check-in desk. Rich ducked under the cordon barrier.

The attendant noticed him. “Sir? Sir? You have to board the plane.”

“Left my glasses in the restaurant.” Rich did not look nor stop.

He dodged people as he moved through the terminal and took the down escalator.

As he went down to ticketing, he heard the announcement: “Air India Flight 1503 final boarding, all passengers please board the aircraft immediately.”

He avoided cameras and found a blind spot. Sitting in a corner, he slid low in the seat and searched on his laptop.

The announcement was repeated.

Two heavily armed Indian military walked through the terminal, flanking a much shorter Air India attendant with a very angry look on her face. The young woman searched faces left and right.

Leisurely ambling behind the trio were two young very white faced westerners wearing dark suits.

Embassy men, Rich thought.

He tugged the hood of his sweatshirt low, hiding his face. He raised up the laptop screen higher. The group passed to his right. Rich closed the laptop, gathered his daypack and turned left. His foot ached, but he walked and walked to a dark area of the terminal under construction. He slipped behind a dusty, plaster stained plywood wall and sat.

Among the stream of announcements Rich heard, “Air India Flight 1503 final call.”

An hour later, he roused himself, returned to the main terminal and fell in line at Lufthansa ticketing.

He handed his passport to a blonde agent. "A ticket for Flight 7501 to Frankfurt."

She took his passport and, looking at the computer screen, said, "You are aware that Flight 7501 lays over in Odessa, the Ukraine."

"How long is the layover?"

She squinted and leaned to a computer screen under the counter. "Three hours. That's not too bad."

"Would it be possible to extend the layover and perhaps catch a later flight? I have friends in Odessa."

"I can book a later flight."

Rich pulled out his credit card and handed it to the agent.

"How long did you want to lay over?"

"Eight or nine hours."

The agent glanced up quickly, surprised. "That's a very long layover." She keyed in the information. "I do have a flight from Odessa to Frankfurt around midnight. It's closer to nine hours."

"That'll do."

She talked and typed. "If you don't have a visa, you won't be permitted to leave the airport."

"Maybe they'll give me a temporary visa."

"Well ... that's worth a try." She tore off the tickets from a printer under the counter. "The Ukrainians can be accommodating...occasionally." The agent swiped Rich's credit card, handing it across. "More often...not." She slid a receipt for Rich to sign.

"I'll just have to take my chances on the visa." Rich said, pushing back the receipt.

"There's your passport, tickets and boarding pass. Flight 7501 to Odessa is boarding at C31 in about an hour. Your flight from Odessa to Frankfurt is 753. You'll need to check in and get a boarding pass in Odessa."

"Thanks.'

"You're welcome."

Rich passed a pair of police as he went into the men's room and closed the door on a stall. They didn't follow. There was an odd porcelain squatting toilet on the wall. Rich pulled out the contact lens case and wet his finger. He placed a brown contact lens in each eye. Then he hurried to his gate.

The twin jet airliner descended out of blue skies and sunshine over the Black Sea and the old seaport of Odessa. Sunlit diamonds dazzled across the water, just beyond a stretch of sandy beach. Were this summer, that beach would be packed with umbrellas and bathers. Banking left, the plane leveled off, passing over the docks and piers. The landing gear cranked down and the flaps ground to full just before touchdown at Odessa Aeroport. The plane taxied past rows of olive-painted military air transport to the undersized terminal, where the ground crew pushed forward mobile stairs.

Through the small window, Rich noticed the heavy presence of patrol police and military. His left foot stung with each step down the outside stairs. Pairs of blue uniformed *politsiya* armed with PP2000s guarded the passengers as they deplaned. *Militsiya* in mottled green camo and field caps patrolled up and back. Both police and military went about their tasks in a bored fashion.

A stiff cold wind blew as passengers crossed the tarmac and lined up at the door into the terminal. Rich hung back. He needed to think. No way could he go back into the plane. The line inched forward. The *militsiya* went into the terminal while passengers took out documents. They were silent and compliant, used to this procedure. He got herded toward the terminal; with no visa, he'd be stuck in the airport. The line shuffled. He didn't want to get stamped in, and then try to leave. They might buy him not understanding he needed a visa. He'd get sent back to Delhi. He wouldn't get sent to the states, not if he had any value. Rich did his utmost to disguise his nerves. He shivered. *Just the biting breeze*, he thought. He had to think how to get out of the aeroport. And if this didn't work, he'd have to find another way.

The line pulled him near the door. A *politsiya* used his compact submachine gun to urge the passengers through the door. With his youthful face, he seemed but a boy. He had no rank; his shoulder boards were clean. He wore the red badge with the four-pronged anchor of the Odessa department of Patrol Police.

Then Rich remembered. He rifled through his daypack and came up with the half-crushed pack of Winstons. Why the hell had he kept them? But it was worth a shot. He smoothed out a crooked smoke and tucked it in the corner of his mouth. He had no matches or lighter.

Rich stepped out of line.

"Eh!" the police said, nudging Rich's back with the short barrel of his PP2000. "*Nazad v liniyu.*"

Rich turned, pointing to the cigarette and held his hands out as if to say, *What can I do?*

The young *politsiya* eased, smirking.

Rich pointed to the terminal. "*Ne pas fumer.*"

"*Frantsuz'kyy*?" the youth asked.

Rich offered the Winstons with one stick pushed out. "American."

The patrol frowned, nodded and pinched a cigarette from the pack. He slipped it into his shirt pocket. He pointed to a dirty area of wall on the terminal with *Dobre Kuryty* written in red.

Rich made a *need-a-light* motion with his thumb and half-fist. He could smell diesel and petrol, but it was apparently okay to smoke by that wall.

The young *politsiya* pulled out a plastic lighter. Rich shielded the lighter from the wind and bent to the small blue flame, puffing. "Ahhhh, *merci, mon ami.*"

The end of the passenger line was almost inside the terminal.

He gave Rich a nod and went back to the line. He said something in Russian, waving toward the terminal.

Rich held up his cigarette. "*Oui, monsieur.*"

The *politsiya* trailed the last passenger into the terminal.

Casually, pretending to smoke, Rich moved away from the door. Twenty yards down the terminal, there was an open garage. He meandered around, smoking, getting closer.

The *politsiya* stepped out of the terminal, pointing for Rich to come.

"*Un minute, monsieur,*" Rich said, holding up the smoke.

Shrugging, the *politsiya* went back in.

Rich threw down the cigarette and broke for the garage. His first step was like a knife stuck up the arch of his foot. He ducked under the wing of a plane, dodging tool cabinets. A mechanic in gray overalls came through a door in the back. Rich brushed past him and was out the door. Head down, he hustled through a parking lot and out a gate to the front of the terminal.

He debated about commandeering a car, getting on a bus or taking a cab. He needed to get away from the aeroport and get lost in central Odessa—fast.

A driver was talking on his mobile phone when Rich opened the back door of his cab and jumped in. "Downtown Odessa."

"*Tak Pobachymo's.*" He clicked off from the call and put the phone on the seat. "*Amerikans'ka*?"

"Yes. Can we get going?"

The driver pulled out. After a minute, he asked, "Why you come Odessa?"

"Work." Rich looked back and saw *politsiya* running out the front of the terminal.

"And you want go?"

"Chorne More Hotel, Rishelievs' ka 59. I'm in a hurry."

"Is not far. What business you do?"

The driver's inquisitiveness annoyed Rich. "Security."

"What that?"

"Ensuring your safety."

"What this?" the driver belly-laughed. "Maybe you spy. You CIA? Jimmie Bond?"

"Just a business man."

"You say."

They entered Odessa, a resort town known as the Pearl of the Black Sea. The central communications tower, like a spear probing the blue sky, marked the city center. Buildings in French and Italian styles from classic to Art Nouveau marked the entrance to the old section.

"Is Potemkin Stairs," the driver noted.

"Nice," Rich responded, scanning the streets. This was the off season, but lots of people walked along the sidewalks, window shopping.

The driver slowed and stopped outside the green-striped awning and steps up to the Chorne More Hotel.

"What do I owe you?"

"Five hundred *hryvnia.*"

"Five hundred? I'm not paying five hundred."

"Fine. You not think I see *politsiya* running out terminal as we go?" He offered a nasty little chuckle.

Rich pulled out his wallet. "Five hundred, then. But you shut your mouth."

The driver grinned. "I have shut mouth. You no worry."

Leafing through the bills in his wallet, Rich saw that he didn't have five hundred UAH. "I don't have five hundred."

"That you problem."

"Tell you what. How about a fifty dollars American?"

"Ahhh," the driver's eyes went to the ceiling and his face mashed up, calculating.

"That would be more than fifteen hundred UAH."

"You give me fifty dollar," he smiled. "You invisible American."

Rich kept his UAH notes. After handing the cabbie two crisp twenties and a ten, he got out.

Next to the hotel was a DHL and Ukrainian Express package delivery office.

Three overly made up, weary-looking women in tawdry red and blue satin dresses, clutching fat down coats closed, stood off to the side of hotel entrance. They smoked and gave Rich their best come-hither expressions. He glanced away and climbed the steps into the old hotel. In the reflection of the glass doors, Rich saw the cab drive off. He watched. The vehicle stopped at the intersection. The light glowed green. The cab didn't move. Rich entered the hotel lobby. The plush red carpet, gold brocade wallpaper and polished wood accents gave the lobby an old-world look. He crossed the lobby and went to the back. Something was written large and bold in Ukrainian on a door; Rich figured that it read *No Admittance.* He did not stop. He went into a small office and store-room, startling a young blonde housekeeper idly thumbing through her phone. He found the back door and was in the alley.

Cars, yellow and red DHL vans, along with blue Ukrainian Express vans, were parked in the lot behind the office. The DHL vehicles were new, while the blue vans were older and dented, needing a scrub and showing signs of rust at the seams.

Rich checked the alley. It was deserted. He clicked on the Taser.

The back door to the office was locked. He banged hard on the door. A shadow moved on the inside of the glass.

Rich turned his back on the door.

A middle-aged man in a blue polyester Ukrainian Express zipper jacket opened the door. "*Tak*?" He chewed, a half-eaten sandwich in his hand.

"Come here."

"*Shcho ty kashesh*?" He stepped out, chewing.

The Taser crackled on skin just under the man's jaw. Flesh smoldered and smoked. He dropped the sandwich and crumpled to his knees with a groan. Food spilled out his mouth. Rich let off the Taser. The man was dazed not dead. Rich went through his pockets. He had a ring of keys with a tag. The tag matched the license of a UAZ Ukrainian Express van. Rich stripped the blue jacket off of the unconscious man and started up the van. He glanced back; the man was still down. He dropped the stick to *D*, pulled out of the lot and drove down the alley.

City traffic was light as Rich drove north. He knew the route from memory, having studied the map on his laptop all the way from Delhi to Odessa. After a couple of turns, he drove east on M14. The van engine ran ragged but seemed okay. A steel mesh separated the driver's seat from the back of the van. There were packages piled there, though not many. The packages slid around with each curve in the road.

He needed petrol but had to get out of Odessa.

A few kilometers later, the wide road merged onto E58, a four-lane divided highway. Out of Odessa, he headed north, where the cultivated fields and surrounding farmlands stretched on and on. This being autumn, the fields were mostly fallow. The sun was going down slowly. It would be dark in a couple of hours—perfect for Rich when he reached Ochakiv.

Past the town of Nechayane, the road turned south off of E50 toward Ivanivka. There were piles of sandbags surrounding a statue in the center of town.

Down the highway, Rich spotted an OKKO refueling station. He pulled in and climbed out. The pump looked nothing like an American gas station, and the instructions were in Ukrainian. He took the nozzle and opened the tank.

"*Ay ay, sho ty Rubysh*?" shouted a rough-looking pudgy man smelling of sweat, walking up.

"*Parle Francais?*"

"*Ne maye*," he replied, taking the nozzle and ringing up the pump. "*Frantsuz'kyy pider*." He hesitated for a second.

Rich, guessing from the intonation that this was an insult, took out some UAH bills. The man smiled broadly. He was missing teeth, two uppers and two lowers. He hummed while pumping petrol.

The pump shut down, and the man replaced the nozzle. Rich glanced at the numbers on the pump. He pulled out UAH bills.

"*Dya kuyu*."

Rich peeled off a one hundred UAH note featuring the picture of a mustached old man in a Cossack hat and pocketed the rest. His hand up indicating *keep the change*, he passed the bills to the man, whose eyes lit up. He grinned like an open cave and saluted Rich. "*Yty ebat' seber*."

Back on the road, Rich drove south through the darkness on T1513. He had the Bug Estuary to his right and Kamyanka ahead. All the maps on computer models had timed the drive from Odessa at two and half hours, but it seemed far longer to Rich.

Signs on the roadside told him Ochakiv was a few kilometers away. A town smaller than the ones Rich had driven through, Ochakiv was a sleepy Black Sea village. He entered the quiet, brightly lit streets. Suvorova, a wide four-lane road, broke off to the east. This was a private and ex-government official resort town. Gated enclaves in tree groves and hedging branched off from the street. He drove slowly, not wanting to miss his landmark. There, ahead, were the three buildings of the *Mykolaiv'ska Oblast*. His heart was tight in his chest, beating quickly. His breathing was shallow. It was a cool night, yet sweat rolled down from Rich's temples.

The first right turn after *Oblast* and then the second left. He pulled off the road and went around to the back of the truck. He sorted through the packages, finding one that was light enough and the right size. From his pocket, he took a Vicodin and swallowed it dry. Back in the van, he stowed his daypack and laptop on the floorboards. He didn't want them rattling around if he had to make a fast getaway. Finally, he checked the Taser in his right pocket.

"Here we go, Gisele," he muttered, starting the engine.

Nicky Franko's notebook had General Ivan Franko's dacha address as *Svetlana Enclave, number 242*. The iron gate was drawn back. Rich eased down a dirt track with overgrown brown grass on either side. There were small houses, some dark, others lit up, on either side. A forest green dacha, built in a sort of gingerbread-house style, had it lights on. Parked alongside were two cars, a beat-up small gray sedan with its front bumper held in place by a bungee cord, and a shiny black Mercedes sedan partially covered by a brown tarp. He slowly motored past. A rectangular shaft of light fell on the front lawn as the door opened. A small shadow walked through the light then shut the door. By shape and gait it was probably a woman. Rich drove to a dirt circle at the end of the track. In the outside mirror he watched the figure open the door to the gray sedan. The interior light revealed a middle-aged woman, getting in. Easing around the bumpy dirt turnaround, Rich saw headlights dim then brighten as the car started, backed out and drove off.

Rich pulled the van to the front of the dacha, leaving the engine running. He slid back the side door and took a clipboard with forms and the right-sized package. The door slammed closed.

A curtain parted, and a shadow looked out.

Cold, damp air, salty and fishy, came in from the sea.

His legs were wobbly as he opened the wooden gate and walked to the front door. It might have been the Vicodin or his nerves, but he couldn't feel his legs. That was a good thing, given the condition of his left foot. The lawn was wild, overgrown and needed a scythe.

Look out, wolf, here comes Peter, Rich thought.

He clicked on the Taser and stepped up to the door. Rich knocked, maybe a bit too hard.

"*Da. Kho ty*," said a young man in a black mock turtleneck as he jerked the door open. He had a newspaper tucked under his arm and an automatic holstered on his belt.

"*Paket.* Ukraine Express," Rich responded in a Russian accent. He held the clipboard up, obscuring half his face.

"*Myne zakazat paket.*"

Rich held the clipboard toward the man, who came out of the door. He reached for the clipboard. As he did, Rich jammed the Taser into the man's neck. Surprise filled the Russian's face as he dropped the clipboard and fell forward in a spasm. Gargling sounds came out the man's mouth as he fought the Taser. But he was out in a few seconds. Rich pocketed the Taser and pulled the automatic from the man's holster. He clicked off the safety and chambered a round, slipping through the door.

He entered a small living room lit by table lamps on either side of an overstuffed couch. Many pieces of furniture cluttered the room. Bookshelves lined one side, with a small desk in the middle of a wall. Family pictures and knickknacks were on shelves and tables. The room was uncomfortably warm. Boiled cabbage and corned beef smelled like tonight's dinner.

"You must be Rice," said a low, gravelly voice from the dark before a bay window in the back. "You are not unexpected."

"General Fra..." Rich started to say, but he was interrupted by the tased man stumbling through the door. Rich sidestepped him. The automatic lit up the room with a yellow flash as Rich put a bullet into the side of the man's head. He tumbled to the floor. Rich wheeled, covering the general.

His ears rang, but he clearly heard the voice from the window.

"You are a most ingenious man."

"Shut up." Rich crept toward the figure. A folded wheelchair leaned next to a short back upholstered chair.

"Let an old man talk." The general clicked on a lamp, casting an amber glow that half-lit his hawklike face. He wore black silk pajamas. "When I heard there was a terrorist attack on the old villa, I knew. I didn't believe it was those ideological fools." He sighed. "And now, my sweet Irina ... killed."

"Suka killed my wife."

"Ahhhh," he shrugged. "You kill me. I kill you. We swear we will kill you. You swear you will kill us. We kill each other...over and over." The general coughed and laughed. "You think it was Irina who killed your wife?

"She ordered it. I'm certain of that."

"No, Rice ... it was me. I ordered your wife eliminated."

"You?"

"*Da*. After you kill my grandson Nikolai. After corrupt American court was going to let you go."

"Nicky came after me.'

"*Da*...that, I know. We could not stop him. But you did not have to kill him."

"It ends here."

"No," the general shook his balding head, raising his right hand from beneath a blanket, aiming a Pistole Parabellum at Rich. "This is what you Americans call a Mexican."

"You mean a Mexican Stand-off. Doesn't change a thing. I came to kill you. If I die doing that, I'm okay."

"You're not scared?"

"People are scared when they believe they have something to live for."

"You think these toys," Franko held up the Pistole Parabellum, "...are the only way to kill a man?"

"Fuck you and your Russian riddles."

"But you know people can die without being killed."

"You murdered my Gisele."

"*Da. Da*." The general nodded in agreement. "Let me tell you my dream. I am a young boy again. I am agile and so full of excitement. I wear oversized boots. I carry a Schmiesser, climbing over a mountain of naked, writhing human bodies—bloody bodies in a vast pit. People scream, wail and cry. '*Hodick, bubbick, chichinitchka,*' I sing. There is a line of men wearing field gray uniforms on the rim. They have smiling skull faces—like the silver skulls pinned on their collars. They point. They laugh. I machine gun the necks of the moving bodies. Blood spurts and splashes. '*Kookawitchka...chook chook chook.*' Soon, I too am covered in blood." He paused a moment. No emotion showed on his ashen face. "I lie to you. That was Babi Yar. It is a memory, not a dream. I have many, many Babi Yars in my life. I have been *vory* and a *zek*. I survive Gulag, purge, pogrom, cleansing, whatever you want to call it. I have walked among devils and demons as their better. I am ready." The general cocked the P-08. "You will die and wish you had been killed." He opened his mouth—and stuck the barrel in.

Rich lunged for the pistol, falling at the general's feet.

The shot was muffled in the general's mouth. White fire belched out his mouth, and lit up his eyes and nostrils. Bone, brains and blood splattered around the bullet hole in the glass behind. The general's head fell back. The P-08 clattered to the floor. A brass shell casing tinkled on the hardwood and rolled away. Smoke curled slowly out of the general's mouth and the hole in the top of his head. It appeared as if he were laughing.

Rich kneeled in the quiet, staring at the general's body. He had been cheated. It took him a couple of seconds to gather his thoughts. Cheated. What to do next? Cheated. Where was he going?

He dragged the young aide's body across the floor, laying him out near the general. The shoulder of his mock turtleneck was wet on one side. His glazed eyes appeared alarmed. Rich wiped down the automatic and put it in the aide's hand.

Rich went around the house, closing windows, shutting curtains, buttoning it up. He took in the scene. It might pass at first glance. Blood spatter glistened in the low light, with clumps of brain and hair. Forensics would sort out entry and bullet trajectory and concluding that the aide had not shot himself. That would take time. Time that Rich needed to get away. He picked up the clipboard and package, leaving a single lamp lighted and slipped out, careful not to track into the blood. He pulled the door closed, wiping and checking the lock. The van's engine idled. He got in and made a three-point turn, driving away from the general's shadowy dacha.

Perhaps it was adrenaline or the residual effects of opium and Vicodin, but Rich was woozy as he drove. He saw ghostly shapes running along the roadside. Shadows tried to catch him. Bodies crawled out of the ditches. White lines were hands grabbing for the van. Around the headlights, there was no light. He could not tell the difference between earth and sky on an endless road. All was darkness for kilometers and kilometers. He retraced his route. Ivanivka was deserted but for a few dimly lighted houses. Again, nothingness and darkness, with faces suddenly to his left and then his right, and eyes way in the distance. He screamed, just to hear if he was still alive and sane. Well, he was alive.

"You cheated me," he bellowed again and again. "You son of a bitch."

After Nechayane, heading south, civilization slowly reappeared. He drove past small clusters of houses. On the horizon, the outline of Odessa stood out against city light.

The bent white hands on the old dashboard clock read: 22:45. His flight was scheduled for 23:50. He had to put the pedal down on the beat-up UAZ van to get the hell to Odessa. A rusted sign marked the exit to Odessa Aeroport. He got there in good time. Passing a pair of green *militsiya* deuce-and-a-halfs with soldiers casually clustered on the sidewalk gave Rich some concern. A symbol of a stationary car at the entrance to an expanse of patched and potholed asphalt indicated a parking lot. Vehicles were scattered about. Rich pulled up to a gate and took the ticket it spit out, driving slowly over a speed bump. The overhead lights in the lot were not all working. He parked between two SUVs in the darkness under a broken lamp. He opened each eye wide and took out the hazel contact lenses and flicked each out the open window. Then he walked around to the side door retrieving his daypack and laptop. His foot ached as he moved. He checked all the locks and surveyed the interior, ensuring that he'd left nothing with which he could be tracked. Slipping off the blue Ukrainian Express jacket, he thought--*That's everything.* He left the jacket and keys on the floor on the driver's side and shut the door.

A steady wind gave the cool air more bite.

Walking hurt, but he struggled to disguise his limp.

The small terminal was brightly lit, with a fake green tree decorated with bulbs and tinsel and strings of colored light. There were piles of wrapped presents about the base. A month before Christmas, and even the former Soviet Republic was ready. Electronic music, with occasional Ukrainian rap verses, played low throughout the terminal. People went in and out the doors, though the crowd was not large.

Rich located the lavatories and slipped into the men's. The stall doors were bent, dented, and covered in graffiti. Not all the urinals worked. No one was in the restroom. He went to a basin at the back and twisted on the tap. Rusty water flowed out. Pipes in the wall vibrated. With his free hand, he took out a plastic razor from his daypack. He pushed on the wall mounted dispenser until he had filled his palm with soap. Lathering up, he quickly shaved his month's growth. The razor stung and dragged on the stubble. He wiped his chin and neck with a coarse brown paper towel. His face showed red marks but no bloody nicks. He wadded up the wet paper and threw it and the razor into an overflowing waste bin. Cupping his hand under the faucet, Rich slurped down a Vicodin. It was only a couple hours since he took the first one, but his foot throbbed and he knew he might have to run. The water tasted like diesel almost making him gag. He tucked the remaining capsules into his sock.

He dipped his head into his sweatshirt, pulled his arms through the sleeves and casually strolled out into the terminal. Knowing cameras were everywhere, Rich looked down. As he did, he saw a maroon stain on his right sleeve. Christ, it was dried blood. Too late to do anything. Knowing that, if he took off the sweatshirt, it might look suspicious, he pushed up his sleeves instead. Keeping his cool, he crossed the terminal, past patrolling *politsiya*. Nearing midnight all the shops were shuttered behind metal screens, except for a small kiosk. Russian and Ukrainian newspapers, glossy magazines, candy, gum and souvenirs were displayed. Rich took down a black Ukrainian National Football team baseball-style cap. The cap featured a blue and yellow emblem with trident, sign of the princely state. He adjusted the Velcro strap and tried on the cap. A small woman sat slumped in a chair, snoring. Rich pulled out a hundred and fifty in UAH notes from his wallet. He cleared his throat. The woman woke with a start.

Nodding, she took the bills and went to her apron for change.

"*Nyet*," Rich said, waving his hand.

She smiled, slouching forward, slipping back into her doze.

Rich plucked ten crisp US twenties and folded them into his front pocket. Just in case.

He worked the stiffness out of the cap as he crossed to the Lufthansa counter. An older man was working the late shift solo.

"*Ya mogu vam chem-nibud' pomoch*?"

"Speak English?" Rich fitted the black cap to his head.

"Certainly, sir. How may I help you?"

"Checking in, Lufthansa Flight 753 to Frankfurt." Rich handed over his passport with his left hand and then let his arms hang down, hiding them behind the counter.

"Any bags to check?"

"No."

"Okay, Mr. Rice." The agent gave Rich his passport and boarding pass. "Downstairs departure lounge. You'll be boarding in fifteen or twenty minutes. Have a good flight."

"*Dyaku...ya.*"

The agent grinned. "No. *Dyakuyu*...and you are welcome."

There seemed twice as many blue shirt screeners at security. That worried Rich. Though he noticed the screeners looking through bags and waving a metal detecting wand were talking across the room to each other, joking and laughing; while those standing behind them were solemn-faced. Good fortune, he'd caught a shift change. Friendly and beaming, Rich breezed through security.

"*Dyakuyu*," he said.

On the other side of the metal step-through a talkative fellow moved the wand up and down Rich. Glancing back, Rich noticed a thin sheet of paper taped to the side, showing the blurry image a man outside the terminal, in the smoking area. Large letters in Ukrainian were written on the top.

The agent motioned for Rich to take his cap off. Smiling, he did so, and was gestured through.

Rich stepped out of security and started down one of two long descending stairways to the flight level. *Politsiya* roamed about the loose knot of passengers mingling before the double doors to the tarmac. Rich took a place at the back of the group of German speaking tourists, staring straight ahead.

Large heaters hummed in the rafters overhead.

Ground crew opened the doors, and wind swept through the departure lounge. Agents started to check boarding passes. Rich moved forward. He could smell the airplane engines outside.

Politsiya lurked.

"Boarding pass?"

Rich gave his pass to the agent.

"Thank you."

A young *politsiya*, carrying his PP2000 in front, locked a hard squint on Rich.

"*Aaaaaaa, Frantsuz'kyy. Frantsuz.*" He pointed and approached.

Rich kept his eyes focused ahead.

Another *politsiya*, burly and older, with a crew cut and three bent stripes on his shoulder boards, came up. "*Ye problema*?"

"*Vin odyn, Frantsuz.*"

"*Ty upevnenyy?*"

"*Sortez la ligne,*" the sergeant said to Rich.

He did not acknowledge them. Eyes front, he shuffled forward. The Germans near him looked around.

The senior *politsiya* poked Rich in the arm. "*Vous, sortez la ligne.*"

Rich started, acting confused, turned to the two police. "I'm sorry, what?" He stopped.

Both *politsiya* drew back hearing English.

"*Frantsuz,*" the younger *politsiya* said, making a smoking gesture with his free hand.

"I don't understand what you're saying."

"*Frantsuz'kyy*?" He narrowed his eyes, peering into Rich's face.

"What are you asking me?"

"*Vin odyn,*" he said again.

"*Ty upevnenyy po-frantsuzskiy*?" the sergeant asked as the younger man pled. "*Vin odyn.*"

"I don't understand."

"*Suce ma bite,*" he spat out, keen for the reply.

Rich shrugged, his face expressing incomprehension.

A German woman drew in a breath with a shocked expression.

"Passport," the sergeant said with an exasperated air, wiggling his fingers to say *gimme*.

"Yes, certainly." Rich handed over his passport.

"*Vin odyn,*" the younger *politsiya* hissed over his superior's shoulder.

The senior turned, opening Rich's passport to the light. "*Amerikans'ka.*"

"*Ne maye ... Frantsuz'kyy.*"

"Yes, I'm an American."

German tourists edged out to the tarmac.

"No French?"

"No, not at all."

The sergeant fumed and then roughly shoved Rich. "You go room."

Rich yielded to the push. "Is there a problem?"

"You go room," the sergeant repeated, attempting to shove Rich again. But he had moved beyond the length of the sergeant's arm.

Rich exaggerated his limp. "I don't want to miss my flight."

"Room, there." The sergeant indicated a side room with colored glass. The man had that wary, sideways walk of a tired old cop.

The young *politsiya* stepped over and opened the door. The sergeant muscled Rich into a room with a table and two chairs. It was unheated.

"You sit."

"What's the problem, Sergeant?" Rich sat, acting compliant, but not passive. An embroidered patch above sergeant's pocket read: Yelenyuk.

The young *politsiya* closed the door and stood by. The sergeant put a black boot on the other chair. "Let me see ticket?"

"Sure." Rich handed up his ticket. The name patch above the other *politsiya* was obscured by his rifle harness.

"You smoke you want." He reached out.

"I don't smoke."

The sergeant gave a quick glance over his shoulder. "He no smoke."

"*Vin odyn*," the other quietly responded.

Preoccupied with his predicament, Rich hadn't noted the visible tension between Yelenyuk and the young *politsiya*.

"You done with my passport?"

Was the friction because they were ending a long shift like gate security? Or was it something else, like an old *politsiya* dealing with a young patrol?

"No," Yelenyuk shot back. He riffled through Rich's ticket. "You fly from Delhi, change plane nine hour later here in Odessa. What you do for nine hour?"

"I read, ate, took a snooze on a bench."

"Nine hour?" The sergeant jerked his thumb back. "He say, you French who leave airport with no visa."

"I'm not French. I'm an American."

The sergeant nodded. "*Tak. Tak.* We have taxi man who say he take American to Odessa."

"I don't know what you're talking about. Was I the only American on the plane?"

Staring at Rich's passport, Yelenyuk's mouth clenched, and he breathed hard. "I don't know."

"Frenchman? American? I think you fellows have me mixed up with someone else."

"*Vin odyn*." The young *politsiya* pulled out something from his front pocket. He unfolded it.

"Shut you mouth," the sergeant barked. He grabbed the flyer, gave it a glance, then wadded it up and threw it in a corner.

Rich studied the two behind a calm, smiling exterior. Yelenyuk's irritation went up a notch, as if put upon with the whole situation. He seemed unwilling to trust the younger *politsiya*.

"Taxi man say American have beard." He swayed, looking back. "This one say Frenchie have beard. You...you have no beard."

"*Vin...*"

"Shut...mouth." The sergeant dropped his head and then twisted his face, staring at Rich. "He say you have brown eye."

The young *politisya* had a tense expression, his eyes glaring.

Rich shrugged, with open palms. "That's not me." He casually scratched his temple. Sweat wet the tips of his fingers. He hoped the sergeant did not notice.

"Final boarding Lufthansa Flight 753..." echoed outside in the terminal.

"*Tak*. Taxi man say he take you to hotel in Odessa."

Rich braced himself, but the sergeant said no more. They hadn't connected the theft of the Ukrainian Express van to him. "He didn't take me. I was in the terminal waiting for my flight."

Yelenyuk pulled in a deep breath, standing. He exhaled through his nostrils with a nosy whistle. He turned on the young *politsiya* with a look that made the younger man avert his eyes. "*Tup yy Rosiyi.*"

The young *politsiya* was *Rosiyi*, Russian. That was why the sergeant did not trust him. Rich focused on how to use it.

"Open bags," the sergeant moved to the table.

"What do my bags have to do...?"

"Just open bags."

"Certainly." Rich unzipped the laptop case and slid it in front of his daypack. He pulled out dirty laundry and spotted the crumpled red pack of Winstons. He pushed it to the bottom. With his back to the *politsiya*, he surreptitiously picked out the ten twenty-dollar bills and laid them on the pile of laundry just under the laptop case lid. The Taser clattered out.

The sergeant pulled off Rich's cap and looked inside and felt around the inside band. Then he leaned over, poking through the clothing. There was a faint odor of petrol. He picked up the Taser. "What this?"

"You know what that is."

"*Ne maye,* a flashlight?" Yelenyuk put the Taser to his nose.

"Personal protection."

"You cook with it?"

"Someone tried to mug me in Delhi." Rich decided to push. "I don't want to miss my plane. Are we done here?"

Not completely satisfied with Rich's explanation, the sergeant tossed the Taser and cap into the pile of clothes. "You pack up." The older *politsiya* adjusted his belt, then went to his pocket, finally resting the heel of this hand on the butt of his side arm.

Rich hurriedly stuffed his daypack. The two hundred dollars was gone. "My passport, boarding pass?" He had the Taser in his right hand, hidden in his sweatshirt pocket.

The sergeant slapped his passport and tickets into Rich's open left hand. He shouldered his daypack and zipped his laptop bag.

"I not say you can go." The sergeant's voice was low.

"Sergeant Yelenyuk, we're not going to start all over, are we?" Rich sounded smooth, chummy. "You're looking for a bearded Frenchman with brown eyes. Am I right? I'm an American, clean shaven, with blue eyes."

The sergeant unbuttoned the holster strap on his automatic. "I could arrest ..."

This was all Yelenyuk's ego. Rich edged very close to the man. They were nearly the same height. They locked eyeball to eyeball. "You could fall into a deep shithole if you shoot an innocent American," Rich hissed. Then he added, under his breath, "You will have a hard time explaining the American money in your pocket." He spoke through clenched teeth, the Taser ready. "You want to trust your career, maybe your life, on that little Russian?"

Rich and Sergeant Yelenyuk stared silently at each other. The man smelled of leather and honey, or just the *horilka.*

Slowly, with menace in his voice, Rich said, "Shoot me. Go ahead. 'Cause I don't give a fuck."

They glared a second longer. Then Yelenyuk's face twitched.

"I not waste bullet. You go. You go."

"*Vin odyn...*"

"*Pysok.*"

Rich sidestepped between the two and was out the door, across the terminal, to the tarmac. Behind, he could hear the sergeant berating the young *politsiya.*

"Vin dura." Yelenyuk bellowed inside the room. *"Ni vin odyn. Ni kari ochi. Ni Frantsuz."*

The ground crew were about to pull the mobile stairs from the plane's door. Over the noise of the jets, Rich yelled, "Wait!" Pain, like stepping on burning coals, shot up his leg from his foot. But he ran.

He climbed the stairs to the plane. "*Vous sale*," he muttered. "*Suce ma bite*." He slipped the Taser into his daypack. Wheeling at the top of the stairs, he tucked his thumb between his index and middle finger, raising his fist.

The flight attendant had a hand on the cabin door as he got aboard. Rich flashed his boarding pass. She closed and armed the door after him.

Finding his seat, stowing his daypack in the overhead bin and sliding his laptop under the forward seat, Rich collapsed. He did not in any sense feel safe. The German airliner taxied to the end of the runway. Rich would not look out the window. The turbines roared and they raced down the runway. A shiver from the Vicodin and he sighed, as the plane's nose rose skyward.

Frankfurt Airport, a busy international hub, was a most welcome sight. The first light of day made the canopies of trees in the surrounding forest glow green as the airliner came in for a landing. Rich limped through the terminal to American Airlines...the last leg of his journey back to the states. His seatmate on the flight was a talkative business executive from Bozeman, Montana. Rich nodded and listened as the man explained what was great about German business and what was shit about American business. He took another Vicodin with a gulp of red wine and let the businessman extoll the virtues of the German miracle. Gisele's father, Wilhem, had been a prudent and smart businessman. He had often spoken of the German miracle as being more of a General George Marshall blessing. Rich was about to contribute to the conversation when the memories of Gisele and her family flooded his thoughts. He missed her so much. He could grieve for her now without the anger and determination to avenge her murder spoiling his sadness. General Franko had cheated him of his vengeance. He would brood on this for a very long time. He should see Gisele's mother in Glencoe when he landed. That would be good. The executive droned on. Rich realized that the German businessmen whom the Bozeman businessman thought so wonderful were Albert Speer, the Krupps, Messerschmidts from the 1930s and 1940s. The American government should take its cue. Rich politely excused himself, pleading sleepiness. The businessman pulled out an oversized yellow hardbound volume of the Bible. His finger slowly skimmed beneath the New Testament.

They touched down at O'Hare, and Rich carelessly lined up for customs. He longed to get back to Omaha and The Ordinary. A hard knot clenched at his gut. Bitterness boiled in his heart. He gazed on the world with only mistrust. Gisele would not love a man such as he had become. Once he could close and lock the door of their upstairs flat, he would let it all loose and cry for his Gisele.

Coils of silver tinsel looped along the white walls above glimmering red letter cut-outs wishing all a happy holiday. Holiday music, the elevator variety, played throughout the terminal. Through a large window, Rich noticed a dusting of snow and frozen blacken mounds from an earlier storm.

What should I get Gisele? he could not stop himself from thinking.

Weariness dogged him. His foot ached. He shuffled out of customs and Terminal M, hoping to find a moving sidewalk and his last flight to Omaha.

At the juncture, where customs opened to the domestic terminals, stood a small, thin man in oversized gold lens aviator shades, and wearing a tan belted trench coat. The man had a sticky bun in one hand, a white cup in the other as he watched the exiting passengers with a detached air.

Rich spotted him right off. "Shit."

His Montana seatmate, now wearing an oversized gray felt cowboy hat, passed. "Lord be with you," he said.

Rich smiled and mumbled, "Thanks."

The oversized cowboy hat and man in the trench coat made eye contact and exchanged nods. The trench coat stepped out, blocking Rich. Two large men in dark suits flanked the smaller one.

"Welcome back to the states, Cowboy."

"Cousin Ogg. What a coincidence. I think the Cowboy just passed you."

"No, you're the Cowboy I'm looking for. We looked for you yesterday, since you were listed on the passenger manifest and scanned for an Air India flight." Ogg popped the last of the sticky bun into his mouth.

"Pilot error."

"I'm sure," he said, smacking his lips. "We had a couple of fellows waiting on the plane for you."

"What for?"

"Wanted to make sure you got out of Dodge...and in good shape."

"Do you mind? I want to get a flight back to Omaha." Rich grimaced, starting to walk.

Ogg noticed. "What happened?"

"Stepped on a nail."

"Sure you did."

Rich stopped. He looked down on the shorter man. "Can I get rid of you?"

"Not easily."

"Give Bertoloni a call. He's got a FedEx coming with info from the villa." He bent down. "Listen, if you're quick, if you maybe have a team close by, there's a dacha in Ochakiv, at the mouth of the Dnieper River in the Ukraine, occupied by Federation General Ivan Franko. It contains a wealth of NKVD, KGB and FSB intelligence."

"Would the general object to our visit?"

"None, whatsoever."

"You?"

Rich heaved a full breath. "I did not have the pleasure. I left the light on for you."

"Hmmm ... very thoughtful. This is a tale you must tell me." Ogg took a quick sip from the cup and handed it to one of the agents. The agent leaned his head down, and Ogg spoke quietly in his ear. The agent nodded and nodded.

"You need the address?"

"We know it," Ogg replied over his shoulder. "Nicky Franko's phone, the one you gave us, was quite useful in confirming some key locations."

The dark suit pulled out a phone as Ogg stepped over to Rich.

"We're done, then?" Rich wanted to know.

"'fraid not. We're buddies for a while. Let the government give you a ride to Omaha. Save yourself some money."

"That would be a first."

An electric cart beeped and stopped. "Come on ... take a load off your foot." Ogg waved a hand to the cart.

Rich struggled to his seat. Ogg sat next to him, and the two agents climbed in behind.

Ogg poked at Rich's sweatshirt sleeve. "Spill some wine?"

"Russian claret. Not to my liking."

"Why didn't you contact the embassy in Delhi?"

"What? Did I miss an embassy party?"

The cart weaved through the terminal, beeping. A large blue, green and red aluminum tinsel tree with colorfully wrapped boxes about its base stood quite tall in the terminal rotunda.

"Don't be so sure we would've interfered." Ogg swayed close to Rich. "I was highly amused by it all."

"Glad I provided you with some entertainment."

"I relish the irony. We have elaborate electronic surveillance, drone and satellite, intel from colon to throat. There are legions of anonymous-looking men and women following anonymous-looking men and women. Believe me, they practice looking anonymous. Moles and sleepers are everywhere. There are dead drops in graveyards, on bridges and in chinks on brick walls. They have flame-haired swallows to give pleasure and steal your pillow talk. There are lithe young boys that don't bite, but blackmail. Oh, the money, piles upon piles. And above it all, this entrenched bureaucracy of espionage, spying and catching the bad guy with his ass hanging out. And you...you...one pissed off guy whose wife they murder...you...with an agenda of unadulterated revenge...you, armed with what? What did you use?"

Rich hesitated, then rummaged around the bottom of his daypack, pulling out the beat-up Taser. "Assuming I did any of it."

"What the...?"

Rich pressed the button. The Taser crackled as thin blue lightning jumped across electrodes—and died.

Ogg burst into a girlish-sounding giggle. "A fucking Taser?" He giggled anew. "A crappie flopper? You just go and do what needs be done. Our laws, constitution, government, diplomacy, senate oversight, tradecraft and fear of reprisal prevents us from doing squat."

"I thought you didn't mind if I settled some old Cold War scores."

"I'd give you a medal, though someone would want to know what for." Ogg raised his brows. "You're going to have visitors..."

Rich angrily interrupted. "What kind?"

"Not that kind," Ogg assured him. "You'll have some inquiries from my congregation, and Jejune's brethren will want to ask questions. But I don't think the bad hombres will figure it out for quite some time. You didn't leave a business card, did you?"

"Skipped my mind."

"By the way...nice touch at the villa...blaming ISIL. It was just off enough to make the Indians think it was a Pakistani ruse."

'How'd you know where I was?"

"Once your name came up on a passenger list for Delhi, we had you on Alert Status. That's why we were concerned when you weren't on the return flight from Delhi."

"I figured every time my passport was swiped or I got a boarding pass scanned, it went to some accessible database."

"And when you showed up on a flight laying over in the Ukraine, I had a fair idea what you were up to—but my bosses were freaking out."

"Why would they care?"

"Mr. Rice." Ogg turned serious. "You survived." He looked down at Rich's foot. "Relatively unharmed. Imagine what would have hit the fan had you failed? American citizen killed in Ukraine attempting to...murder a hero of the revolution: Order of Lenin recipient, ex-Soviet General Franko. If they'd captured you alive, that's all kinds of bad."

"That would not have happened."

The electric cart turned down a long, narrow corridor.

"We couldn't help you. That's another level of bad. If we'd participated in your adventure—and failed as well—you can guess what a cluster that would be."

"So am I under arrest?"

"Noooo." Ogg drew it out and paused. "And you won't go through a staged grand jury hearing. You did nothing in U.S. territory."

The cart entered through wide doors into a cold hanger where a small twin-engine jet and black SUV were parked. They climbed out of the cart.

"I have to tell you. You have shown yourself to be quite useful."

"Lucky me. The general said I was *ingenious*."

"The general's dead."

"So I hear. That and ten bucks will get me a sticky bun and some coffee."

"They told me you were a regular guy with a sense of humor, who could handle himself." Ogg said. "And then, at the FBI headquarters, I thought you were a loose cannon. You've turned. You've got a helluva book to write someday."

That remark irked Rich. He glared at Ogg.

A dark-suited agent whispered in Ogg's ear.

"There's a team coming out of Turkey to see what's what in the general's dacha."

"Nothing to do with me anymore."

"Climb aboard. We'll fly you back to Omaha."

Rich balked at the steps into the executive jet. "I am so goddamn sick of flying in airplanes. I just want to get back to The Ordinary." He ducked his head and entered the narrow cabin.

ALGONQUIN

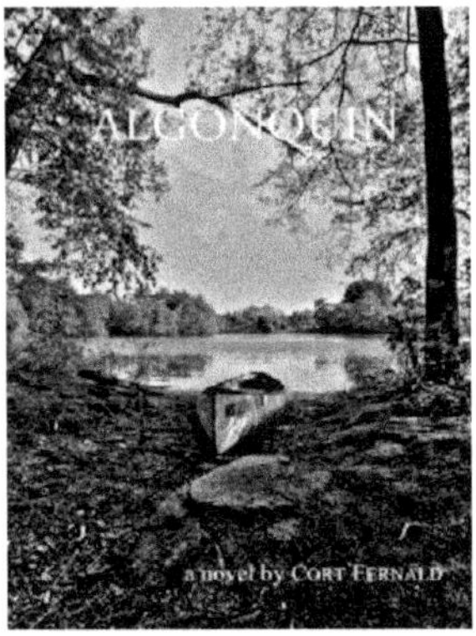

When Royce Partridge learns his boyhood pal Toby Bergman is dying of cancer he returns to the small town of Algonquin, Illinois on the Fox River where they grew up. Royce left Algonquin 40 years ago. Progress in the form of strip malls, subdivisions and congested traffic, has changed the once bucolic river town. Royce surprises Toby in the hospital and slipping fast. Royce stays in Algonquin at a quaint Victorian bed & breakfast.

Despite of the heavy hand of progress Royce can see the small town he and Toby raced mopeds around as teenagers. But it is down on the banks of the Fox River that Royce relives the wild adventure he, Toby and two other friends had the summer of 1964 before they started high school.

SISTERS' SECRET

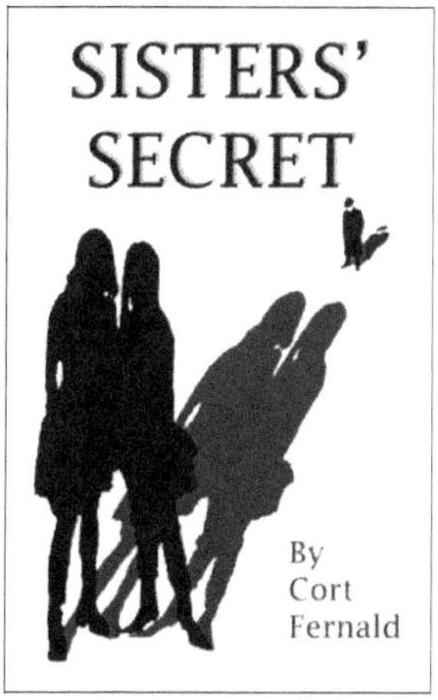

Sisters' Secret is a novel of grief and obsession. Mike Smith's beloved wife, Rebecca, is raped and murdered by unknown assailants. The police haven't a clue. Mike tries to lose himself in his work. He tries to get on with his life. Months later, he attends his high school reunion. There he learns his high school girlfriend and her younger sister were abducted and gang raped. The crime was never reported.

Mike is horrified, but moreover, he believes he knows who among his classmates committed this crime.

Mike sets out to expose the criminals. But in so doing, he puts his life at risk

Available from Amazon and Amazon kindle, as well as www.cortbooks.com

KEEPER of an ORDINARY

Rich pulled out the Glock and aimed into the black. Blam... Blam... Blam... light flashed and brass casings spit out the receiver.

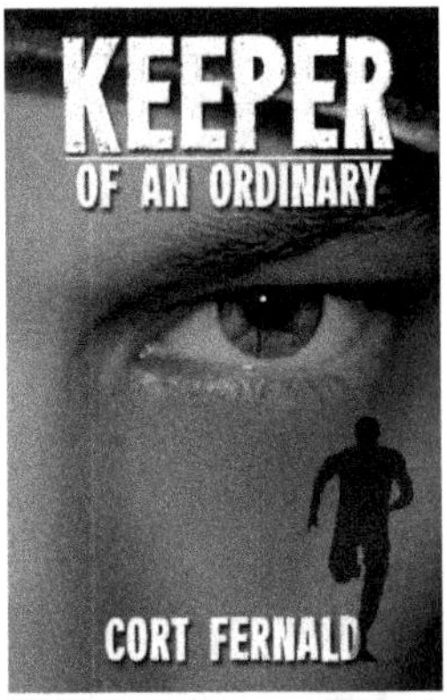

Some problems can only be solved by a gun. Investigative reporter Rich Rice learns this when the Russian mafia comes after him for writing about their sex slave and human trafficking in Chicago. An assassin's bullet wounds Rich, forcing him to flee. Known as The Keeper, he hides out in South Omaha. Despite his best efforts to remain invisible, the Russians find him. Only then will the gun end it – dead or alive.

Available from Amazon and Amazon kindle, as well as www.cortbooks.com

Reader Comments

"They say the first sentence makes a book. The first sentence grabbed me." R Jas

"Loved the book. I started and didn't put it down until I finished. I was surprised at the great ending!" R. Hendley

ABOUT THE AUTHOR

Cort Fernald is a professional writer with newspaper and magazine publishing credits spanning more than 30 years.

Keeper: Trial & Vengeance is Cort Fernald's fourth novel, and sequel to **Keeper of an Ordinary**, his third work of fiction. In 2013 Cort Fernald published the Vietnam era coming-of-age novel **Algonquin**. **Sisters' Secret** and **Algonquin** are available in paperback and Kindle ebook through Amazon and other internet retailers.

Cort Fernald has a degree in English from Southern Oregon University, and did graduate work in journalism at the University of Oregon.

A member of the Nebraska Novelists, as well as Nebraska Writers Guild, Cort Fernald is very active in the literary scene in Omaha, Nebraska, where he resides.

www.ingramcontent.com/pod-product-compliance
Lightning Source LLC
LaVergne TN
LVHW051108080426
835510LV00018B/1962
9780692908327

The Earthly Paradise by William Morris

A Poem

Part II

William Morris was born in Walthamstow, London on 24th March 1834 he is regarded today as a foremost poet, writer, textile designer, artist and libertarian.

Morris began to publish poetry and short stories in 1856 through the Oxford and Cambridge Magazine which he founded with his friends and financed while at university. His first volume, in 1858, The Defence of Guenevere and Other Poems, was the first published book of Pre-Raphaelite poetry. Due to its luke warm reception he was discouraged from poetry writing for a number of years.

His return to poetry was with the great success of The Life and Death of Jason in 1867, which was followed by The Earthly Paradise, themed around a group of medieval wanderers searching for a land of everlasting life; after much disillusion, they discover a surviving colony of Greeks with whom they exchange stories. In the collection are retellings of Icelandic sagas. From then until his Socialist period Morris's fascination with the ancient Germanic and Norse peoples dominated his writing being the first to translate many of the Icelandic sagas into English; the epic retelling of the story of Sigurd the Volsung being his favourite.

In 1884 he founded the Socialist League but with the rise of the Anarachists in the party he left it in 1890.

In 1891 he founded the Kelmscott Press publishing limited edition illuminated style books. His design for The Works of Geoffrey Chaucer is a masterpiece.

Morris was quietly approached with an offer of the Poet Laureateship after the death of Tennyson in 1892, but declined.

William Morris died at age 62 on 3rd October 1896 in London.

Index Of Contents

WILLIAM MORRIS – A CONCISE BIBLIOGRAPHY

MAY

O love, this morn when the sweet nightingale
Had so long finished all he had to say,
That thou hadst slept, and sleep had told his tale;
And midst a peaceful dream had stolen away
In fragrant dawning of the first of May,
Didst thou see aught? didst thou hear voices sing
Ere to the risen sun the bells 'gan ring?

For then methought the Lord of Love went by
To take possession of his flowery throne,
Ringed round with maids, and youths, and minstrelsy;
A little while I sighed to find him gone,
A little while the dawning was alone,
And the light gathered; then I held my breath,
And shuddered at the sight of Eld and Death.

Alas! Love passed me in the twilight dun,
His music hushed the wakening ousel's song;
But on these twain shone out the golden sun,
And o'er their heads the brown bird's tune was strong,
As shivering, twixt the trees they stole along;
None noted aught their noiseless passing by,
The world had quite forgotten it must die.

Now must these men be glad a little while
That they had lived to see May once more smile
Upon the earth; wherefore, as men who know
How fast the bad days and the good days go,
They gathered at the feast: the fair abode
Wherein they sat, o'erlooked, across the road
Unhedged green meads, which willowy streams passed through,
And on that morn, before the fresh May dew
Had dried upon the sunniest spot of grass,
From bush to bush did youths and maidens pass
In raiment meet for May apparelled,
Gathering the milk-white blossoms and the red;
And now, with noon long past, and that bright day
Growing aweary, on the sunny way
They wandered, crowned with flowers, and loitering,
And weary, yet were fresh enough to sing
The carols of the morn, and pensive, still
Had cast away their doubt of death and ill,
And flushed with love, no more grew red with shame.

So to the elders as they sat, there came,